Books of Merit

To MY dear Friend, Morteza Farzaneh,
who I love Brotherly.

Best wishes

Jadi
April 30th, 2010
Vancouver, Canada

The secret of Happiness is Freedom,
and the secret of Freedom, Courage.
(Thucydides)

THE FLIGHT OF THE PATRIOT

THE FLIGHT OF

THE PATRIOT

(ESCAPE FROM REVOLUTIONARY IRAN)

YADI SHARIFIRAD

with PJ REECE

THOMAS ALLEN PUBLISHERS

TORONTO

Library and Archives Canada Cataloguing in Publication

Sharifirad, Yadi, 1946–
    The flight of the patriot : escape from revolutionary Iran / Yadi Sharifirad.

ISBN 978-0-88762-526-8

1. Sharifirad, Yadi, 1946–. 2. Iran—History—1979–1997—Biography.
3. Fighter pilots—Iran—Biography. 4. Iran-Iraq War, 1980-1988—
Personal narratives, Iranian. 5. Torture victims—Iran—Biography.
6. Escapes—Iran. 7. Political refugees—Canada—Biography. I. Title.

UG626.2.S49A3 2010   955.05'4092   C2009-907221-1

Editor: Janice Zawerbny
Jacket design: Sputnik Design Partners Inc.
Jacket images: Liv friis-larsen/Shutterstock, Alexander Vasilyev/Shutterstock

Published by Thomas Allen Publishers,
a division of Thomas Allen & Son Limited,
145 Front Street East, Suite 209,
Toronto, Ontario M5A 1E3 Canada

www.thomas-allen.com

ONTARIO ARTS COUNCIL
CONSEIL DES ARTS DE L'ONTARIO

Canada Council
for the Arts

The publisher gratefully acknowledges the support of
The Ontario Arts Council for its publishing program.

We acknowledge the support of the Canada Council for the Arts, which
last year invested $20.1 million in writing and publishing throughout Canada.

We acknowledge the Government of Ontario through the
Ontario Media Development Corporation's Ontario Book Initiative.

We acknowledge the financial support of the Government of Canada
through the Book Publishing Industry Development Program (BPIDP)
for our publishing activities.

10 11 12 13 14   5 4 3 2 1

Printed and bound in Canada

CONTENTS

THE FLIGHT OF THE PATRIOT

UNDER THE GALLOWS

Flying again! High above the hills of my youth, riding the thermals, it's like being held in God's hand! Now I'm on the ground, tiny, frightened—a hare! Suddenly, I'm the hunted, my heart pounding as I run like hell from the shadow of the predator blotting out the sun. Any second I'm going to be impaled by talons and plucked off the face of the earth. Run, Sharifi, run . . .

"109! Blindfold on!"

Maddar-jen—son of a bitch! How many times had this happened? Woken by the guard to a nightmare more horrendous than anything I could have dreamt.

Tehran, Iran (early April, 1988)

Ninety-three days since my arrest. Another line scratched on the wall of my cell, a space no roomier than a grave, and almost as dark. The guards and I, we hadn't reached an agreement about my crimes, which perhaps explained why I was still alive to scratch and dream. My

1

former life outside these walls was becoming so hard to remember that I wasn't sure I even believed it anymore. The last memories to desert me were some of my very first, as a kid, running after those rabbits and dreaming of being an eagle. That explained the dreams. Eagles reminded me of the many times I'd risked my life for my country. But for what? Look what it had got me. A dungeon. Not even a name to go by.

"109!"

Often it was "Hadji" (pilgrim), meant to remind me that I was destined for a journey to the next world, once they'd tortured a confession out of me. My stubbornness earned me a steady routine of solitary confinement, interrogation, and torture. The worst part was listening through those endless nights to the cries and screams of others who, like me, refused to invent lies to save their lives. Their voices, brave at the start, eventually became pleas for mercy. The only response I ever heard was the dull snap of the hanging rope, or a volley of shots from the firing squad. Each bullet meant one less father or mother, one less brother or sister, parents lost to their children, children torn from their families. Who in Iran could have imagined such a thing? A government destroying its own society of families. Destroying not just love but thought. Imagine being denied the right to believe what you believe, or think what you think. Imagine the sun gone forever, along with any promise of the future, except for a sadder and deeper darkness. Imagine knowing nothing but fear until the day you hear that special tone in the guard's voice as he shouts your number, "109!" Finally, blessed, terrifying relief. And you begin that last walk out into the night. I remember. There were three of us, side by side, our hands tied behind our backs, nooses fitted over our heads. My two sad companions, they went first. I saw them struggle against the rope, a frantic, impulsive reaction against the end that was exclaimed finally in the drop of a slipper that fell from a dead foot onto the cold ground below. At that moment, something inside me refused to die.

"You can't hang me," I commanded. "I'm an officer. I have the right to be executed by firing squad."

2

"As you wish, Hadji," came the dull reply. "Tomorrow."

That night as I lay on the cold floor of my cell, the shadow of Death fell over me, invading my heart and soul, evicting the last ghost of a hope for the coming of another day.

1

EAGLES

———————

I was born in a village in the hills of northern Iran. My ancestors had cultivated a family tree with roots that drew nourishment from the Persian qualities of strength, patience, and compassion. Proud families like ours lived freely in a string of settlements along the Shahroud River, herding sheep and growing wheat and barley. We would raise children to grow up to raise more children to tend more sheep, and on it would go and on it had gone since before Cyrus the Great, 2500 years ago.

From my family I learned about loyalty and love, honour and duty. But from nature I discovered my imagination. The dry etched hills behind our village were the source of those magical eagles. I was addicted to watching them soar above the valley, even clambering to the highest point within sight of the village to be closer to them. A kid was on top of the world, looking down upon the shepherd with his dog, while the sheep grazed on the freshest sprouts of grass the season had to offer. Wherever I looked upon those hills, at the riots of wild-flowers or the thousand shades of green, it was all an extension of me, it all issued from my happiness. My happy river wound its way from the mountains in the east to nourish our valley, then continued on its way westward into the blue hazy world beyond, about which I knew absolutely nothing. As for the eagles, they were deeper inside me, yet, like religion.

One day, a rabbit startled me by jumping out of the bushes. I watched it run across the contour of the hill until the shepherd yelled and his dog barked and bolted after it. The rabbit cut sharply uphill, but that sheepdog was a thing of beauty and I could see that it was no contest unless the rabbit found an escape hole, and quickly. A shadow crinkled across the hillside and I looked up in time to see the eagle tuck its wings and give itself up to gravity, and in the blink of an eye it snatched that hare right out of its dilemma, and then rose again with that furball in its clutches. The dog stopped and whined, trying to make sense of his prey becoming a dot in a blue expanse of sky. The shepherd pointed his stick and cursed, either at the eagle or his dog, I wasn't sure.

Poor rabbit, I thought. But not for long. I was too much in awe of the eagle's speed and timing to feel sorry for the rabbit. That bird of prey sent a thrill up my spine, and I expect that dog had the same longings, because we had witnessed an action that wasn't of this world. What the eagle had, I wanted, and from that day onward my life's course was set.

I would fly.

For better or worse. Both, as it turned out.

I have my father to thank for making many things possible. First he sent me to Gooran, a village about four kilometres away, then to Tehran, the capital of Iran, to Pahlavi, a school that introduced me to the larger world. Soon, I was a teenager, dreaming of being an officer and a pilot. But my father's death in September 1968 suddenly put the responsibility for the family on my shoulders—my mother, Ozra; three sisters, Mahin, Shahin, Nasrin; and one little brother, Horma-tollah (nicknamed Akbar). The grief stayed with me for a long time because he was like a friend to me, and one who often made me laugh hysterically. But our last time together was anything but funny. I returned to our family home in the village of Taleghan to find him suffering cancer of the brain that had numbed the right half of his body. He gripped me with his left hand, his eyes fixed to the ceiling, as he told me he was going to die.

"Today or tomorrow," he said. "Nobody can do anything about it. I can't talk too much, only to say that I wish I could be alive until you get married. I'd love to see your children. But, as you see, God has a different plan for both of us. He wants to make you a responsible young man. I know it won't be easy for you to accept being the man of the family, but you must now look after your mother, sisters, and brother."

That was it, my final meeting with my father. He pushed my hand away and said nothing further. He passed away soon after that, but I'd left the village by then. My father, dead at the age of forty-eight. He was buried two days later without me there to say a final goodbye.

Two years later I was in the Air Force Academy. I was not a war-monger, in fact I was a peace nut. War made no sense to me; it was an archaic concept. Soldiers got killed or wounded, and that was the furthest thing from my mind. No, I wasn't thinking of war at all, just of becoming a pilot and flying like the eagles above my village. And so I did, and by my twenty-sixth year, I was guarding the skies over my homeland.

In the academy, they did their best to turn me into a fighting machine. I didn't resist, but I was smart enough not to let their brainwashing scrub me too deep. My head was in the clouds, where it belonged. I had no mind for politics, and even less enthusiasm for the violence that politics generated. My training was an extreme sport, and one in which I never lost faith even when I screwed up and for-got to put the landing gear down prior to landing or entering the traffic pattern before calling the control tower. These errors made me look like a complete idiot and mostly it happened when I was flying with my instructors. Success didn't mess me up, either, which I credit to being a village boy at heart, never apologizing for having moral principles, always respecting others before expecting them to respect me, never straying far from the middle of the road. I guess I was what you'd call square.

Pilot training had its own special ways of humiliating the cadets, but I never once thought of giving up, even in the face of some early flights that caused my instructors to question my choice of career. I persevered until I got my wings and moved on to jets and flew solo, at the speed of sound. And I remember landing and climbing out of the cockpit and setting my feet back on solid ground, and never in my whole life feeling more proud of myself.

Those years, I was blessed with the greatest gift a human being can have. It's called "enthusiasm." Then, later on it was "good fortune" that enriched my life, finding myself, in fact, wealthier than I ever thought I'd be, and not just with money but with the respect of my fellow officers and the love of my own family. But in all the excitement of my training, I may have forgotten that my freedom made me richest of all. And I would have to lose it to finally appreciate it. It's an old story, "You don't know what you've got till it's gone." I lost my freedom along with everything else to the Islamic Revolution that saw the Ayatollah Ruhollah Khomeini return to Iran in 1979 after fifteen years in exile. At the time, people were praising him for bringing a purer form of Islam to Iran, ending the poverty and extending love, freedom, mercy, forgiveness, and harmony to the life of the nation without any discrimination but "pure" really meant "simplistic." It became an excuse to ignore the Koran's compassionate teachings in order to mete out vengeance, which became a plague of indiscriminate slaughter. I saw it as revenge against anyone who had been a patriot in the time of Shah Mohammad Reza Pahlavi. No group was more thoroughly "cleansed" than members of the Armed Forces, fighter pilots in particular, since we had reputations as "glamour boys." How far the eagles had fallen!

In my tomb, I had little else to do but wonder how it happened. How had Iranians allowed our nation to be hijacked? How could one group tell us how to dress, how to behave, how to think? Dissenters were dealt with swiftly, their voices silenced behind stone walls, or at the end of a rope suspended from a crane in public places. Had we seen this kind of abuse of power before? Sadly, yes. Everyone knew of SAVAK, the Shah's secret police. The Shah may have been paranoid, but

Ayatollah Khomeini took it to another level. Took us all the way back to the Dark Ages. That's what fanaticism does; it breeds an ideology born of ignorance. You suppress anyone who doesn't subscribe to your perversions, you torture and execute them in the name of God, a total rejection of compassion that underlies all the great religions, including Islam. So, how did we let it happen? What kind of hypnosis blinded us to the intentions of these zealots? After all, the Revolution didn't come in the form of an invading force, didn't arrive as an alien horde on horseback. It was far more frightening than that. It came through the ayatollahs, Shiite religious leaders, guided by Ayatollah Ruhollah Khomeini. They used to be the most compassionate, holy, and respectful figures in the country, especially among their follow-ers. After they established an iron grip on Iran politics, they turned to the gangs of criminals.

I will tell you how it happened.

2

A SHORT HISTORY LESSON

_____

We Persians know plenty about invasions, beginning with those of the Assyrians and Babylonians. We have a long history of being bystanders as our nation changes shape around us. More recently, the role of conqueror was played by the Russians, the British, and finally the Americans. Attracted by Iran's strategic position in the Middle East—not to mention our natural resources—these foreigners repeatedly altered the course of our history, which explains why Iranians were so enthusiastic about the Islamic Revolution at the outset.

In the early years of the twentieth century, Iran was living under a kind of constitutional monarchy, having shed the archaic notion of the Shah being the "shadow of God on earth." Hopes of actually running our own ship were dashed by the Anglo-Russian Convention of 1907, which divided Iran into three zones. We were outraged, all but the Shah's supporters. Nationalists continued to assert our independence, even briefly recapturing Tehran in 1916, but were brutally suppressed by British and Russian forces who occupied Iran until the end of the First World War. Britain continued to use Iran as a staging ground for exiled White Russians to launch attacks against the Bolsheviks. The Brits were also protecting their interests in the

Anglo-Persian Oil Company (today's British Petroleum). Iran's oil could fuel the British empire forever, if only the political situation could be stabilized. Iran needed a powerful leader. Enter a junior Cossack officer named Reza Khan, who, with British support, staged a *coup d'état* in 1921. No more National Assembly. In 1925, Reza Khan Pahlavi was proclaimed Shah, and his son, Mohammad Reza Pahlavi, was dubbed Crown Prince and heir to the throne.

Reza Khan attempted a comprehensive national make-over. Huge infrastructure projects were commissioned. The judiciary was reformed, also health care and primary education. Travelling abroad for post-secondary education became fashionable, all of this giving rise to a professional middle class. Secular dress codes were introduced, western-style for men, while women were forbidden to wear the chador, the veil worn by Persian women to cover their hair and whole body. The mullahs, the religious leaders, interpreted this as a direct attack upon Islam.

Although indebted to Britain for Iran's progress, Reza Shah turned to Germany and other European nations for assistance in developing further megaprojects. But with the arrival of the Second World War, Britain demanded that the Shah expel all Germans from Iran. Reza Shah refused and declared Iran neutral. As postwar allies, Britain and the Soviets invaded Iran on August 25, 1941, arrested the Shah, and sent him into exile. When the Americans joined the occupying force, there we were, a neutral country under the thumb of three foreign armies. Mohammad Reza Pahlavi, son of the exiled Reza Khan, was installed as the new (more co-operative) Shah of Iran.

Mohammad Reza Pahlavi soon found himself struggling for control of the government against the popular nationalist leader, Mohammad Mossadegh, who became prime minister in 1951. Mossadegh quickly attained hero status by nationalizing the British-owned oil industry. Predictably, the foreign press denounced him as a threat to world peace, leading to a showdown at the UN Security Council where Mossadegh delivered a winning speech on October 8, 1951, and returned home an even greater hero. Britain and America might have been expected to support an emerging democracy like Iran, but such thinking would prove extremely naive.

It appeared as if Mohammad Reza Pahlavi couldn't take the heat, because he left the country on August 16, 1953. The following day, we were surprised to find we had a new prime minister in General Zahedi. Apparently, before he fled, the Shah had signed decrees dismissing Mossadegh and designating Zahedi as prime minister. The CIA publicized photos of the signing. Nationalists demonstrated, but after a bloody battle in the streets of Tehran, Mossadegh was arrested on August 19, 1953. Once again, the British, backed by their American buddies, were in control and Mohammad Reza Pahlavi returned to Iran on August 22, 1953.

The Shah continued the social reforms begun by his father. Peasants became landowners, factories started up, and roads, dams, and railroads were constructed. Health services were enhanced, and an illiterate generation was educated. The city of Tehran took on a western persona with the usual trappings—from liquor stores to movie theatres to high-end fashion boutiques. In 1971, the Shah spent a hundred million dollars to celebrate the 2500th anniversary of the Persian empire (and to glorify his own reign). The entire world took notice. At the same time, the mullahs began to openly criticize the Shah. The exiled Khomeini denounced the Shah as "an enemy of Islam."

While petro-dollars enabled the Shah to continue spending, much of it looked extravagant and even irrelevant to the country's needs. Inflation and economic disparities were causing such widespread resentment that in 1975 the Shah created a one-party state. The secret police (SAVAK) quelled all political dissent. U.S. president Jimmy Carter warned the Shah not to suppress civil freedoms. With the relaxing of press censorship, the Shah began to be seen less as a god and more as a mere mortal. President Carter paid the Shah a visit in 1977, hoping to bolster his status, praising his "great leadership" and giving him credit for making Iran an "island of stability" in a "troubled region of the world." Then, on January 7, 1977, Ayatollah Khomeini was denounced in the press, inciting a religious backlash in which dozens of people were killed, many of them mullahs. That was the tipping point.

Religious fanatics fought back, trashing every symbol of westernization they could find—foreign banks, cinemas, luxury hotels. The Shah proclaimed martial law, resulting in more bloodshed, which not only fuelled more protests throughout the country, but incited Ayatollah Khomeini to call for the overthrow of the Iranian monarchy. From his exile in Paris he appeared on BBC television promising Iranians a government that would embrace the Koran. He promised religious and political freedom, and he promised a free ride for Iran's poor—free rent, gas, electricity, even public transportation. The Shah had to respond, and he did, making his own television appearance, and in a breaking voice he claimed to understand the "revolutionary message" coming from the people, and he supported it, he said, and was ready to atone for past mistakes. It felt like a classic case of too little, too late. The monarchy was finished, I knew it, and in my heart I said goodbye to the Pahlavi dynasty.

Excuse this history lesson. It was typical of me while in prison to spend endless hours rehashing the past. Perhaps I was trying to escape out the back end of my life. All the way to ancient times would have been wonderful, to the days of its great poets and to the enlightened reign of Cyrus the Great. These daydreams were a last defence against the stench of death in that prison, against the hopelessness that lay heavy over me the minute I started to feel sorry for myself.

I had to keep reminding myself who I was.

3

NO GLASS OF SAKE

———

At the time of Ayatollah Khomeini's return to Iran, I was a squadron commander. It wasn't long before he had us doing his dirty work, fighting his personal battle with Saddam Hussein in Iraq, next door. My fighter-pilot training was put to the supreme test against that madman. As pilots, we were living out our purpose in dramatic fashion, and getting high on the adventure of it, I admit. But every time I brought my F-5E Tiger II home upon completing a mission, I reflected upon my many friends whose lives had been snuffed out, not by an honest Iraqi missile barking up their tailpipe, but from the firing squads of our own glorious revolutionary government. Our crime? We had once pledged allegiance to the deposed Shah. Of course we had! It was his air force. He had purchased the jets and sent us to America for pilot training. But that was then, and the brand-new now was the Islamic Revolution. We were living for the present as before, and were no less ready to take off at a moment's notice to repel any and all invaders. In one of the saddest ironies, the life expectancy of Iran's fighter pilots increased proportionally to the pounding we got from our mortal enemy in Baghdad. The more Khomeini needed us to repel Saddam, the longer our lease on life.

Caught between the devil and Khomeini's deep seething mistrust of human nature, we pilots simultaneously loved and loathed that war. Somehow, I survived missions that grew increasingly suicidal. I began to suspect that my missions had no purpose beyond finishing me off. It was Khomeini's twisted take on the once-honourable Kamikaze. Except for us there was no ceremonial glass of sake, no final word to our loved ones, no salute to the flag and to the rising sun, which we'd see no more. With our backs to the wall, we had no choice but to continue doing our duty and hope that our patriotism would shine through, and that it would inspire the regime to forgive us for having flown for the Shah, and would earn us the right to continue defending our country. But I guess they didn't see it that way. And I took the blame for allowing myself to be so bamboozled as to believe that it would be possible to live as a free thinking man in the midst of a fundamentalist revolution.

The more I defied death, the more of a fighting machine I became. One day, however, God must have decided he was spending a ridiculous amount of time keeping this one crazy pilot alive. I was returning from a mission when I found myself committed to a dogfight with Iraqi MiGs. I shot down two of them, but the third one got me. Flying at hundreds of miles an hour and only a few feet off the deck, I had to eject. I should have been killed. Maybe I was meant to be killed—I was certainly at death's door—because from that point on, my life took so many bizarre turns that I became convinced God was making it up as he went along. Lying there in a bloody heap in enemy territory—let's call it the end of my innocence. What better time to realize what those skies actually meant to me. Knowing what a prison Iran had become, the wild blue yonder was not merely symbolic of freedom, it was my only freedom.

While I was having my religious experience (in a state of total paralysis), Iraqi Kurds found me. That was miracle number one. They were rebels, freedom fighters who recognized that we shared a common enemy. They hid me by absorbing me into their midst, and delivered me after a month's trek through the mountains to the Iranian border. In welcoming me back to life, my base commander, Colonel Farzaneh, addressed me as a hero of heroes, "a living martyr." Sounded impossible, but I guess it was true because I had already been officially mourned as dead and gone. The press can never get enough of heroes, and likewise the political propaganda machines. I was brought before Ayatollah Khomeini at Jamaran, his residence located in the northern part of Tehran, and feted as the latest poster boy for the armed forces. Soon afterwards, I wrote the story of my crash and subsequent survival against all odds. *Crash on the 40th Mission* was published and sold out in days. By then, I had been assigned the prestigious position of military attaché to Pakistan, in Islamabad. At the same time, filmmakers went to work dramatizing my book, calling their big-screen production *Eagles*. How appropriate! But I wasn't in Tehran to enjoy celebrity status. The revolutionary government didn't need one more cocky fighter pilot basking in glory.

My sojourn in Pakistan had a three-year time frame from 1983 to 1986, after which I was required to return to Iran. And once back in Tehran, it was a shock to see that Khomeini's Revolutionary Guard was still purging the regime of Shah loyalists. But I was a military attaché and former war hero, almost a pop culture icon; surely I was beyond suspicion. In my own mind, I was still flying high with those eagles of my youth. That is, until the early morning of December 30, 1987, when I kissed my wife and three children goodbye before heading to work.

At that time of morning it was mainly us military types getting a jump on the day. I was on foot, and I remember it was damn cold, but I loved walking. Rush hour hadn't started yet, the shops still shuttered tight, and the stars still crisp in a cold sky. At the end of the lane I would have arrived at the main street, but before I reached it, a car pulled up. A young man got out. He was good-looking with a trimmed beard.

"Are you Colonel Sharifirad?" he said.

I was wearing my flying suit with my rank staring him in the face. "I am."

"I'd like a few words with you." He was polite, but I could see a walkie-talkie antenna sticking out from under his jacket. "Just a few questions," he said, stepping over the gutter.

"What kind of questions?" I asked. "Who are you?"

"We'll explain everything, Colonel, if you'll just get in the car."

The whole polite scenario began to feel eerily familiar, like I'd seen it in a movie or a dream. Was I suspicious? Yes, I was. Was I innocent of any wrongdoing? Yes, absolutely. I was a national hero.

I did as he said. I got in.

4

A TERRIBLE MISTAKE

"Subject is arrested." The driver was on his mobile. "We're heading towards Gisha Bridge—over."

As I feared. But was I worried? Not a bit. My self-esteem was indestructible. A man was innocent until proven guilty, wasn't he? And I was utterly innocent. A stupid mistake, that's all this was. There was absolutely nothing to worry about. Look how willingly I climbed into that car, entirely of my own free will. What more proof did anyone need of my innocence? That's how catastrophically naive I was!

"I want to know where we're going," I said.

They ignored me until we stopped under the bridge, where another car met us and I was transferred into the back seat.

"I'm going to be late for work," I protested.

"Don't worry. We'll drive you there later." In the meantime, I was to wear a blindfold, and suddenly this wasn't a tea party anymore. "Put this on," he said, handing me a bomber jacket that covered my rank. Then it was, "Lie down with your head on my knee."

As the car started up and began to move, I recalled with horror the stories of other pilots who had been arrested. The procedure was identical. I couldn't believe it was happening to me, and my first thought was of my two sons and how I would explain to them the way I'd got into this mess. Would they understand? Would they ever forgive me for not fighting back? All pointless anxiety, because this was nothing but an embarrassing mistake. Somebody was going to lose their job.

We turned left, right, left, right, confusing me. I had no idea what part of the city we were travelling through. When we stopped, I heard a chain rattling through heavy metal bars and a gate opening. We continued forward into what must have been a military base, or a prison of some kind, but I couldn't visualize it. When the car came to a final halt, I was ordered out. Someone pulled me by the hand and led me off. Through an opening beneath the blindfold I could see a few details— my guard's trousers and feet. His feet were bare, in worn-out slippers. I caught a glimpse of a section of old wall, dark with grime. The air was sour with the ingrained stench of urine.

"Duck your head!" he said as we entered a more confined space, which smelled even worse. "Blindfold off."

I was surprised to see how young he looked, despite a full beard. The room was the size of an average apartment bedroom, but dingy, vile, and dark. Overhead, clothes hung from a line, civilian and military articles, and on the floor were pairs of shoes, dusty, ragged, and worn, as if they'd been sitting there a long time. I felt sorry for the guard, a kid, really, no more than twenty-one, and I remember thinking, what a waste of youth. His jacket and trousers were ill-fitting and badly made and shabby brown and blue. No pride of regiment there. His eyes were slightly crossed, poor kid, but somewhere deep down I couldn't help feeling he must have been intelligent. But in a place like this, a person would never find out how smart he was. How strange that I would feel sorry for him.

Then it was, "Boots off," and "Suit off." And on with a striped prison uniform.

"What about shoes?" I asked.

"Only slippers," he said.

They were oversized and mismatched and filthy like everything else, not even the same colour, one of them ripped along the side.

"Do you have something smaller?"

"You'll need large," said the misfit, with a little smirk.

Once I was dressed, he ordered my blindfold back on, and pulled me by the hand through door after door and along what I imagined to be a narrow tunnel at the end of which I heard a heavy door heave open, and he pushed me in. "You can take your blindfold off," he said. "Welcome to your new home."

The space was no more than two metres square, with a high ceiling, maybe four metres. One feeble light bulb in a wire cage, but so high up that its dim light hardly illuminated anything.

"Someone will come," he said, "to brief you about the rules around here. Until then, no noise." He kicked at a piece of cardboard stuck to the floor. "In case of emergency, put it under the door. If somebody sees it, they'll help you."

"And if they don't?" I said.

"Then, they don't," he grunted.

He seemed uncomfortable answering questions, so he retreated, closing the door with a bang, and then making a hell of a noise locking it.

Words like "small and claustrophobic" and "filthy" fall short of describing that cell. I could take two and a half steps, that's all, before hitting a wall; two and half back, another wall. Two and a half, two and a half, nothing but walls. They were etched with lines, some of them small and straight in nervous little rows, obviously meant to keep track of time. Some writing was plain enough, but most of it was obscure, with equally obscure pictures carved into the crude plaster walls. Deciphering the messages was difficult because it was so gloomy in there. But there was no mistaking the images of men with turbans looking like Dracula. What bothered me most were the images I couldn't interpret. No meaning, nothing, just shapes drawn by someone to keep busy. I understood already, and it horrified me. I was in a crypt, crowded by the ghosts of others who'd been here before me, with all their pain and sorrow.

An hour, that's all my incarceration process had taken, but not a second went by that I wasn't examining my past for an explanation for why I deserved to be there. Now that I was in that dungeon and left on my own, that's all I had to do, plus count those lines on the wall and speculate how long I could expect to be in that hellhole. More than a hundred, that's how many were in one batch of scratches. I heard someone outside the door.

"Blindfold on!" It was a different voice this time. A few seconds later it asked me if the blindfold was securely on. I heard the door open, and it was a different person who entered. Through that ragged blindfold, I could see him from his pant cuffs down, another young man, I was sure about it, but this one larger and duller. He started in with the house rules. "No speaking, no yelling, nothing," he said. His voice was rough and uncultured, and also sick. The guy was ill, wheezing, as if with asthma. "No disturbances of any kind in here." Maybe he was getting over a cold. Or perhaps his breathing difficulties were due to a weight problem. He spelled out the bathroom rules, which proved just what a spiritual place this was. If I prayed three times a day, bathroom privileges came three times, otherwise only two. Feedings were three times a day. And during washroom visits, that's the only chance I'd have to wash my dishes. I got two blankets, one to serve as my pillow. "Any questions?" he said.

"Yes, where's the bed?"

He didn't even answer me, just snickered, but before he left, he remembered something else. "Nobody knows who you are in here," he said. "Not your name, your job, nothing. Nobody cares, either. And telling anybody who you are is forbidden."

"If I don't have a name, how will I know if anyone is calling me?"

"You have a number," he said. "Or they'll call you Hadji."

Hadji, pilgrim; he who has been to Mecca. I'd been there. But I had a strong feeling it wasn't going to bring me any special treatment.

"Then, what's my number?" I asked him.

"What time were you arrested this morning?" he said.

"Around five-thirty, six o'clock," I said.

"You're an early bird," he said on his way out. "You're probably 109." He closed the door behind him and slammed shut the small square window in the door as well.

109. There must have been a method in this madness. According to the Iranian calendar, it was the ninth day of the tenth month—that must have been it. I learned later that subsequent arrests on the same day would be labelled 109a, 109b, and so forth. So, I was the first catch of the day!

I paced back and forth until boredom set in. About ten minutes. When I sat on the floor, that's when anger overwhelmed me. What was I doing there? How had I allowed myself to get sealed in this death trap? What was I thinking? The freedom I had been enjoying—it was all an illusion. They'd had me in their sights for years, of course. It was only a matter of time. Of course! There was no place for anyone like me in revolutionary Iran. Cyrus the Great, himself, would have been abducted and imprisoned by the ayatollahs. The thought of it— of realizing how far Iran had fallen from its days of glory—it made me nauseous. For two thousand years that great man had been dead and gone, yet he was our touchstone for all that was true and good. It was a bad time for Iranians who yearned for such greatness, for the kind of morality that grows from a heart free of dogma. I knew this but had kidded myself, chattering on endlessly, naively, about liberty, truth, and respect. You'd have thought that Cyrus the Great was still watch- ing over his empire, a community of nations that willingly laid down their arms in advance of Cyrus's army, waiting to be conquered, for all the humanity he brought to his rule. Since I studied him in grade school, my heart had beat to the rhythm of his wisdom, because after 2500 years he was still alive in those isolated villages. Taleghan, my home. How far I'd come; how quickly I would have returned, if given the chance. Scenes played out on the screen of my mind, episodes in our simple family life, how my mother had confided in me her happi- ness on the day I was born. No wonder I was optimistic! Who wouldn't be? And how proud my father was when I showed an interest in reading the holy books. And the shock I got after asking him what he was saying to God when he prayed. My father had no idea. He didn't know what the words of his prayers meant! They were in Arabic, and we spoke Farsi.

"Doesn't God understand Farsi?" I asked.

"God understands every language," he said, "even the language of birds and four-footed creatures."

"Then why don't you pray in our language?" I asked.

"Because Arabic is the language of the prophet Mohammad," he said. "Our holy book, the Koran, is written in Arabic, and all Muslims around the world must be able to read and write it, so that they can read the Koran."

"Then why don't you understand it?" I persisted.

"No one in our village knows Arabic," said my father, "so no one has taught me."

It was logical, what my father was saying, but still it was crazy. I tried to be respectful, but it wasn't easy. "But, Father, I don't understand why we speak to God in a language we don't understand."

"You're right, my son. Everything you say is absolutely correct. I am ashamed to have no answer for you. Perhaps I am not so curious as you. Someday, your children will interrogate you, and you will do a better job than I did, answering these questions."

From that day forward, I never questioned him about his praying five times a day, and my father never bothered me about religion or God. Cyrus was compassionate in the same way, allowing his subjects to worship as they wished. As for my beliefs, I never mentioned them to anyone. Yes, I continued reading the Koran, hoping it would help me develop a workable belief system, but all it did was breed greater doubts about fundamentalism, leaving me in two minds about religion: to believe any of it or not?

Suffering often brought people to religion, everyone knew that, but what does an enthusiastic child know about that? The peasants in my home village of Taleghan treated me with affection, and in return

I helped them out whenever I could. Love kept us from being poor. Caring for one another, my father's brand of Islam, that was our real religion, and in that I was a believer. A religion based on kindness, on sharing with your neighbour, where people exchanged a smile for a smile and where forgiveness was well known to be better than revenge—much harder than revenge, but much better! In all this I was a believer.

I also believed in luck, because how else to credit my good fortune in being called to take my fighter-pilot training in Phoenix, Arizona? I couldn't have dreamed of anything more exciting. Then my return to Iran and my marriage to Akram and the births of my children, Shahram, Shahrokh and Mahrokh. If there was any doubt that I lived a charmed life, it was shot down in flames when I escaped certain death in the Iran-Iraq War of 1980–1988. Imagine being found by rebel Kurds in enemy territory. As I recounted earlier, they gave me sanctuary until I was strong enough to be secreted back to Iran, where I became a hero, an icon, a symbol for our nation that meant we would survive against all odds. And off to Pakistan I went, as the first Iranian military attaché after the Revolution. All these blessings I remembered, and nothing about them added up to a crime against my homeland. So, I sat there in that stinking cell, expecting at any moment someone to enter and apologize from the bottom of their heart for this horrible mistake. I sat there and sat there. For a long, long time I sat there.

5

NO ROOM SERVICE

I was going to be shot, I knew it. Eyes were watching me through holes in the walls. Eyes behind rifles that were trained on me, waiting for me to make one wrong move. The air was steamy and hard to breathe, even on the floor. Then I realized that the ceiling was low, so low that I couldn't lift my head, could only move it left and right. Searing heat moved from my feet up my body, a burning nauseous wave that filled my heart and head. Someone was pulling my legs, pulling me out of the crypt, then dumped me into a pool of icy water. They made it clear that, this way, I would survive longer to be tortured further. I found that the veil of steam rising off the water hid me, and I could move undetected, and I escaped towards a nearby hill and began to scramble upwards, but not before the guards started chasing me. I made it to the summit, where I faced a precipice, and a thousand-foot drop to a river that emptied into a vast black ocean. I hid in bushes that overhung the cliff and hung on to the thickest branch to avoid falling. I buried my face in the earth so I wouldn't see the enemy approaching, but then I heard the shrubs snapping and the roots giving way, the whole thing disintegrating, and I felt myself falling and I screamed. . . .

I woke up sweating, terrified. The guard opened my cell.

"Why are you groaning? We haven't tortured you yet."

"Nightmare," I said.

Who knows what time it was?

"109! Blindfold on!"

The door heaved opened. Someone grabbed my arm and pulled me out. Down the hall we marched, then up a few stone steps and into another cell.

"Sit!"

He shoved me into a seat. I got the feel of it—a student-type desk you find in schools, with a writing arm attached, but for a left-hander.

"Don't move," he said. "Don't touch your blindfold; don't even tilt your head back. Not a single move. Someone will show up and tell you what's next."

I sat there for hours. Then, more hours. It must have been twenty-four hours that I sat there, and still nobody showed up. Twenty-four hours! Fear of what might be coming kept me from falling into a sound sleep, but twice I dozed off and fell out of the chair. Eventually, I heard some kind of chattering going on in a nearby room, questions and answers, then some crying. Then screaming. Crying to God for help. I could hear the interrogator clearly saying that the only God in there was the God of right answers. The poor guy had no shortage of answers, lots of them good ones, but of course they weren't the right answers. More screaming. From another part of that deadly labyrinth, a woman began a woeful wailing. I could hear them threatening to hang her upside down. If that was supposed to frighten the hell out of me, it succeeded. Fear and fatigue, I had no idea what a deadly drug it was. I was shaking, on the verge of losing it, totally.

My mind began racing backwards again in search of reasons, why, why! Because I spoke my mind? My mental wheels kept spinning but

I could see they were stuck there. Yes! That was it. I had a tendency to stand alone in the truth, it was who I was, I'm sorry, but it seemed to work. That must have been it. So, then it was, What had I said? I had always stood up for my rights as a free man. Big mistake. No ayatollah ever preached individual freedom. Suddenly, I blamed myself, hated myself. Their tactics were working. In my altered state, the past became one vast panorama that I could see in one eyeful, and at the far end of which I saw my birth in that perfect poor village, all the way to this shithole that loomed like the opposite end of anything that could be considered good and fair and just and natural. Perhaps there was a limit to how much grace a person was worthy of in a single lifetime. Maybe I had exceeded my limit. Was this some kind of equalizer? Was this a test?

Two men arrived, finally. I felt dizzy, close to throwing up, and numb all over. What sounded like a leather briefcase landed on what sounded like a table. One of them mumbled something, which I took as a greeting, and I tried to politely answer back. Something being drawn from the satchel, then dropped on the writing arm of my desk. My blindfold suddenly yanked up to my forehead, and in front of me lay a pad of paper with the Iranian Judicial Emblem imprinted on the top, and below it the words "Interrogation Form." The men kept out of sight behind me. I would never see them. Blank paper and a blank wall, that's all I would see. And my chair, which reminded me of elementary school. Actually, it reminded me of final exams. I remembered our supervisor, a real sadist. I even remembered his name, Akbarian. He had what you call an anger management problem. I was terrified of him. I could hear my heart, that's how much it was pounding, just thinking about him. If you turned your head, no matter how innocently, and he thought you were looking at the student beside you, you got thrown out. And flunked on the spot. I had a prayer I used to say—more like wishful thinking—praying that I was smart enough that I wouldn't need to look anywhere. I couldn't tell if I was remembering, or hallucinating.

"Start writing, Hadji. About your life."

"What part?" I said.

"From the time you were born, everything."

Everything? Were they kidding? My life, short as it was—forty-two years old—was already a very long story. "But what in particular?" I asked.

"Everything," he said.

"That'll be a book," I said.

"Let it be a book, then," he said.

This was nuts, but at least it was better than sitting there hallucinating. Perhaps if I started, they'd let me sleep. So, I got set to start. I tried the pen.

"Why was I arrested?" I said.

"Start writing, Hadji!" he yelled. "You'll understand soon enough."

I rested my aching head on my hand. It felt like a sandbag with a slow leak. And my spirit, it was the size of one small grain lost somewhere deep inside. Under pressure, I started thinking, just like at exam time. I was good at exams, and was surprised at what clear recall I had. But first I repeated that child's prayer, then I began.

"I was born on the 24th of March, 1946, in a village named Nesa-Olya, one of a group of villages strung out along the Shahroud River in the Taleghan area of northern Iran."

I immediately thought of how my mother would have chastised me for writing by such a dim light.

"At the age of five I went to a private school and learned to read the Koran and other holy books. Mullah Esmail, that was my teacher's name, and the next year I was taught by Ali-Akbar, Roohel Amin, and after that by Kali Mollah." Names and places, they sprung to mind as if it was yesterday. "At eight years old, by the advice of a close friend of my father's, Bagher Honarpour, I was sent to a regular school in Gooran, a village about four kilometres away. Being so young, it wasn't easy travelling to school and back alone, especially in the winter when snow drifted thick, and foxes and jackals and wolves ran wild. Not that I ever saw a wolf, but I was helpless in the face of bandits. Not that I ran into them either, but one spring day I was forced to run from the

Shahroud River when it roared down from the mountains, thick with mud and carrying boulders until it flooded as high as the branches of the poplars.

"After completing six years of elementary school in four years, it was off to high school, which was located even farther away, a seventeen-kilometre journey back and forth each morning and evening. I remembered the name of that village, Shahrak, as well as the name of the school, Mohammad Rastegar. With the onset of winter it became necessary for me to rent a room with another family until late spring when the roads thawed and drained and dried up and became passable again. Keep in mind that at that time there were no automobiles or buses. Such things I'd only seen in pictures, and I couldn't believe that machines that large could run on a single engine and would actually obey the driver's commands.

"During my time in Shahrak, I somehow managed a weekly visit with my mother and siblings. As for my father, who was a tailor, he was most often away from home, on business in the capital city of Tehran, or off to Abbasabad on the Caspian Sea. Summer was my favourite season because my father hung around home. He and I were very close. I know he loved me because whatever I asked for, he gave. I knew of no other kid whose father had never disappointed him.

"After grade eight, they opened a government high school in Mangolaan, closer to home. But it only had grades seven to nine, so a year later I was sent away again, this time to Tehran, to the home of Amoo Mohammad, my father's cousin. What a different world that was. Though located in the poor district of Shoosh, Uncle's house was a seraglio, a regular sultan's palace, compared to our humble abode in the village. My school was twenty minutes away on foot, which for me, was nothing.

"Uncle Mohammad and his family spoiled me. Had they wanted to adopt me, I was willing, but after a year of this special treatment I was called back to my village. My father had opened a tailor shop in nearby Shahrak, and he decided to supervise my education, himself. To a tailor, an education naturally included tailoring lessons. In my free time, of course. Because I loved him, I grew to love sewing and making alterations, and I guess I learned his lessons well, because when I got married, my wife found I could alter dresses better than she could!"

"Sewing machines! Why are you writing about sewing machines?" He'd been standing behind me reading all this.

I turned around. "You wanted my life story," I said.

He cuffed the side of my face. "Face the wall! And don't write garbage. You're wasting my time."

"I'm sorry. You wanted my story, and that's part of it."

"Keep going, then," he said. "On second thought, give it to me." He snatched away my writing. "I want to see what you've done." He took a few seconds to flip through the pages, during which his shit breath just about knocked me out, as if his bowels were backed up. No wonder they put him to work in a shithole. He left with my pages and came back about two hours later carrying more paper.

"Keep writing," he said. "It wasn't bad."

I began again, centimetre by centimetre, an account of my life:

"For grade eleven, I was back in Tehran, this time billeted with a family in an old house on Ray Street. The landlady was a woman who treated me like her own son, and her son, Mohsen, and daughter, Shekooh, became my best friends. Her daughter and I hung out like two infatuated teenagers. At that time, there was another girl, Noori, whom I liked the most, and if I hadn't been a student, and not so pre-occupied with sports and school work, I'd have asked her to be my girl-friend. But I didn't have time for her and I never asked. We remained friends, though, until I became an air force cadet. Noori must have had some kind of psychological problem about flying, because she imme-diately broke off our friendship, for good. It was weird; I never saw her again.

"In grade twelve, I wound up living on Boozarjemehri Street near the Grand Bazaar of Tehran, only fifteen minutes by foot from Pahlavi High School at Shah Square. I was living with my friend Khodaverdi (who later married my sister), and his brother and one of his cousins. The owner of the house was an old lady who lived with two huge cats in one part of the mansion. The rest of the house she rented out, and I can tell you she spent no money on upkeep. It was such a crowded house that we used to call it *Khaneh Ghamaar Khaanoom* (*The House of Lady Ghamaar*, the name of an old Iranian TV series). We were lodged on the second floor, where we could see everything going on in the yard. One of the residents, Fati, had a steady stream of men and women coming and going from her place. I felt sorry for her nine-year-old son, Reza, who didn't know what was going on, or who the visitors were. But he knew perfectly well they weren't relatives!"

My interrogator returned and slapped more blank pages on my desktop and disappeared. This time, I caught a glimpse of him—overweight and awkward. He reminded me of a film clip I'd once seen—a coroner was holding up a human colon, the large intestine, freshly extracted from an obese corpse. The point of the show and tell was that it contained seventy-five pounds of old shit. You have to understand how vividly I was remembering these things, something close to hallucinations. My headache became suddenly worse, and my mouth drier and my stomach churning. I couldn't hold a train of thought for more than a second, and I was crazy for even a few minutes' sleep. The problem was, I would have passed out for hours.

I woke up to a whack on the head. I must have dozed off.

"What do you think this is?" he yapped. "Your aunt's house?"

He ordered me to finish my story, and quickly. I said that I was done with my school years, but he didn't think so. He wanted more. More about my relations with girls. He definitely wanted me to focus on women, even if it meant jumping ahead to the juicy parts. According to his logic, if I was in the Shah's air force, I must have had unrestricted access to women. I explained that when I returned from pilot training in America, I had married soon thereafter, and was always faithful to my wife.

"What about in the U.S.?" he demanded. "Or before that?"

Did my arrest have something to do with a suspicion of infidelity? The very thought made me relax, because I had a clear conscience. My record in that regard was spotless. Well, almost.

"We know about you," he said. "You and your womanizing in America and here in Iran." The way he said it, and the way my brain was malfunctioning, I wondered if I'd forgotten something. "Tell us everything," he said. "Names included. Then we'll be finished. If not, you'll be here for a while."

The truth was that I'd had girlfriends in the United States, two of them. In San Antonio, Texas, there was Leonore, and in Phoenix, Arizona, it was Karen. The relationships never got too serious because we weren't allowed to marry American girls. Otherwise, there were girls around all the time, but we were just friends. But this was none of their business. What especially bothered me was having to explain myself according to the Islamic Revolution. It's not that I wasn't a Muslim—in fact, I had a great fondness for the kind of Islam my father practised, a religion based on kindness. To him, revenge was easy, and forgiveness the difficult and rewarding practice. These animals were fixated on nothing but revenge. That's not a religion, it's a mental illness.

"That's it," I said. "You know everything about my love life."

I had a feeling that my teenage adventures weren't going to satisfy his perverted curiosity. I thought about inventing something a little juicier, just to satisfy him. That's when another memory stuck its head out of my deep past. It wasn't so much a repressed memory as a protected one—about one more girl back in my village; she smelled like God's perfumed rain. She had always stayed with me, like a second sun in the skies of my youth. To hell if I was going to titillate those bastards by telling them that story.

"There's nothing else to say," I said. I was totally exhausted.

"When you were the military attaché in Pakistan," he said, "who was your closest friend?" He was wheezing and getting short-tempered. "Who did you meet most often?" I couldn't stand his shit-stained breath.

"Other military attachés," I replied. "Occasionally I met ambassadors when headquarters asked me to."

"Tell me about them," he said.

"That'll take a month," I said.

"Take a year if you have to!" He kicked the leg of my chair. "All of them! I want to hear about every meeting you had. Every detail."

My mind started playing tricks on me—it went blank. How many days had I not had any real sleep? Three, maybe four.

"I really need to sleep," I said.

"Sleep? You want sleep? Where do you think you are? In a five-star hotel? Shall I call room service? Have your shoes shined? Answer my questions! That's all we do in this hotel, Hadji—you answer my questions! Do you understand?" He kicked my chair again.

My neck couldn't support my head, that's how heavy it felt. And my fingers fumbled the pen and it fell to the floor. It occurred to me, out of nowhere, to surrender. Death was preferable to being led down this road. I knew I was coming apart. I couldn't even understand what he was saying anymore, but the pressure to provide answers didn't let up. He kept threatening me, but his words were distant and meaningless. I shrunk within my own little cocoon, terrified, wondering what would happen if he kept making these demands I couldn't understand, and what kinds of demands they might be. My nervous system couldn't cope with it. I felt myself weak and powerless, trapped in a hole with no exit as if I was dying slowly.

"Our intelligence reports indicate that you were in contact with American diplomats in Pakistan, and that you agreed to spy for them."

I got it—they were throwing out any accusation they could invent, barking up any old tree just to see what they could scare out of it. His claim didn't deserve a response, so that's what I gave them—nothing.

"Are you going to tell us about it?" he asked. "Yes or no? Yes, and we'll let you sleep. Is it a deal?"

That kind of bait didn't work on me. I couldn't confess to something that wasn't true. I wasn't made that way.

"No thanks," I said.

They hauled me up by the arms and led me off to another cell, one already occupied by an old man, and proceeded to hang me upside down by my ankles. I guess it was torture for him as well, since he started crying like a baby at the sight of me hanging there. Time had lost all meaning—all I remember is that I hung there until I passed out. When I came to, again, I was on the floor, alone but for that kindly old man who encouraged me to fall back asleep.

I was kicked awake and hauled off again and thrown into a cell with another older man, an army colonel by the name of Soltani. He had recently been the adviser to the chief of staff, General Zaheer-Nejad. Soltani was interested in knowing what I'd been accused of and why I was there. Before I had the chance to talk, he recounted the torture he'd undergone, both mental and physical. He'd been caught trying to escape over the border into Turkey. For more than a year and a half, he'd been in solitary confinement, sick and unable to see properly, and of course they'd taken away his eyeglasses.

His story horrified me, since the charges they'd trumped up against me of spying were potentially more serious than the colonel's crime. I knew very well that in the armed forces, spies get a bullet to the head. Or worse, a public hanging. From a construction crane. I began to wonder if perhaps I had responded too proudly to the interrogator's questions. But I didn't take it lightly, being falsely accused and humiliated. I was innocent, so my confidence came naturally. And what's more, I expected to be freed at any moment. But after three or four days without sleep, and the constant pressure of all that writing, I knew I could easily lose it, and if I fought back, well, that would be the end of me.

After some sleep, and after hearing more of Soltani's story, my mind emerged a little clearer. I challenged my memory of the Iran-Iraq War, searching for better reasons why I had been arrested. I reflected on the friends I'd lost, pilots who had not hesitated to risk their lives to strike well-guarded targets deep in Iraq. I recalled the first day of the war, moments before Iraqi planes surprised us with an attack on our base in Tabriz. . . .

I was in the command post preparing the schedule for the next day. It was early afternoon, about 1:45 on September 22, 1980. The building shook with a massive explosion. Ceiling tiles crashed down, and phones bounced off tables. I tried to call Base Commander Colonel Farzaneh, but the line was dead. All the lines were out. I rushed for the door, curious to see what had happened, when I ran into Colonel Farzaneh storming in. He was shaking, his voice breaking as he, too, tried all the phones.

"The lines are down, sir," I said.

He was angry, but I was angrier. We'd had no warning! Nothing! How could our intelligence have been so—hell, it was non-existent. And, more important, why hadn't we received the order to take off after the Iraqis?

"This isn't the time for recriminations, Sharifi," he said. "Just get every available pilot in here."

I did as he ordered, sent soldiers to roust pilots from their homes, although I was sure they must have been mobilizing already. Within minutes we were arrayed in the command post, at attention, and waiting for orders. You could sense the uncertainty about us, all of us—because it was war! Here, finally! We collaborated on a quick plan for retaliation in which I was selected to lead the first attack. We were suiting up when the order came down from above to hold off any action until early in the morning.

A faint sound outside the cell door brought me back to the present. I stiffened, expecting my number to be called out. That fat bastard! My nervous system was chafed down to the bare wires, and I'd been anxious about having to walk because my feet were still painfully numb from hanging. My heart was pounding at the thought of being taken back to the interrogation room. I didn't think I could handle any more sleep deprivation.

"You can do it, man," the colonel said. "I know you can."

But I barely heard him. My mind was already racing ahead, but it couldn't outrun the grim reality.

"109! Blindfold on!"

The door opened. The guard grabbed my arm and led me out.

6

SPY LIKE ME

———

It was the guard with a head like an eggplant. Don't blame me if that's not accurate, but that's what I conjured up, since I'd only had the briefest glimpse of him. My imagination took over from there. I actually felt sorry for that guy. He led me down the corridor to a room that looked much the same, with a school-type chair with the writing arm on the wrong side. He left me alone for an hour or two, until I heard the faint but rising rustle of approaching evil. The door opened and I sensed that same fat bastard who had interrogated me previously. When he dropped more sheets of paper in front of me I noticed a soup stain on his sleeve. Even a grain of rice lodged under a button at the cuff.

"Hello," he said. Sounded like he was my best friend, suddenly.

"Hi," I said.

"Did you have a good sleep?"

"If you can call it sleep," I said.

"Hadji, I'm trying to be nice. You co-operate, and this will go off without a hitch. Otherwise, I could become my old self again."

His words were punctuated by a scream from a nearby cell. Someone else being politely encouraged to co-operate. If their battle plan was for me to feel that fellow's pain, it worked like a dream.

"Are you listening to me?" he asked. I nodded. "So, are you going to co-operate and tell me the truth? Or are you going to give me answers like you're hearing in the next room?"

"I am co-operating," I said. "I don't have a reason not to, because I have nothing to hide."

"Then how do you explain what we found in your house?"

"What?"

"What your wife told us."

"You've arrested my wife?"

"At least *she's* working with us. She told us everything."

"You have my wife in custody?"

"We had no choice," he said.

Suddenly, I understood the meaning of torture. Nothing that had happened so far was as painful as the suggestion that Akram was in their hands. All I could do was suffer through listening to that asshole. He told me that she'd confessed. "Confessed what?" Something I'd been keeping from them? It wasn't possible.

It was a relief to know she was taking the course of least resistance, and I didn't blame her, almost admired her intelligence, because I was pretty unsure about mine, suffering like this. But I couldn't imagine what she might have said, since she knew next to nothing of my military life. I had a strong feeling to hold the course, and continue defending myself.

"Why would I lie?" I asked.

"Only you know that, Hadji," he said. "We found a digital radio at your house."

"What radio?" I asked.

"And lists of names and telephone numbers."

"What radio? All we've got at home is a plastic radio," I said.

"You're not the first spy to use such a thing," he said.

I was speechless. I mean, if they were planting evidence, then I was doomed. They could say anything they wanted.

"You don't mean that black plastic radio?" I said. "You can buy those at every second shop in the bazaar! If it can be used for espionage, nobody told me." The idiocy of this accusation totally threw me off my optimistic dream of getting out of that crypt by telling them the truth. "Spy on who? And why? Why would I need to spy?"

I could have strangled that moron, and almost did, until I sensed that if I kept on talking about my military career, he would be convinced.

"I was the military attaché in Pakistan," I explained. "My work was monitored. I was being watched. Everyone was, by internal spies keeping a sharp eye on everyone. It was a condition of employment. If I had acted suspiciously, they would have dealt with me. Take a look at my record. During the war with Iraq I was a top fighter pilot, and I became a war hero after surviving a crash in Iraq."

"Saved by the Kurds," he said.

"Yes!" I responded. "And God bless them!"

"Are you sure it wasn't the Americans?"

Suddenly, it hit me—there was no point in arguing, no point in lying, and no point in telling the truth. They would hound me until they got a confession. It didn't matter how long it took. They were totally in charge of a horribly sick game.

"I'll sign whatever you want," I said. "Just write it out, and I'll sign it. You win."

"Not that easily, Hadji," he said. "Tell us what you know, then you can go. Like your wife."

"You let her go?" I asked.

"We kept her here one night only. She understands."

"Where is she now?"

"In a better place than you," he said, smirking. "And you can count on staying here until you decide that you want to be back home with your wife and children."

I was highly suspicious, since Akram knew next to nothing about my military work. Wives never did. It was a condition of military life, and they accepted it. These assholes knew that, too.

"You invited an Argentinian to Iran," he said.

"The Argentine chargé d'affaires," I said.

"Why? Why him?"

"We became friends in Pakistan," I said. The answers were so simple, and I gave it to him in all the detail I could. How, for instance, this Argentinian had arrived in Iran after his tour of duty in Islamabad was over. He wanted to visit this country as a tourist before returning to Argentina, which, you have to understand, was halfway around the world, and not a trip he was likely to ever take again. While he was in Tehran, he dropped around to bid me a final goodbye. But, of course, for my interrogator, the truth was just more grist for his mill. How did he become my best friend? he asked. Didn't I know he was a CIA agent? I shot back that I wasn't responsible for what that fine fellow was or wasn't, but that from the first time I met him at a reception at the Iranian embassy during our National Day celebrations, he struck me as being a highly professional diplomat. But everything I said was undermined by more pseudo-intelligence, such as reports that this supposed CIA agent and myself had met on many occasions, including in my own home. At the risk of repeating myself, I reminded him that I was the military attaché, and therefore had the authority to meet with anybody who might benefit Iran, sometimes many times, especially if I thought they had goods for sale that might upgrade our armed forces, or could provide information that would assure our victory over Iraq.

"Did you buy anything from him?" he asked.

"He offered some kind of military tent," I said. "Quite cheap too. So I passed the specs along to headquarters. But they turned it down as we were well supplied in that department."

This fat, shit-breathing moron kept on me about this friendship, this special friendship I had developed with the Argentinian, and he wanted to know how we could have become such bosom buddies in such a short time. I told him that if he didn't believe me, there was nothing I could do about it. I was exhausted.

"You played tennis with him."

"Yes, so?"

I had the urge to call him what he was, an imbecile, but provoking him couldn't possibly help, so I continued as calmly as possible, and even enjoyed describing my job in detail, since I'd had to keep it entirely to myself, over the years. I described how, as a diplomat, I'd had excellent relations with many government representatives, especially from countries that had a supportive relationship with Iran. Argentina was one such country. When diplomats were invited to my house, there was no reason why the Argentinian wouldn't have been invited as well, so that would account for the many occasions at which we met.

Unfazed by anything I said, he referred to a sheet of paper upon which were listed everybody I'd ever known in my life, or so it seemed. "Brigadier General Tirmezi," he said.

"Pakistani military attaché in Iran," I said.

"Correct—how did you meet him and what do you think of him?"

I began to wonder if it might be possible to actually bore this guy to death by telling him the details of our first meeting, the only strategy I could think of. So I slowed down, collected my storytelling wits and explained where I'd first met General Tirmezi, who was my counterpart here in Iran. I met him in Tehran, in one of those high-class restaurants on Fereshte Street, accompanied by Colonel Beigi, the head of Iranian Foreign Protocol Affairs. It was a cool night with the threat of rain in the air. We both ordered steak, since the restaurant was a steak house, and I distinctly remember it being very delicious, the most delicious I'd eaten in a long time, streaked just the right amount with fat, and done perfectly, seared on the outside and red on the inside. I carried on describing this meal in ridiculous detail, until my interrogator switched to the Australian military attaché. He'd sent me a personal letter after my mission in Pakistan was over.

"That's right," I said. "It's called friendship. Would you like me to explain it to you?"

Apparently—now, follow closely—while introducing me to their ambassador in Tehran, the Aussie had called me by my first name. From this insignificant detail, this fat baboon concluded that I was a double agent, conspiring with international intelligence against Iran. Once again, the truth was just so tediously boring that I couldn't help obliging this sorry excuse for a human being.

"When I left Pakistan, most of my fellow military attachés came to Islamabad Airport to see me off," I explained. "But the Australian you're trying to incriminate wasn't among them, because he was out of town. So, that's the reason for the letter—to apologize! And to thank me for my co-operation within the attaché corps while I served in Pakistan."

"We'll break you, Hadji," he said. "We'll break you wide open and pick the truth out of your brain, word by word."

With those words of encouragement, he left the room.

7.

NO GOD IN HERE

As hard as I tried, I couldn't figure out why they'd arrested me. Not a single memory caused me a ripple of guilt. The questions of my interrogators provided no clue, either, since they were inconsistent. From an adjacent room a woman's scream paralyzed me. She was calling to God for help.

"No God in here," came the answer. "And if there is, he doesn't listen to a *moshrek*." Infidel. "You are *mofsede fel-arz!*" he snarled. Crap on earth, that's a close translation. "The truth or else!" Or else he'd hang her and feed her carcass to a pack of wild dogs.

Goons torturing a woman—how barbaric! How inhuman! Nothing brought me closer to losing faith than that. Nothing that happened in that hellhole sickened my heart more than that. Of all the pain I suffered, nothing was less forgivable than that, and I swore to hold the ayatollahs responsible for it, no matter how much I may have taken blame for my own misfortune.

Somebody brought me *adass polo*, rice mixed with split peas. But who could eat? My mouth was dry as concrete, and my head teetered on my neck like a bowling ball. I couldn't believe the situation I'd crash-landed in. Truly, it was worse than ejecting in enemy territory.

Still, I expected to snap out of the nightmare. Nausea reminded me that this was the real thing, and that the screams were real, and that my wife was in danger as well. That was more real to me than anything.

I tried to eat, but couldn't swallow. My throat felt chapped. I wanted to weep, and not just whimper, but to explode into tears. Then I thought of my two sons, Shahram and Shahrokh, and what they'd think, seeing their father crying. The thought of them sparked a memory of that first day of the war, and my return home that evening and the boys running towards me. . . .

"Daddy, I saw the Iraqi plane!" Shahram yelled. "It was black, the same as the C-130! I was playing with my friend when it dropped the bomb! My friend fell down and hid behind the wall!"

My younger son, Shahrokh, wouldn't be outdone. He'd seen it too! "When it exploded"—he was out of breath—"Mommy was scared, but I wasn't."

Akram remained silent with tear-filled eyes that wouldn't look at me, since she knew what this meant.

"What are you going to do?" she asked, when we were alone.

"Retaliate," I said.

"When?"

"It's better if you don't ask."

Akram went to bed. I followed her shortly afterwards, but I couldn't sleep for the thudding of my heart. She must have heard it. I eased myself out of bed and went to the kitchen, where I wrote her a note. The words are burned into my memory:

My Dear Akram,

As you know, we are at war now, and I'm a pilot trained for days just like this, to defend my country and our people. The Iraqis must know we're preparing to strike, so I don't know how it's going to turn out. But before anything happens, I would like to give you some advice to consider:

1. If I don't return, take good care of the kids. Train them well and teach them to be patriots, and to always be prepared, prudent, and full of energy, and to always be patient and brave.

2. Accept that I'm gone, but rest assured that you won't be the only one who's lost a husband to this war.

3. Don't grieve too much. What's lost is lost. Get on with your life. And remember that if I don't return, your responsibility to live a full life will be doubled—one for yourself, and secondly for me.

4. Don't let the children see my absence as mere emptiness. Remind them that my death is a rich one, full of sacrifice for my country, and for our independence and freedom.

5. Goodbye, my love. Goodbye, Shahram. Goodbye, Shahrokh.

"You're not eating!" It was the interrogator.

"You want it?" I said.

"You better eat something," he said. "We need you alive for a while longer."

"You warm my heart, knowing how concerned you are for my welfare," I said.

He remained behind me, out of sight, leaning over and turning pages that lay on the desk in front of me. He stopped. "Who's Captain Lorry?"

"The American navy attaché," I replied.

"We know you kept his phone number in your personal address book."

"That's right, he was a member of the corps, the military attachés corps. We met together every month, all of us, all the attachés. We discussed how we were being treated by the Pakistani authority. If Lorry couldn't make it, we were supposed to call him later. To brief him."

"Did you show him any information about Iran?"

"No, why should I?"

"You tell me, Hadji!"

And so it continued, just like that, the interrogator trying to over-turn rocks that weren't even there, searching for what? Snakes? Some slippery thing I might have done, digging for information that I must have leaked about Iran. Silence only infuriated him, so I would keep talking, anything, vague memories. For instance, I'd spoken with some officer in the office of the German military attaché, who wanted to know how many Afghan refugees were encamped in Iran.

"Did you provide him an answer?"

"Yes, I did."

"Where did you get the information?"

"It was common knowledge," I explained. "Everybody had access to *Jane's Magazine*, the military journal, and that info had appeared in a recent issue. And in return for this scrap of information, the Ger-man passed me some relevant intelligence that I forwarded to head-quarters."

"I guess we'll have to keep your wife one more day," he said.

"I'm not lying!" I insisted.

"Of course you are!" he shouted. "You're a spy!"

There were two possible courses of action, I figured. Either stran-gle this moron, or continue my strategy of boring him to death. So, I continued to paint a detailed picture of life as an attaché, describing my everyday contacts with diplomats, and how it had always been carried out in an open and public manner, with no secrets at all, with every encounter written up and duly reported to headquarters. All they had to do was check my file to verify the truth of what I had been saying.

"You lied to everybody," he said.

I fought hard against caving in. I would have regretted it forever. But it took all my willpower, especially when he brought up that little radio again, and wanted to know on what frequency the Americans had broadcast to me. I took a deep breath and tried to sound like a bureaucrat.

"It was a Sony, sir," I said. "Twelve bands. You've probably got one, yourself."

"Why does every spy have such a radio in their home?"

"Every Iranian has one. In their kitchen, probably. That's where we keep ours. We listen to music and the news, soccer, things like that. Probably all over the world, people are listening to their little Sonys in their kitchens. It's a good time to listen, while you're cooking. Does that make us spies? If a radio makes an Iranian a spy, then our country is crawling with them."

"Do you believe in the Holy Koran?" he demanded.

I guess he'd had enough of radios. "Of course I believe in the Koran," I said.

He started to read *Soreh Maedeh*, a verse about activities traitorous to Islam. "Spying against Islam is against God and his prophet," he said. "Spies must be killed for their wrongdoing. Do you understand?"

"Absolutely," I said.

"Well then, you'll be executed, won't you, Hadji?"

It was like having a rope around my neck. Every time I squirmed, one way or the other, the noose only tightened.

"Such a shame," he said. "The truth could change your death sentence."

"To life in prison?" I said. "No thanks."

He slapped the back of my head.

Up to this point, my belligerence had masked my fear, but I began to hyperventilate and sob uncontrollably. Tears soaked the bottom of the blindfold and trickled to my mouth, and I can still remember the salty taste.

He forced me to my feet. "I make spies talk," he said. "It's my specialty." He pushed me ahead of him into the corridor and on into another room, where I sensed more people present.

Under my blindfold I could see a bed frame, a military type of bed, and a bucket of red water. I was shoved face down on its criss-cross metal webbing. It was hardly a bed, really, just two iron bars, one at the head and one at the foot, and for springs, only a metal mesh, like a schoolyard fence. My shins were fastened to the bar with rope, while my hands were cuffed to the bar at the head of the frame, and I was stretched so tightly that my abdomen only barely touched the mesh. Every joint in my body screamed with pain, and especially all my old injuries. I don't know how or why, but I had a good idea what those sons of bitches were going to do, those *maadar Jen...ha—sons of bit...es.* (I didn't have an arsenal of profanity foul enough to describe my feelings.) To distract myself from the suspense of what was coming, I recalled my friends who were killed in the war. They were luckier, I figured, for having been killed in action. They didn't have to suffer this slow death. I appealed to God, asking if my sins, whatever they were, deserved this much punishment. But I couldn't concentrate, not even on God, so I tried simply to remain quiet, but that too was impossible. I made them a deal.

"Untie me and I'll write you whatever you want!"

They laughed. "The American spy wants to make a deal!"

"I'll sign anything. You can even shoot me!"

It was just the encouragement they needed to start flogging the soles of my feet with a rubber cable, all in the name of Allah, if you can believe it. Those bastards! Allah, the beneficent and merciful! The blows found every nerve ending and laid it bare, sending my body into shock, and automatically I started calling God to help me.

"No God here, Hadji!" they yelled. "Better you ask help from the Americans. A little louder! They can't hear you!"

I pleaded my innocence. What a useless effort that was. I lost track of the number of hits to my feet and ribs. I couldn't take it anymore. I lost my last shreds of self-control, and cursed them without end. *"Ahmagh-ha—Idiots! Haraamzadehaa—bastards!"* Of course, they weighed into me all the more until the pain was beyond anything I could have imagined, and my limbs went numb and I was unable to even identify the boundaries of my body, which I took to mean that I was dying. I remember howling defiance until someone sat on my back and gagged me with a filthy blanket. The body went cold. More dying. Between each lashing, I felt vomit rising in a body that was not only freezing but drifting off into fainting, and everything flattened out into a two-dimensional mosaic of pain and noise and memory, all upon a vast plain of disappointment. In this altered state, I couldn't possibly have cared about anything.

When I opened my eyes, I was in a strange cell. Alone. My feet were swollen to twice their size, and bright red with monstrous blisters on the soles, and unbelievably painful. I was raw all over, worn right through the veneer of my character. Whoever I used to be, superficially, was gone, burned off like a thin layer of fog, leaving me cynical about anything my mind might come up with, especially notions about being a hero. For whom was I trying to be a hero? Tears streamed down my face. Thinking and feeling had given up vying for my attention because I had surrendered. Is this what the Revolution was about? Is this what our leader was about? I must have not quite hit rock bottom because I still had the wherewithal to despise this so-called revolution. I was thinking again about what a freak the Ayatollah Khomeini was, a mutation who had grown like a fungus upon the stumps of his arrested development, from his utter failure as a human being. Drained of spirit and hope, I lapsed into dreaming of another time.

The war against Iraq, I always came back to it. It was a time when I loved my country and willingly risked my life. In the beginning I was full of respect for the main principles of the Revolution (independence, freedom, the Islamic republic). Ask anyone. Sure, they'd also tell you that I spoke my mind, that I didn't hesitate to state my opinions, and as time passed I turned critical of our political leaders and openly shared my suspicions. Things like that have to be aired out, or you go crazy. I spoke out about Iran's fighting men, pilots in particular, who should have been treated with more respect. I didn't want to hear any more bullshit claims that we were rebels or insurgents. The few of us who remained alive worked harder than before, harder than before Khomeini's purge of the Shah's sympathizers. Our duty as pilots had doubled, since we were half as many. I appealed to the government to be more careful when sending its pilots on missions. But they couldn't forget that most of us had earned our wings in America.

For a short while we'd enjoyed a privileged lifestyle—officers' clubs, complete with bars. For having tasted these freedoms, many of my buddies were considered rebels, and executed without trial—thirty-one of my fellow pilots in the summer of 1980—hung in public, like social scum. To give credit where it's due, President Abolhassan Banisadr tried to save some of the pilots, but the clerics rushed most of them to their executions before the president could bring his influence to bear on the situation. Those not killed were re-educated in the evils of the Shah and America, the "Big Satan," then ordered back into their cockpits to fly suicide missions against Saddam Hussein. Some of those pilots defected at the first opportunity, but the rest continued to fly mission after mission, until their luck ran out, their patriotism completely overlooked, their true martyrdom uncelebrated. What more proof did they need that we, as a fraternity of fighters, loved our country?

Would better treatment of pilots have served the Revolution? I thought as much and said as much, because I was optimistic that things would turn around, and that as the Revolution matured, things would get better. But my arrest changed all that. The courts didn't care who you were, or how well you carried out your responsibilities. "Judge Blood" found everyone guilty, over six thousand, according to one report—men, women, and children. He was one of Khomeini's revolutionary prosecutors, Sheik Sadeq Khalkhali. When asked how he would rationalize an innocent person dying on his gallows, he said, "An innocent executed by my judgment dies for the cause of the Revolution and Islam, and goes to paradise." International human rights organizations protested these executions without trial, but Ayatollah Khomeini gave them a legal lesson: "Criminals should not be tried," he said. "The trial of a criminal is against human rights. Human rights demand that we should have killed them in the first place. In our belief, criminals must be killed without a trial."

Clearly, our own leaders were more lethal than the Iraqi army— that's what you call "the enemy within."

8

TA-ZEER

Days passed, I lost count. Only by our dismal little rituals did I know roughly the time of day. At four o'clock in the morning, the radio blared with *Azan,* the call to prayer. Every day it was another mournful tune designed to break the heart in two. Sadness saturated me to the soul. The guard would then show up with the blindfold prior to my stepping out of the cell, where I'd stand outside the door. I could hear the others going through the same motions until the order was given and we'd hold each other's shirttail or put a hand on the shoulder of the man in the front for a march to the washroom. At one point along the hallway, I would occasionally see a shred of sunlight through the blindfold. It made my heart beat harder and renewed my desire to see the sun and the sky and all of nature. It was such a fleeting pleasure, yet it nourished me greatly.

One by one, we took our turns entering the filthy latrine. Inside, we could remove the blindfold to complete our ablutions in preparation for morning prayers. With cold water and the same dirty bar of soap, we would wash our dishes—a red plastic bowl, a mug, and a spoon. A few minutes were all we had to accomplish these tasks, since the lineup had to keep moving. Any delay and the guards would clobber us. Back on went the blindfold, back into the line again, hanging on to another anonymous prisoner. No one spoke, or moved. We only breathed. Sometimes I could hear them, those poor wretches, heard the pain in their breath, sometimes seeing their feet from under my blindfold. What heart-wrenching affection I felt for them. When the last prisoner finished, we marched or limped back to our cells in the same manner as we came.

Soon after the cell door closed, I would hear the sounds of two young food servers beginning their rounds. My little window would open and a portion of *barbari* bread would appear, with a small piece of *paneer* (cheese) and four *ghand* (sugar cubes). The second server retrieved my mug and filled it with chai. This was breakfast, and we were allowed to eat it before or after *namaaz* (morning prayer). No one was checking to see if I was praying, but I liked it. It was like having someone to talk to, and it led to an exploration into the possibility of God. If such a force existed, I didn't want to be entirely without faith. Just that small amount helped me regain some hope for my situation.

Lunch and dinner went the same way. The most common dish was *aabgoosht* with broth, an almost tasteless mash of potatoes, peas, and beef, sometimes lamb, often left over from previous leftovers. At other times we had *khoresht*, a more highly spiced mixture of rice and meat.

After a week or so, my feet shrunk back to their regular size, but the blisters remained like walnuts. Unable to put weight on them, I moved mainly by walking on my toes. One day, I was ordered to face the opposite wall while someone entered, the usual drill. He had a gift for me—another pad of blank writing paper, a "gift" from my interrogator.

"Answer the questions," he said. "He'll be back for them later."

"What questions?" I asked.

"You know the questions," he said.

This pointless exercise actually became a pleasant diversion for me, keeping me busy for the best part of the day, even though I only explained everything all over again. I was careful not to write any less or any more than I'd written before. Something missed or something added would have made trouble for me. So, I filled the pages and waited, and waited, and waited. Twenty-four hours passed and the interrogator didn't show up. Naturally, I couldn't sleep. During this wait, I had an unscheduled urge to use the toilet, so I slipped the appropriate piece of cardboard under the door. The guard approached, and speaking with a Turkish accent, I heard him say, *"Na, nemishe."* No toilet for me.

"It's urgent," I said. "I can't hold it."

"Two hours," he said.

"I can't wait for two hours," I said.

"Be man marboot neest." Not my problem. And then it was *"Aghaa, ziyaad harf mizani!"* And you talk too much.

I talk too much? It must have been a joke. Or else he'd been listening to my prayers. That was okay with me. He closed my window, leaving me alone and knowing that I couldn't wait for two hours, not even two minutes. I yelled for help, which only loosened my bladder to the point of leaking down my trousers. I pissed right there, but from the smell of that place, I wasn't the first to foul his cell. What upset me, though, was wetting my blanket—it couldn't be helped in that tiny space.

Next morning, after breakfast, I was led to the interrogation room and sat facing the wall. I heard my interrogator approach. I knew him by the heavy footfall and the wheezing. His shit breath had become as oppressive as bad wallpaper.

"You pissed in your cell—why?"

"Why?" I would have laughed if my feet hadn't been in so much pain. Anyway, expressing emotion wasn't recommended in there, and I was one frayed nerve away from strangling that asshole.

"I couldn't hold it," I said.

"Do you piss in your home?" he asked.

"At home, I have a toilet," I said. "If I have to piss, I use it. I don't need permission from anyone."

What could he say to that? Such a fat idiot. He reverted to his usual complaints, that I was giving him the same old information, the "same old garbage."

"Sorry," I said.

He accused me of wasting my "free time," the time he'd so graciously allowed me to "rest and think," as if I'd squandered some sort of god-damn holiday.

"Sorry," I said.

Predictably, he demanded the "right" answers, and warned me how serious my situation was becoming, and how I was heading for a long stay in there, probably forever.

"I'm sorry," I said. "Sorry that you can't appreciate the truth."

"You're going to be sorry," he said.

"I'm sorry I can't invent the story you want to hear. If you give me an outline, I could fill it in. I'll even sign it."

He seemed almost happy to play this stupid game, such a charge he got out of accusing me of lying. He especially loved all that phony-goodwill b.s., explaining that he'd done all he could to give me the opportunity to reduce my death penalty to a long-term prison sentence. But apparently, I didn't want to help myself. Or my family. Apparently, I didn't even care about my wife. Apparently, my life was filled with extramarital sex. What could I do in the face of this madness? I remained silent. So, he moved on to another subject—videotapes.

"You have a movie collection," he said. "Why?"

"I like movies. You don't like movies?"

"Movies from the time of the Shah? No. But you, you like every-thing about the Shah. And the way things used to be then."

"If I was such a fan of his," I said, "I would have left the country when he did."

"Your wife," he said, "why didn't she cover her head in Pakistan? Cover her head in public, why?"

"Ask her yourself. You say you have her here."

He accused me of failing as a husband. A good husband is respon-sible for educating his wife about how to appear in public. I explained that I didn't have time for such things, since I was fully occupied with official business, acting as Iran's representative in Pakistan for our armed forces, and for my country as a whole.

"And as a spy for the CIA," he said.

I laughed, couldn't help myself, his accusation was so absurd. "No, sir, I am not a spy."

"You are the follower of Reza Shah, King Reza, who had stolen the *hejaab*, the veil, stolen it from our women in 1933! You and your wife are not only anti-revolutionary, but you're anti-imam, anti-Ayatollah Khomeini and Islam! We kill people like you, don't you know that?"

He left the room, but returned minutes later, and this time he was all business. He grabbed my arm and pushed me into the corridor and along to the cell I dreaded most—the one with the two-man goon squad whose specialty was fastening people to that bed frame. They took even greater delight in doing it again, and slashing my feet as before. As you can imagine, it didn't take many hits before the blisters opened and the puss splattered out, then the blood. They untied me.

"The bucket! Stand in the bucket! And walk!"

As I walked on the spot, they demanded the truth, or it would be more of the same.

"I've told you everything I know," I said. Those chalk-heads, those sons of bitches! "Isn't it obvious that there's been a mistake!" I yelled. "You're torturing an innocent man!"

One of them stepped towards me, but I figured he was bluffing, so I continued my walking in the bucket, one foot at a time.

"Torture?" he said. "But, Hadji, this isn't torture, this is *ta-zeer*."

Ta-zeer, the Koranic word ordained by the clergy for this kind of "persuasion."

"It feels like torture to me," I said.

"Your feelings aren't important."

"I'm beginning to understand that," I said.

Back to the bed, shins tied to one iron bar, hands cuffed to the bar at the head end. They laughed, trying to decide which gauge of cable to use on me. Then came Allah, the invoking of Allah as one of my torturers started to thrash my feet, and all I could think of was that nothing on earth could possibly be more evil and unpardonable. Torture in the name of God? The thought gave me strength, knowing that my belief in Allah, however basic it may have been, was profound compared to that held by these animals.

They gagged me when I started screaming.

"If you're ready to talk, move your finger," the interrogator said.

With that dirty blanket halfway down my throat, I thought for sure I was going to die. With each hit, the pain exploded out every nerve ending. Then an especially sharp pain flared under my fingernails. My left hand must have been on fire. I wiggled my fingers in surrender, but I guess it was too late for that. Too late for everything that related to the outside world. But inside, it was all confusion and hopelessness, more punishment in places where whips couldn't reach. But I kept going deeper—I had no choice—receding until I was able to view this madness as if from far away. At which point, of course, I passed out.

I woke up feeling sick and dizzy. I was in my own cell. Every body part ached. My feet! They were in plastic bags. The thought of resisting any longer was unthinkable, absolutely impossible. My innocence? What a useless concept that was. Did I think of killing myself? Yes. My days were clearly numbered. To them, I was a spy, and nothing was going to change their minds. My death by hanging or firing squad seemed imminent.

I thought of my pilot buddies, classmates of mine from pilot training in the United States, who were shot for plotting a *coup d'état*, immediately after the Revolution. Shot the next day, and their corpses plastered across the front page of the paper. It was better for me to commit suicide than be tortured and then executed, but I had no idea how to do it. Nothing in my cell could serve as a weapon, with the exception of my own teeth. I thought of biting the veins in my wrist and bleeding to death. Funny how, with that very real possibility available to me, I began reflecting on life again. My family. Being with them—what a joy it would have been. And catching the full sun on my face, seeing birds in flight and smelling the rain before a storm hit. And snow falling at night, and seeing my wife's smile again. And embracing my daughter and playing soccer again with my sons—all this distracted me from thoughts of ending my life, until the P.A. system in the hallway brought me back. *Do-aa-ye komail,* an hour of music that seemed to come from a graveyard.

Every Wednesday night, the same sad solo by the singer, "Aahang-araan." Not once did they ever play a happy song in that place. Everything was a downer. The words of the song reminded us of the wrongs we'd committed against God, and to ask for forgiveness. It was a reminder of the martyr Imam Hossein, grandson of the prophet Mohammad, and his struggle against Yazeed, son of Moaviyyah, Ommiad caliph. He was the enemy of Islam, and it was by his order that Imam Hossein was martyred. He was responsible for the loss of Imam Hossein's family, including his six-month-old baby, Aliasgar. This mournful story filed the prison and started many prisoners howling with grief. Hearing them, I sank so deep into despair that I began to see that we were all to blame. All Iranians guilty! It was true! We'd allowed a bunch of religious fundamentalists to turn the calendar back fourteen hundred years. We allowed ourselves to be ruled by law that was centuries out of date. We'd even fought for it! Risked our lives for it, some of us did, over and over again.

I remembered the last time I had the pleasure of risking my life. My final flight. They were becoming more and more like suicide missions. This one, you might as well call it murder.

9

IRAQUI AIRSPACE

I had been ordered to lead a mission to knock out the power plant at
Debis in northwest Iraq, near Karkook, close to the Turkish border.
Installations like Debis were well protected, and it wasn't the first one
that I'd been sent to destroy. I knew I was living on borrowed time, and
that I was alive only because I was good at my job. But we were valued
so little that they sent us without backup, without protection, without
nothing.

I briefed my three wingmen on the task at hand. After our pre-
flight checks, and after we'd fired up our engines, Lieutenant Baghai
reported engine problems. He requested another F-5, but I told him
to forget it—the three of us would proceed without him.

Within minutes of taking off, we were in Iraqi airspace, and making our standard descent, racing into enemy territory at an altitude low
enough to avoid radar detection. I'd become expert at this manoeuvre
since it was our standard strategy all through the war. This time, however, I found myself strangely anxious, even reluctant. I was becoming
far too conscious of the growing number of pilots who never returned.
These pilots, all of them were my close friends, you understand. But
never mind, emotions or hunches or feelings of any kind pack no

punch in the decisions a soldier makes in carrying out his duty. I'd been trained to act without hesitation, to get out of my own way and carry on defending the country, even if it meant surrendering my life. That day, we were eagles like every other day. But unlike birds of prey, we weren't under the influence of any primitive urge to survive, not out looking for food or concerned for our young. We'd learned to fly with an unearthly confidence and a single-minded attitude to destroy our target and return home safely.

We were a tight little triangle, myself leading, and my wingmen slightly behind and only three feet off each wing tip. Everything was going according to plan until approximately fifteen miles short of our target when thick, low-lying stratus cloud forced us to descend even lower. I dropped as low as I dared, and still couldn't see a thing. Very dangerous. I risked radio communication with my wingmen, telling them to dump their payload and head home. The way I figured it, by flying alone I'd more quickly locate a break in the cloud, establish a new course on the target, and get the job done. And I did, attacked the power plant from an unrehearsed angle and got the hell out of there. But, by now anti-aircraft fire had turned the sky into a fireworks display, with me slicing a course right through it. The problem wasn't just avoiding the flak, but at the speed I was flying, I could overtake the shells and hit *them*! Luck was with me, as it had been so often, and with only eighty miles to home base, I was already celebrating.

Two planes in front of me were the only visible aircraft—must have been my wingmen on their way home, I thought. I tried hard not to lose them, but when I got closer, I noticed they were Iraqi MiG-21s. Before I could think my way out of the situation, I found myself in a dogfight. Those Russian-made fighters had a high-altitude manoeuvrability advantage, but at low altitude they weren't quite as good as our American-made F-5s with their manoeuvring flaps. Before we had a chance to lock on to each other, one of the MiGs was shot by his own wingman. It was a piece of cake for me to finish him off. My missile nailed him from behind, right in the engine, and he exploded. I saw a parachute open, fortunately, and the pilot heading for safety. What a relief. In my mind, he wasn't the enemy, nor was I his. We were both fighting for someone else, two heads of state who loathed and despised each other, who would never meet face to face. Two cowardly tyrants whose style it was to leave it to innocent soldiers and pilots to fight it out.

I was relieved to be heading safely towards Iran again, and was only twenty-seven miles from the border when two more MiGs fired on me. No way I wanted to get involved in another scrap so close to home, and what's more, I was short of fuel. It was easy to get on the tail of one of them, but that left the other MiG time to find me in his sights. I quickly launched a missile, but it failed to fire. A machine-gun attack was my only recourse, but for that I had to get much closer. I started firing 20mm rounds, but before I could determine what damage he'd sustained, I was struck from behind. *KABOOM!* A missile up my backside. The stick went limp in my hand. There was nothing I could do with it. It felt like a spoon in a cup of coffee. I was on a collision course for the ground, with no choice but to do what no pilot ever gets a chance to practise. Eject! I pulled hard on the handle.

When I opened my eyes, I was on the ground. I felt nothing. The left side of my face was in the dirt. Bloody, dirty. I was still locked into my harness, and couldn't move. I must have fainted. How long had I been lying there? What had happened? I'd never heard of such a thing— ejecting so low to the ground—at 450 knots. Lots of blood. About the pain, I don't think I felt much. But I heard noises. Many people approaching. Men and women, even children. I knew very well what happened to enemy soldiers. I'd seen pictures. Tied to a truck and dragged around, coming apart piece by piece, scattered across the countryside for the vultures to pick at. I saw Akram as a widow, and my children growing up without a father. And my mother, she'd have the toughest time of all. I heard the group come to a halt and saw three men approaching. Young strong men, armed with some kind of big gun, and swords hanging from their belts. They spoke in Arabic, which I don't understand, so all I could do was wait and see what they had in store for me. Was I in pain? I don't remember.

They couldn't figure out how to separate me from the chute. With a mix of Farsi, Turkish, and English, I tried to explain how to unlock the clasps, which is when they realized I wasn't Iraqi. They broke into Farsi.

"We are Kurds," they said. "Don't worry. You're safe with us."

Once my guard was down, I realized how bad I was hurt. I couldn't even smile without pain. But I did smile, and through plenty of tears, with thanks to God.

"We have to move you quickly," they said. "Iraqi forces are nearby."

They rolled me over and slipped a blanket beneath me, which served as a kind of hammock to carry me to a truck, where I was hidden from view in the back as we motored through the mountains. It was cold, I tell you. One of the coldest Februarys. We were in the vicinity of Lake Dokan, as far as I could tell, not far from the city of Ranieh, and it was at a little house in the middle of nowhere where we finally stopped and took shelter.

An old man showed up. He had been summoned to come and check me over. His beard was white, his head turbaned, not in the way of Sikhs or the Iranian clergy, but more loosely. As he studied my condition, hardly touching me, he reminded me of my uncle, a kind and quietly confident man with compassion in his eyes. He spoke Kurdish, which I didn't understand, then Turkish. He explained that he had to get my clothes off. With scissors, he cut my jacket open, then freed me from my flying suit by slitting it open, too.

By then, I could discern one injury from another; my left elbow seemed to be the most complicated, dislocated for sure, maybe broken too. My skull felt like it was busted open. With one sure but brutal move, he reset my elbow, but the pain was too much, and I fainted.

I awoke to find myself bound from head to foot, wrapped tightly in makeshift splints of willow branches. I was aware of my knee throbbing. The only movable parts were my eyes. And my heartbeat; for some reason, it seemed to be located in my back, and it was beating a cruel rhythm, up and down my spine. Around me were seated a dozen people talking loudly, and smoking. I learned it was three o'clock. By my reckoning, I had crashed at 11:15 a.m. I was thirsty and hungry.

A group of men entered, armed to the teeth with guns and knives. At the arrival of their leader, the residents of the house were quick to offer him their seat. I wanted to stand, too. He was a big handsome fellow with a thick moustache. He paid no one any attention, just came directly towards me and bid me welcome. *"Be kheyr bee."* He spoke in Kurdish. He had one wildly undulating eyebrow, and cheeks as red as apples. His name was Sowar Agha and he was the commander of the Kurds in that area.

Another well-respected man entered, this one younger but just as tall and strong, Sowar Agha's brother, Kaak Aako, I discovered, and the vice-commander of the martyrs known in that region of Kurdistan as the *pishmargan*—the members of the Patriotic Union of Kurdistan.

"You are lucky to be alive," he said. "We pass here only once a week to deliver supplies to our men fighting over that way."

I asked him where he'd learned to speak such good Farsi, and he explained that during the time of the Shah, many Kurds in that area including his family were pushed all the way into Iran by Saddam's forces. The Shah had given them refuge in Isfahan and Varameen, where they remained for a few years. Through words punctuated with painful groans, I inquired about the old gentleman who had doctored me. I learned that he was neither a doctor nor an officer, but someone who had patched up so many goats in his time that his skills as a sawbones were second to none, anywhere.

"I'd like a glass of water," I said.

"Sorry," they said. "Not yet. Not until we're sure you haven't suffered any brain damage."

So, I *had* cracked my skull open. Eating or drinking would be deadly, they explained, if my condition was serious enough to require an emergency evacuation back to Iran. I asked why that wasn't their plan, in any event.

"Too risky. The countryside between here and the border is thick with Saddam's forces," said Sowar Agha. "We'd be risking everyone's lives."

"Where to, then?" I asked.

"Somewhere safe. And more comfortable."

Sowar Agha organized a team to load me onto a stretcher. It was made from a ladder. Eight men hoisted me up, lifting the rug I was lying on, and very carefully lowered me onto the makeshift platform. Supporting me on their shoulders, we trekked into mountainous country. I wasn't sure if it was intentional, but my rig was identical to those used to carry corpses to the pyres.

I'd never experienced such biting cold. Lying on my back, I appreciated how magnificently clear the skies were, a high-pressure system having entrenched itself over Asia Minor. The February moon was bright, and the stars! I'd never seen such stars. Nor had I seen mountains that loomed so forbiddingly, so impenetrably. I remember the night as eerily quiet. But, back to the cold—I could feel it breaking its way into my cocoon, entering through my toes and ears. My teeth chattered like typewriter keys. I didn't know how I was going to survive that cold, not to mention my wounds being jostled every which way, no matter how carefully the men tread that icy trail. To make matters worse, I couldn't help moaning. It was embarrassing. I tried synchronizing my moans with the rhythm of their footfalls. Then it was my tears, turning my face to a mask of ice. But I was in no position to complain.

How much farther we had to go, I had no idea. Or even if I'd make it. But what was the use of speculating? What good was self-pity? Being utterly helpless, I had no choice but to surrender, even to the point of watching myself die, if that's what fate had in store for me. I must have lapsed into some kind of altered state, because I remember thinking that the countryside reminded me of Taleghan, the valley of my ancestors. And that these people who were caring for me were like the people back home who loved me. The memory of my childhood—what a treasure it was.

We arrived at a village, a few shelters built of dirt and sticks. The doors were so low that the men had to bend over to enter. They set me down in a small room dominated by a wood-burning stove and a loudly hissing kerosene lamp. The place wasn't exactly toasty, but I wasn't complaining. What's more, it was clean and colourful. The walls had a floral motif. On a closer look, they were covered with plastic, the small window, too, covered by colourful plastic.

"What kind of bedding you prefer to sleep on?" Sowar Agha asked me. I couldn't believe it. These people were so kind.

"Whatever's available is more than fine with me," I said.

They had two mattresses, a foamy and a woollen one. Quickly, they set up a bed, and then they laid me down upon it. It was the kind of care and attention you would only expect from your mother or your sister. Over me they laid a new blanket and provided me with an extra pillow to support my broken arm. I felt like a baby being put to sleep. Sowar Agha and his brother sat on one side of me, and eight other *pishmargan* sat on the other side of the room.

An hour or two passed. Most of the talk was about me and the best way to conduct me safely to the border. Sowar Agha translated for me much of what was said. At midnight, he and his brother slipped away, leaving the others to tend me. Two guards kept watch outside, while one fellow slept close by and met my needs as best he could. His name was Ghader, but I called him Dr. Ghader because he had some pain-relief pills to help me get through the night. And he brought me a tin can to piss in, but I was too self-conscious. My bladder wouldn't co-operate. There was nothing more to do but sleep. . . .

I heard the guard coughing. Morning. I expected to hear the cock crowing, but instead heard the prison's brittle P.A. system inviting everyone to prayer.

"*Allaho Akbar!* God is great! *Ashhado anla elaha ellallah!* I believe in no other God but God the great . . ."

10

DANCING WITH THE DEVIL

The prayer call really grated on my nerves. Head aching, feet throbbing, and my left hand still burning. The next musical offering was a sadder song yet, "Do-aa-ye rouz," "the song of the day." My crash had done my body worse damage than my prison beatings, but somehow that pain had been easier to bear. The friendship of the Kurds was a soothing balm. But in prison, there in my own country, I had no place to turn for relief.

Time to be blindfolded and trooped off to the washroom for ablutions, followed by *namaaz*. I used the door to hold myself up until the guard handed me my crutches, which were leaning against the wall outside my cell. I was so broken up that I couldn't walk without crutches.

"You need crutches, why?" he asked.

I cursed him silently, the son of a bitch: *"Maadar ghahbe."* Two steps was all I could take. Good thing I was at the end of the line.

"Hey, Hadji! You with the crutches! Move! Hurry up! We're late! You think this is a hotel? Move, move!"

I couldn't go any faster. I grabbed the shirt of the guy in front of me and carried on to the washroom entrance. When the guard escorted the next prisoner into the washroom, the prisoner beside me asked how long since I'd been arrested. I told him I'd lost count of the days. Then it was my turn to use the washroom. I sat on the bowl but couldn't piss. Eventually, blood leaked out, a scary sight, let me tell you. Were my kidneys failing? The beating on my feet must have done it, but I didn't know why.

Back to my cell for prayers, which I practised from a sitting position, since I couldn't stand up. The remainder of the daily routine awaited me, starting with breakfast, consisting of bits of apples and oranges. I was peeling the orange when a familiar voice hailed me from behind the door. The interrogator. His arrival meant only one thing—my blindfold had to be in place when he entered.

"How are you doing?" he asked.

"What difference does it make?" I said.

"If I didn't care, Hadji, I wouldn't be here right now," he said. He looked at my feet. "If you'd confessed everything, this wouldn't have happened. You could be home with your family. But now we have to wait until you heal up. What a shame. Anyway, look what I brought you. Some more paper. I know how much you like to answer my questions."

We bantered back and forth like that, pretending to be friendly, me assuring him that I'd rather just go home as I was, never mind the healing.

"I promise I won't tell anyone," I said. It was becoming almost funny.

"Sorry, Hadji, can't do that," he said. But he gave me a counter-offer—provide him with some written answers, and he'd let me speak to my wife.

"She's still here?" I asked.

"And in far better condition than you, my friend."

"Who's looking after our kids?" I demanded.

"You worry too much," he said. "Everything is under control."

He left me alone with those same stupid questions, the same old stuff about my relations with the Argentine chargé d'affaires in Pakistan, and about other people with whom I had contact as military

70

attaché, especially Americans. I had to explain why they'd become my friends, and what my official business with them had been. Other questions were sprinkled in, like how much money I had, and why I wanted to send my oldest son to an "American" school. They wanted to know about certain friends of mine and their opinion of Ayatollah Khomeini and the Revolution. Although I had nothing to hide and nobody to rat on, nevertheless I wasn't interested in providing them with information about any friend of mine, but of course I had to commit something to paper, and so I did, especially because this writing helped pass the time. It probably saved my sanity, replaying my life in this way. It might even have saved my life.

As I wrote, I became increasingly anxious. The Americans. I'd come to know plenty of them in their military attachés. Despite our countries' differences, we related well, as well as anyone. The problem lay with them being Americans. In the eyes of the Revolution, merely conversing with agents of the enemy was a crime. Ayatollah Khomeini had proclaimed that conspiring with the United States was equal to fraternizing with Satan, which amounted to treason of the worst kind. But, my meetings were sanctioned by my very position, and I began to wonder if I had been intentionally forced into a Catch-22 situation. Did it matter that my business with Americans amounted to nothing more than a few cups of tea? Probably not. How could they kill me for a cup of tea? Could they? It was unimaginable.

I finished eating my orange and reread the questions, trying to determine what it was they really had against me. Why had they found me to be such a threat against the regime? After all, I was a popular figure. I was in the newspapers, I had written a book about my crash and survival in Iraci territory, which had become a major motion picture. These were not insignificant cultural events in Iran. I had thought I was the source of some inspiration at a time when the country desperately needed it. So why did the regime want to arrest and torture me? It made no sense

In that confusion, I recalled Koranic verses that advised the faithful not to worry too much about a negative turn of events, since no one ever knew how things would ultimately turn out. Perhaps it was all for the better. And likewise, a blessing could become a curse, tomorrow. You never know. For a moment I let myself picture a happy ending to this ordeal, a beautiful life for me and my family sometime down the line. Unfortunately, it only made the reality of that stinking cell even worse, and I began to feel like a misguided fool. Not to mention, I must have looked like a wild animal.

I began answering the same old questions with the same old answers. I was careful not to say more or less than I had before. New questions about my friends and co-workers had to be treated carefully, so as not to incriminate them. While they had no love for Khomeini or the Revolution, I wasn't going to risk them or their families by putting words in their mouths. One careless word from me could have spelled trouble. Perhaps it was best that they kill me before I became the cause of someone else's nightmare. So I wrote only about my work, about the missions my colleagues and I undertook together, hard-fought battles against the enemy, avoiding any criticism of the ayatollah or the Revolution. The whole day I wrote, wrote to the point of exhaustion. Just as I was about to fall asleep, they announced that prisoners could take a shower.

"Blindfold on!"

I felt nauseous, yet I desperately needed a shower. Since my arrest, I hadn't had one. We were constantly in the dark during those months, seeing no one and never being able to take proper stock of that place. Leaving the cell for even a few minutes was a welcome change, and it reminded me of freedoms I'd enjoyed and a time when I could go anywhere and avail myself of the washroom whenever I wanted, to take a bath at any hour. But who ever takes a moment to feel grateful for such gifts? I knew then what freedom was, and what price I'd pay to have it back again.

With a great deal of pain, I struggled to engage in the usual way with the usual lineup in the corridor outside the cell.

"Heads down! And move slowly! Hadji! You coming with us?"

The voice was new. I sensed a person more friendly than the others. I sensed that he was taking stock of my feet sealed in plastic bags and my attempt to reach the crutches standing outside the door.

"I'm coming," I said. "If you're not in a rush."

The guard surprised me with his intention to help me out, but as the line of prisoners shuffled down the hallway I was quickly left behind. He must have suddenly realized what a liability I was to the orderly carrying out of his orders.

"Hadji! You can't take your crutches!"

"I can't walk without them!" I said.

I was stunned by a whack on the head, which caused me to teeter.

"No talking!"

He grabbed the crutches away from me and I fell over, grasping for something to hang on to.

"Can't walk, Hadji? Tough luck." He pushed me into my cell and slammed the door.

I'd never felt such loathing for another human being. Never felt such hostility combined with such little ability to respond. One word out of me and I'd only have made things worse. All I could do was try to put it out of my mind, but such anger didn't pass easily. My desperation and self-pity seemed to magnify my filth and itching. And the stench! I would have offended a skunk. I tried to conjure up happy times, since it had worked before. Few things made me happier than my time with the Kurds.

11

BY COFFIN TO NOORZANG

"We're moving immediately."

"Where to?" I asked.

"All the way to Iran. Are you ready?"

Kaak Aako, brother of Sowar Agha, had ducked into my shelter to warn us of enemy helicopter patrols in the area. We'd heard them. Aako reported one *pishmarg* killed and a few others injured.

"I'm ready," I said.

Of course I wasn't, really. I was in agony, but what did that matter, because I was going to see my family again. My spirits had never been higher. But we were wasting time talking about it. I wanted to go immediately, but not so fast that I neglected to express my gratitude to the owner of the house and his family. I couldn't speak much of their language, but with hand signals and body language we made ourselves understood. It's trite to say so, I know, but I loved these people.

I remember, at the time, reflecting upon how this kind of love can creep up on you. Many small kindnesses find their way to the heart, little by little, drop by drop. Slowly, the heart fills with affection and you feel a connection with these free spirits. And though it may not be immediately apparent, wait until you're on the verge of parting company, and suddenly you sense what you'll be missing the minute you say goodbye. My heart has always gone out to friends and fellow soldiers fighting for freedom.

My small battalion of *pishmargan* moved me around the mountain. The terrain was steep, and the trail a series of suicidal switchbacks. Kaak Aako told me that we were traversing the Valley of the Horse, so called because a long time ago a *pishmarg* had leapt one of these chasms on his steed, jumping from one cliff to another, an impossible span of many metres. I remembered an Iranian fable about a horseman named Rostam and his steed, Rakhsh, who had made a similar leap. I wondered how many other mountain cultures possessed comparable legends.

After half an hour's trek we arrived at the village of Palangan, and stopped at the house of Sowar Agha. It was small but clean and tidy inside, with simple peasant decorations throughout. Again, I was made to feel like a special guest. Sowar Agha and his brother provided me a Kurdish outfit, a disguise for the next leg of the journey. As I was fitted into it, I felt cocooned by a strange heaviness, a sense of responsibility growing out of an immense gratitude I felt for these people. It wasn't that their love weighed me down—although in a sense they had heaped tons of it upon me—it was a burden that kept me alive. Never have I forgotten their hospitality, their generosity, and their dedication to my cause, and to the cause of freedom for their people.

It was early evening when we headed out by truck along a cliffside trail so narrow that I wondered how sheep and goats managed to navigate it successfully. The truck stopped in total darkness. Sowar Agha wanted to show me something, and he helped me down. With a flashlight, he pointed across the valley, flicking the torch on and off. On the opposite hillside, a hundred lights blinked on and off.

"Meet your new friends," he said. "They will take you home."

He explained that there were eighty men in that party, all briefed about their mission. "They're good fighters," he said. "Not good in the air, like you, but on the ground, no one's better." He laughed with a fatherly pride in those fighters. "Don't worry about meeting Iraqi soldiers. Our people don't give up. We fight to the last man."

Sowar Agha advised me that I'd be staying for a few days at their headquarters, in a place called Noorzang. But it would only be a matter of days before I'd be with my family again.

It was time to say goodbye to Sowar Agha. He'd be returning to Palangan. This parting wasn't easy. In fact, I was shaking. When he embraced me, I hoped his strength would calm me, but my voice trembled. I felt a great sense of loss, leaving him behind. Kaak Aako looked at me one last time. He tied his shawl like a belt around my waist, adjusted the scarf over my head, and pulled my hat over my ears. I shook his hand. We both got a little dewy eyed. Then my goodbye to all the Kurds who'd accepted me and looked after me for almost a month. It felt like saying goodbye to an entire nation, and it shamed me to think that this was a nation of people with whom we'd often been at war. Our countries had been born at the same time, our people descended from the same ancestors.

Our caravan comprised two horses loaded with luggage and supplies, and one mule with a coffin-like box strapped to its back. That was to be my vehicle for the onward journey, and it took a half-dozen *pishmarg* to carefully hoist me up and set me inside. Sowar and Kaak emerged from the darkness to take one last look at me. I stopped myself before uttering any more unnecessary words of goodbye. I would only have disturbed the silence of that clear, pure night.

The way to Noorzang took us up a steep trail that made me think we must have been heading for the mountain peak. The stars were in their millions, looking down upon this lonely procession. I likened myself to a kernel of wheat being trucked along by a colony of ants. So little we know about anything, I thought. A few words of chit-chat could be heard as we went, but I could tell that these *pishmargan* were already tired. The silence was eerie, especially since my coffin allowed me no view of anyone except Dr. Ghader, who kept close to me at all times. I felt like his newborn child, too vulnerable to stray from the bosom of the mother. I marvelled at the commitment of this man to tend me in this way, and I thought about how self-sacrifice had all but vanished in our society. I also wondered how one repaid a saint like this.

We stopped for a rest. The mule wrangler started singing. He was a short, fat character whose steady smile revealed teeth as black as charcoal. "Do you like my voice?" he asked me.

What could I say? It was a song I'd never heard, words I didn't understand. To this day, I remember his name, Mohammad Saleh Amin. "Yes, Mohammad," I said, "I love it." He sang louder, and just watching him sing was a comfort to me. Seeing how happy his singing made me, others threw their voices behind Amin's. Someone laughed for the sheer relief of it, which triggered other laughter, and I couldn't help laughing, myself, at all this laughing. When we settled down again, I realized how tired and sore and stiff my knees were from not moving for hours. And how cold I was. My knees were like knobs of ice. But what a difference, that kind of pain, versus my suffering at the hands of the Iranian traitors who called themselves revolutionaries. In my Kurdish coffin, I was happy, I couldn't deny it. Happy for being with my *pishmargan*.

I may have been broken into bits, but I was embraced within a community of people who believed in the dignity of human life. In Iran, which was in the grip of the ayatollahs, the meaning of human dignity was foreign. The ayatollahs believed in God, but in the most unholy way. Kindness was unknown to them. Their spirit was hateful to anyone holding a different belief. Death to anyone who thought differently! Who dared to entertain a new idea. Tell me who is the most holy of these two groups? The one who risks its safety to save the life of a stranger, or the one who tortures their own kind for a confession that will only serve as the reason to execute them? Sheer madness.

The weather turned foul, and we found ourselves on the rainy, windward side of the mountain. It was almost a jungle. Foliage hid a series of small caves, each large enough to accommodate two of us, at most, lying down. We were safe there from a long night of cold rain and snow. But no matter how hard I tried to adjust my position, there was no avoiding drips from the ceiling landing on my head. My right hand swelled up, the skin so badly in need of a healthy flow of blood that it turned a dark and hideous shade of blue. I didn't sleep, only fantasized about a cup of steaming-hot tea.

In the morning, the men collected their gear and helped me onto the mule. By the time we were moving again, the sky was showing promise of breaking through. Soon the sunbeams found us and warmed us, as if trying to make amends for a terrible night. The view from my coffin was of a clean sky, as clear as a lapis, an unbroken ocean of blue. With my spirits lifting, I felt myself becoming impatient to reach Noorzang and cross the border and see my own people. Especially my family.

It's hard to imagine, but in prison I often recalled my Kurdish adventure to distract myself from pain. Imagine, living in a beloved homeland and wishing I was back in Iraq, encased in a coffin on the back of a mule on a cold and rocky trail! Sad but true. Sometimes, to pull myself out of depression, I picked up one of the two books in my cell. The Koran was always available, of course. Also, a volume written by Ayatollah Khomeini, himself. It was called *Resaleh* (*A Key to Solutions*). For the longest time I never bothered to examine it. Parts of it were written in Farsi, other parts in Arabic. The book turned out to be as primitive as I'd expected. A bad joke. It dumbfounded me, the power Khomeini had, why anybody heeded him. He had murdered so many of his own citizens. Everyone must have lost friends and relatives to his butchery. He was a madman, lusting for blood according to his perverted version of blessed Islam. I'd met Khomeini twice, and both times he showed little sign of intelligence. Nevertheless, I began reading his book until I fell asleep, only to be woken by the morning *Azan*, the call to prayer blaring from the prison speakers.

Day after day, everything repeated exactly as it was the day before. I remember deciding to reread the Koran, to concentrate on the messages sent by God to Prophet Mohammad, and try to understand the true meaning. After only a few pages, I would fall in tune with the way God was speaking to the Prophet through the angel Gabriel. I was envious of the intimate relationship that existed between God and

Prophet Mohammad. After finishing the Koran, I plowed through *Resaleh*, then read them both again. I could recite by heart some sections of these books, and began to welcome the good advice where I found it, since much of the content was about praying for freedom from life's hardships. But it turned out that I must have been praying all wrong, because nothing improved for me. On one page of the Koran, a previous prisoner had written a few words:

> *These bastards, they can torture you, but they can't kill you. Don't let them think they are stronger than you. They only have so much time to question you. After that, they can't torture you any further. Remember what you are saying, and never give them any new information. Many people who suffered here are now free. Yes, some have been executed, and perhaps they're the lucky ones for not having to suffer further torture. Good luck!*

I was tempted to write up and down the margins of these books just to keep busy, to keep my mind off speculating what the interrogator was doing with my latest answers. I longed to write a political philosophy, a plan for ruling this country in the manner of Cyrus the Great. There would be no more hellholes like this one, and little need for political prisoners, because citizens would enjoy freedom of speech and religion. Politics and religion would be separate realms. An independent judicial system would be based on globally accepted human rights. The income gap between the richest and the poorest would be reduced, ensuring a more dignified society. And, of course, we wouldn't interfere in another country's affairs.

I remembered reading a book entitled *Crime and Punishment*. I'd read it years ago. The author spoke of prison as the "house of justice" and compared its employees to nurses, of all things. What a dreamer! He was a Russian, the author, by the name of Fyodor Dostoevsky. At worst, guards would be required to behave like mothers, slapping their children, not to humiliate them, but to prevent them from straying too far off track. His utopian jails were intended to train wayward people in a better way of life. Solitary confinement was reserved for the worst of the criminals, for traitors and violent offenders. That's where I was, for God's sake, except these psychopaths were the keepers of the keys! They wielded the steel-cored cables dripping with blood. They were my torturers.

I became crazy with all kinds of pointless thinking, like entertaining the notion of retaliating. That was almost as pointless as my next thought—bashing my head against the wall. When I calmed down, I realized I only wanted to go to the toilet. Anything but that cell. The novelty of a faucet and a toilet bowl was pure delight to me. Better yet, on the way to the washroom, I had the chance to feel the presence of other people, to hear their breathing. Sometimes we'd accidentally touch, hands particularly when we were standing in the line for our turn to go to the washroom. What a sensation that was! A sense of being alive, of realizing I wasn't alone, and that others were sharing these same experiences. And surviving along with me.

Don't ask me how, but I became aware of a change in season. Of darker days. Winter had been a time for our family to come together and linger longer over the evening meal. Such thoughts made my situation even worse. I stared at the two small windows up high, totally closed shut, so I would imagine. Talk about imagining—those primitive etchings on the walls? I read entire novels into those sad scratches. Nothing, however, relieved the incessant aloneness, sitting in a cell no bigger than a walk-in closet. It was mental torture that became worse than physical torture, seriously. Interrogators could crush you physically, but mentally you could remain stronger than them. They knew it and you knew it. The interrogators constantly humiliated you. You never laid eyes on the questioner, never knew what he looked like, couldn't put a face to the evil. And worse yet was not being able to ask a question, even for clarification. No cross-examination. Everything they threw at you, you had to suck it up. All that, however, was nothing compared with solitary confinement. That was the worst. It didn't kill you, but it drove you to begging the guard to kill you. The ultimate humiliation.

As more days and nights passed, memories started vanishing as quickly as they arose. I couldn't grab hold of thoughts. They drifted by me like mist. Probably because, by that time, the thoughts themselves knew they were meaningless. And who was there to care about my fading away? Deep down, I knew I was already in the grave. So my whole organism was one big "Why bother?"

Then, a vague and puzzling wave of rising energy found me memorizing a few more verses of the Koran and gaining some self-esteem from getting to know it better.

"Ready for the shower?" The voice of the nameless guard.

Was I ready? I'd been ready for days. But my feet couldn't join me in my enthusiasm. They were still painful. I stood as erect as I could, and affixed my blindfold in place, my little hand towel secure in my waistband.

"Hadji, let's go!"

I managed my position in the prisoner lineup in the hallway, hand on the shoulder of the man in front of me, and off we trudged. I was surprised to find the line still moving as we passed the stone step that led to the washroom. Instead, I found myself outside in the open air. I remember hearing a television, a man's voice, the host of some show, I couldn't remember his name. I only remember thinking what a pleasure it would have been to sit and watch television, any stupid show at all. How pathetic is that?

"Heads down!"

Two or three other guards herded us into a minibus. Okay, it was more like a van, since it didn't have seats, only a piece of carpet.

"Sit absolutely still, or else. One word and you're a dead man."

My mind, always finding a way to escape, conjured up the memory of my Mercedes and my military driver, Safai. Wherever I needed to go, at whatever time of the day or night, Safai would open the back door for me and hold it respectfully until I was safely in, then close it and move quickly behind the wheel. "Sir, where to?" he'd say. "To the Chinese embassy," I'd say. My slightest wish was his command. Or perhaps to the German embassy, or perhaps it was a meeting with

General Rahimkhan and the chief of the Pakistani Armed Forces, or General Aaref, the army commander, or Jamal of the Air Force Command. Or why not the Japanese embassy, to participate in their National Day celebrations? Mr. Safai was right there with an upbeat and willing "Yes, sir!" Now look at me. Herded into this metal coffin, probably not to shower at all. Probably to be taken away and shot. The human mind wasn't built to comprehend this kind of possibility.

Guards started cursing one of the prisoners who had apparently moved his head, or allowed his blindfold to slip. They clubbed him and beat him as if he were a punching bag, and left him groaning. *How can God stand idly by and sanction this kind of cruelty!* If love existed in the soul of the universe, or even any trace of wisdom, how could God justify these crimes against humanity? And if there was a just cause for my punishment, was there not some other way to send me a message? I felt sure we were all going to be dead men, shower or no shower. Then I recalled the handwritten message in the Koran: "They can't kill you here." That's why we were being moved. If our execution was imminent, then, so be it. Better than to be left rotting in solitary confinement until the mind short-circuited and the body's many flowing functions were reduced to trickles, and we became shadows of human beings. Had I perished like that, my most regrettable thoughts would have been of my wife. So much trouble for her, and all because of me. I would have had no chance to say goodbye, or apologize for this catastrophe. What had happened to her? The thought of her fate was an even worse injustice than mine, and it was enough to make mush of my willpower. That always got me.

As I felt my tears soaking the blindfold, the vehicle began a series of left-right turns, causing us to sway and nudge each other. Each accidental touch of a fellow human being felt like a heartfelt hello, or an expression of compassion and understanding for our mutual anguish. It became a silent, blind, but friendly, physical conversation.

The van came to a stop.

"Everybody out!"

12

HOPE AND DESPAIR

Once we were standing outside the van, we knew enough to remain motionless, each with a hand on the shoulder of the adjacent prisoner.

"Don't move!"

We were paraded blind into a large hollow-sounding space. It smelled like a public bath. We were instructed to strip.

"Ten minutes to wash and get out!"

There were twelve shower stalls in a row, one for each of us. We each had soap. What a relief! What a luxury! A godsend! I washed myself well and quickly so that I could accomplish everything, including rinse out my shorts and shirt. It brought back memories of bathing at home, but more than that it was simply the concept of being able to take a bath. I'd never even thought about it. It was a gift from God. Bathing was a gift from God, imagine that. Never mind that guards stood watch outside our locked cubicles. Who cared about that?

"Time's up! Blindfold on!" All down the line of shower stalls, the three guards shouted these orders.

My small towel was the same sad cloth I used in my cell to dry my hands and face, only here it had to do for my whole body. With no change of underwear, I slipped into my prison garb without them, holding the damp things in my hand. The door opened and a guard pulled me out by the arm and led me through a door to benches where other prisoners were sitting. When we were all assembled, the return journey began, into the van and back to the prison we had left an hour earlier. The outing was over. I felt as if I'd been on a trip to the beach.

Back at the prison, we trudged like ants, holding each other's shoulder for our little march back to our cells. With a little finesse, I managed to hang my shorts and undershirt from a notch in the rough cement wall, and hoped that it would dry by morning. The wash had relaxed me, made me feel kind of lazy, even sleepy, so I made a pillow of one blanket and lay down, covering myself with the other blanket. In solitary confinement, sleep was considered a major success. The more you got, the less stress built up. But I had a problem with sleep. I was unable to string many consecutive hours together, which only led to unnecessary thinking and worrying. But that day, I fell into a pleasurable little reverie about my return from Iraq with the Kurds, to Noorzang, the last stopover before the Iran border. Once again, I remembered a big fat wood-burning stove in the corner of the house. The fire inside snapped and crackled as the sparks flew straight up the pipe to escape through the roof and into the sky. A draft from the window forced me closer to the fire.

"It's only four hours by foot to Sardasht," said Kaak Shooman, my new host. Sardasht was in Iran. I was excited because we could have been there before supper; instead, we went nowhere for two weeks! There was always some reason for the delay, some danger that lay ahead. If it wasn't fighting nearby, then it was because more reconnaissance was necessary. I became impatient, and sickly again. It was coming on for mid December, 1980.

A man dropped by the house, Kaak Mostafa. He told me that his grandparents lived in Iran. I asked him if he knew how a letter might be delivered over the border to my wife. She would have had no idea that I was still alive. Mostafa told me to go ahead and write it. He would think of a way to get it through.

"How do I know if you've managed to send it?" I asked him.

"If you don't see me tomorrow night," he said, "the letter and I are gone. I assure you. I'll get it into your wife's hands."

The next night, no Mostafa. I could only imagine Akram's reaction to the letter. She must have already buried me by now.

On my last night in Iraq, we were camped in a shelter that was mostly open to the sky. Only a flimsy piece of nylon shielded us from the elements. It did nothing to keep out the bitter cold, and I lay awake listening to my four companions snoring until 3 a.m., when the owner of this place woke us up. There was nothing left to do but assemble with the eight *pishmargan* who would accompany me across the border. A mule was available to carry me this last leg of the journey, but I felt somehow good enough to at least start the journey under my own steam. I was pumped, keen, even celebrating; I wanted to start without delay.

Snow threatened, and started to fall as soon as we began our trek. Those mountains all looked the same, especially with snow cover. Borders in this part of the country were invisible, fictitious demarcations, political decisions, lines only found on a map. When we stopped for a rest, it was still dark and cold, but I was advised that we'd crossed the border.

I undid my jacket and removed my *jamdani*, my head cover, which was wet with sweat. From that point, I decided to take advantage of the mule bareback, and we pushed on. The roads remained narrow and slippery, but nothing could have made them impossible. I was in Iran and couldn't wait to arrive in the first Iranian village.

Dawn was beginning to lend texture to the snowscape. The single, faint, grey line of road on a field of white reminded me of art classes when I was a child, when I would draw that first hesitant line across a blank page. How odd that I should have felt a special love for these hills, when they were identical to those hills we'd just left behind in Iraq. Something more than patriotism was drawing me onward, something almost mystical. Some love affair with the soil that gave life to my ancestors, and the land where they'd been buried.

A geography of love and passion.

The first Iranian sounds I heard on that early morning were dogs barking. In my mind's eye, these were loyal protectors alerting their masters to approaching strangers, and it made me proud. The truth is, they were a pack of wild dogs that didn't care who I was. Never mind, I was in Iran and everything was perfect. I noticed shepherds leading their sheep to the river, and women drawing water to carry home for morning ablutions. They saw us but didn't stare. I couldn't help seeing them as brothers and sisters and neighbours. Hadn't the Bible said, "Love thy neighbour as thyself"? That's the thought that came to mind, so you can see what kind of ecstatic mood I was in to be back home again. I was in love with everything, from wild dogs to the free fresh air. I inhaled deeply and exhaled with even more vigour so that I could greedily breathe more deeply still.

As the roads improved, our pace picked up, and soon we were approaching the first Iranian settlement, the village of Dolatoo. I could see the people, Kurds again. The same community of people spanned this Iran-Iraq border point. When our caravan came to a stop, I slipped off the mule and dropped to my knees in the snow to kiss the ground. My Iran! My homeland. My complex country of religions, tribes, beliefs, battles, and betrayals. None of it caused me to feel anything but pride to be its servant, its soldier. I remember noticing the Kalashnikov hanging from my shoulder, and thinking that my Kurdish disguise was no longer necessary. . . .

This exquisite dream was not quite over when I heard my number announced from the corridor.

"109! Get ready!"

My response was automatic—blindfold on, stand up, be strong. Ignore the wildly beating heart.

The cell door opened. A man entered and grabbed my arm, and down the corridor we went, past the familiar steps that I had caught sight of many times through an opening in the blindfold. In we went to a room that was unfamiliar, yet all too familiar in my imagination. Dark, a desk with writing arm for a left-handed person. I felt sick at the thought of further endless hours of pointless interrogation.

"How are you, Colonel?" my tormentor asked.

He had no idea how pathetic his feigned politeness sounded, and how much it made me sick. Then he apologized for what had happened to me, followed by his gentle admonition that it had been my fault.

"You could have found it in your heart to co-operate with me," he said.

"I co-operate with my heart," I replied.

"I read your latest responses," he said. "Unfortunately, it's the same old garbage. What can I do, Hadji?"

"You could try accepting it as the truth," I said.

"I try my best to help you, but you don't want a break. You sure don't deserve one. So, someone else will have to convince you. Someone who's a lot better at this than me. He'll break you, take my word for it. Unless you can handle dying three times a day, Hadji. What a shame."

What was I supposed to do, beg for another chance? I was immune to him and his threats. It was all I could do to stop myself from cursing him to his face.

"I was going to arrange that you meet your wife today," he said. "And talk to your kids. But you couldn't care less. The only thing you care about is America. America!" He started lecturing me on America. He knew nothing. He was as thick as brick. "Get up!" he shouted.

He pushed me towards another room and closed the door. This one was bigger and brighter.

"Remove your blindfold," a man said.

It was a real office with a few chairs and a sofa and a big desk. A bearded man was sitting behind the desk. This must have been the director of this shithole.

"Sit down," he said. "What seems to be the problem?" He spoke kindly. "Why not co-operate with us?"

"Can't you tell when someone's co-operating?" I said. "You've got the truth. I've given it to you."

"It's all garbage! Lies! We know everything about you! You're a traitor. Your objection to the war! We purge traitors to the Revolution, and you object to that. You can't hide anything from us, Hadji. You're condemned to death already, so why not tell us everything. Tell us about the CIA! We know you're spying. Tell us!"

I wasn't sure I could handle another long session like this. There was no point in repeating everything to prove my innocence. It wasn't going to happen.

"I'll sign," I said. "Whatever you put in front of me. Your firing squad will feel better about it."

"You were opposed to the Islamic Revolution before the war started? Do you deny that?"

This was something new. I was prepared to talk about that, and I told him so. He accused me, straightaway, of being anti-revolutionary and an enemy of the state. "*Taghooti Kheianatkar!*" he called me. Devil worshipper. That was a new one, way over the top. It was almost funny.

He pulled a report from his briefcase and read from it, some conclusions they'd reached regarding my criticism of leaders of the Revolution for executing pilots. I had lots to say on that subject, and he must have sensed it, because he switched to some bullshit story about having done everything he could to submit a favourable report about me. But no longer. The court martial might have reduced my sentence, but it was too late now. "Blindfold on," he commanded, and called my interrogator.

"Take him away!"

"WHY IS EVERYONE CRYING?"

I'd heard stories of military personnel being executed without a trial, plenty of them, and it looked like I was next, yanked from the room amidst threats of handing me over to the firing squad, one more victim of ayatollahs gone berserk. One more citizen guilty of daring to think for himself.

"You're going to call your wife," they said.

"You freed her?" I asked.

"Why should we keep her? She told us everything."

I'd always suspected them of bluffing, but that proved it for me. As I recounted earlier, Akram knew nothing about my job. Not because she wasn't interested, but because it was out of bounds. Strictly forbidden for military personnel to reveal anything like that. So she never asked. She never made it difficult for me.

He took me to a room and had me sit on a blanket on the floor. "There's a phone beside you," he said.

From under my blindfold I could see two white telephones.

"Sit there until I come back."

After a short time he returned with the good news that his boss had agreed to the phone call. Also, he told me, I had another chance to redeem myself. *Don't these guys ever quit?* I wondered why—when I'd given them nothing more than my original story—they had such confidence that I'd suddenly provide them with critical intelligence.

"When your wife answers, talk normal, the way you always do. Nothing about this place or what's happening. Just 'Hi, how are you? How are the kids?' And be brief. I'll be listening on the other phone."

I didn't know what number he had dialed to reach my wife, but the phone was ringing. What was I going to say? Already, I felt my heart pounding in my throat, but somehow I had to control my emotions. Akram answered.

"*Akram jaan, salaam.* My dear, hello, how are you? And the kids?"

"All right. Don't worry, they know nothing about what's happened."

"Everything is okay, then?" I received a poke in the ribs.

"We're fine," she said. "You know me, as strong as a rock. But anxious to see you. I love you."

"I love you too."

"Bye."

"Bye."

I hung up. That was it. That was it?

Off we went to another room. More written questions to answer. What did I care? Bring 'em on. I'd quit resisting. Every strand of common sense was twisted out of shape in that place. No one understood the rules. It was a perfect place for a monk, someone whose way to God was through surrender. Maybe that's where I was headed. I might emerge from there a saint, who knows? Maybe there was hope for me in the afterworld. Maybe freedom in the next life!

He left me in the next room with the same old desk and another stack of test papers. Right away, I noticed a few names, different people he wanted information about, but all I could think of was Akram and the kids. Her words were kind and reassuring, few though they were. I doubt that she'd been at home. Probably the interrogator playing more games with me, since that's all he ever did. Nothing that happened in there was straight up. More than likely she was speaking from the next room, subject to the same humiliation. I felt sick. Sick and guilty as hell for all the ways she must have been suffering because of me—I couldn't banish the thought from my mind. I recalled our years together, from our first meeting right up to the phone call I placed from Sardasht City, after crossing back into Iran from Iraq. She'd been informed that I was alive, but she fainted, anyway. She had even written back to me, a letter I'd received, miraculously, just before I arrived in Sardasht City. It included photos of the boys. I remember holding both the letter and the pictures, like a kid with two ice-cream cones, not knowing which to devour first. Those photographs of the children—I wasn't just seeing two young beautiful people—I was seeing all the magic that happens when two people come together. It was a magnificent mystery: two strangers meeting and finding harmony in being together. And their coming together produces a miracle—children. All bright-eyed and innocent. Akram's letter began with an outpouring of poetic affection, almost formal.

"Yadi, my love, my power when I feel weak, my shade when I am hot . . ." She really poured it on thick, and I appreciated every word. Both of us felt we were the luckiest couple in the world. In her letter, she went on about the difficult time she'd had in the days after my crash. How difficult it was to believe that I was dead. But a funeral was kind of obligatory, in the absence of any evidence to suggest that I'd survived. And how hard it had been to look at a photo of my smiling face. But now it was just as hard for her to believe that I was alive. "I love you more than you can imagine," she said, in signing off the letter.

"What are you doing?" It was my interrogator.

"Thinking," I said.

"About those questions, I hope. I don't have much more time to waste on you."

"You're wasting your time for sure," I said, "if you're hoping to get different answers."

"The trouble I went to!" he shouted.

Uh-oh, I'd offended him, and off he went on a rant about having arranged the phone call, and now this one last chance for me to write out the truth, finally, because apparently I'd said I'd co-operate.

"You're not stupid!" he said. "You're one of those elite pilots, a hero! A celebrity! Your life made into a movie for the whole country to see. All you did was make a few mistakes. Just admit it. That's all you've got to do. Why you made these mistakes and how you contacted the Americans. Such a small thing. Then you can go home."

I started to feel sorry for him (like hell!). He was obviously failing in his job. Maybe his boss was pressuring him. Once again, I swore to God and the prophet Mohammad, begged him to believe that I'd been telling the truth. He didn't trust me swearing these sacred oaths, and suddenly it was like the last straw for him; he started yelling verses of the Koran and dragging me up, shrieking at me like a madman, and pushing me out the door towards another cell, promising me as we went that I'd quickly learn how lenient he'd been with me.

Now we were in another room, my senses twitching, telling me that more people were there already, three or four maybe. They mumbled the situation over, then joked and laughed as they began to push and punch me as they yelled questions about the CIA. I was thrown onto the torture bed. My blindfold slipped up onto my forehead so that I could see those bastards for a split second before a fist smacked my lights out. They laid me on the bed as before, and handcuffed me to the headrail, legs to the opposite end. And started flogging the soles of my feet. Immediately my blisters puffed up and started bleeding. I could actually hear blood splashing around the room. They only stopped to pour a warm antiseptic on my feet, saying it was a gift from my American agent.

I remember their sadistic laughter as they started the beating again. I was ordered to move my fingers if I wanted to tell the truth. The pain was unbearable, and I twitched my fingers, but they couldn't have cared less. They only wanted to keep beating me, so, okay, I get it, there's no escape from all this, so, it was kind of okay after that. That's the only thought you have when you're more than halfway to losing consciousness. What can you do? It's kind of okay.

I found myself back in my cell, my feet packaged in those plastic bags, right up to my knees. My brain boiled with pain, nothing specific, just everything. I couldn't understand how I could be so crushed and drained of all will to live, yet still be breathing. I couldn't differentiate between falling asleep or fainting, or even between being alive or dead. I responded to nothing, and didn't care, due to my growing relationship with death. I only needed a little help from God. Perhaps if I prayed, but I was too dizzy to even do that. I remember being lifted onto a stretcher and carried away.

I remember an ambulance.

I remember a hospital.

An army doctor examined my heart and found nothing wrong. Some doctor! He wanted me out of there.

"Doctor, listen to me," I said quietly, in English. "Please, I need a few days' rest in your hospital."

He pretended to understand nothing, just looked at me like I was a lunatic, and even ordered me taken to a psychiatric hospital. I was soon back in the ambulance for another ride to the air force psychiatric unit in Qasre Firoozeh. On the way, my guards didn't object to me removing my blindfold so I could gaze out at the streets, at people who were walking free. Can you imagine what a wonderland it seemed to me, out there, a wonderland of simple but precious freedoms. It was like an epiphany, or a religious experience. What had monetary wealth to do with anything that's important in this life? Nothing. With everyday joys like talking to people? Nothing! Watching television, eating in some third-rate café, taking a bus somewhere, spending a night in a tent—what blessings.

We passed the place where I first met my wife, at the old air force hospital. We continued past air force headquarters, where I used to come and go freely, and was saluted as I went. Imagine!

In the Qasre Firoozeh hospital, the head physician examined me. He was given some fictitious name and occupation, but I set him straight—I was a pilot. He became annoyed because he wanted to know which it was, and what the hell was going on here. He needed the correct information for his file. "Okay," the guard admitted. "He's a pilot," and he looked at me like he was going to kill me later.

For eight days I stayed there, at night strapped to the bed so that I wouldn't escape. It was no holiday, but still, compared to the constant and fearful vigil alone in my cell, it was a holiday. Perhaps because it was close to *Nowrooz*, our New Year's, or perhaps because one of my guards was Kurdish. I'd never met a Kurd who wasn't naturally polite and helpful. He looked upon me as a son might his father, or so I imagined. He took me for walks in the yard, for fresh air. He was too frightened, however, to let me phone my wife, but he did promise to get a letter out to her, in which I wrote a brief account of my situation.

Back at the prison, in my cell once again, I started to mend, although, for a long time, the soles of my feet continued to feel as if they were on fire. However much better I felt physically, I was that much heavier at heart. Days passed with nothing but the routine: three times a day the washroom, three times meals, five times prayers. Over and over again I examined the Koran and that bizarre little book by Khomeini. It was full of valuable moral advice for every kind of situation, for example, during an earthquake, if your house collapses and a woman who is sleeping upstairs—an aunt or any other woman who by marriage is prohibited from being with you—lands on top of you, and your penis accidentally finds its way into her, well, God would pardon you for that. What an idiot. The majority of the educated and younger people were laughing behind Khomeini's back, and he didn't know it.

I began an exercise regime, which provided an escape from the constant fear of death. And I wrote about my experiences, writing in tiny script in the margins of Khomeini's book, then carefully tearing them out. I had a small pile of paper strips, which I kept with me in case I could secret them out. Then, one day . . .

"109! Blindfold on!"

The same old terror. The panic of not knowing what next. They marched me in the usual direction towards the torture cell, but instead we veered left, and left again, until I found myself outside, where I was ordered to remove my blindfold. He gestured to a trailer parked in a corner of the yard.

"Your wife and children. You have fifteen minutes. Talk only of family matters, is that clear? Nothing about what goes on here. Nothing of your life here." He handed me a comb. "Fix yourself up. And try to look happy." He looked at me as if that was probably asking too much.

It was the first time since my arrest that I had looked at myself in the mirror. A long beard. My face creased and brown, the colour of a chestnut shell. White hairs popping out of my skull. Despite my swollen feet, I leapt up the three steps to the trailer and opened the door. Akram stood there, holding my daughter, who stared at me, wide eyed. I didn't blame her. Who was this total stranger who was kissing her mother, and crying all over her? My sons waited impatiently for their turn for a hug. Nobody was saying anything. How could they, after this months-long silence. You have to be a parent to understand the sweet sorrow of crying in front of your children. It's kind of shameful, but who cares when you're all crying. Tears conveyed the torment we'd all been through. Shahram could hardly speak, trying to tell me how much he missed me. Little Mahrokh sat on my lap, so frightened of this creature who was supposed to be her father that she peed herself, leaving a spot on my trousers. She was so embarrassed.

"Perfect!" I said. "You're the only one who noticed that this filthy outfit of mine is only good for pissing on." I kissed her.

"Time's up," the guard said.

As I kissed Akram goodbye, I slipped her my little wad of handwritten notes. (She later told me that the guard had become suspicious and threatened to have her searched by a female guard. However she had stood her ground and called his bluff and managed to leave without being searched.)

Back in my cell, I lapsed into a dreamlike state of wishful thinking—perhaps it was praying—in which I imagined being returned to my family. God had bestowed one miracle upon me, why not another? I recalled that day, my return from Iraq, how I was flown by helicopter from Sardasht City to the army base in Oromieh, where I was welcomed by the regional commander, Colonel Taa-jed-dini. That first night I got the full VIP treatment in their officers' club. The next morning, I was escorted back to the airport where an official reception awaited me. On short notice, the military had amassed quite a number of officers. My wife and eldest son were there, too. Shahram stood at attention, holding a garland of red roses to place around my neck, but Akram fainted before he got the chance. She collapsed on the spot. Shahram jumped into my arms, laughing and crying at the same time, and attacking me with a thousand questions: why had I grown a moustache, and where was my flying suit, and why did I look like a Kurd? And most important of all, what had I brought for him? I had to put him down to help Akram to her feet. And hold her. I could sense some real emotion rippling through this usually tough military crowd.

"Why is everyone crying?" Shahram said. "I thought men don't cry."

"You're a man, too," I told him. "Why are you crying then?"

"I'm not a man," he said. "I'm a child."

My commander, Colonel Farzaneh, hugged me as well and welcomed me back. Then we had one more journey to make, a short flight to my home base, back full circle to my point of departure on that fateful day. We arrived in twenty minutes, and were greeted by friends and colleagues who were eager to embrace this ghost, to see that the rumours were true. Of course, in all that squeezing and backslapping they forgot I was still broken in a number of places. But their love and kind words were a healing in themselves.

"Peace to Sharifi!" they yelled. "Welcome home, Sharifi!"

Three F-5 fighters made a deafening pass overhead, completing this touching salute.

That was my past, and not a bad one, either. I stared at the dim bulb high on the ceiling, itself trapped in a little cage, and tried to conjure up an image of my future, but nothing came into focus. Maybe I didn't have a future. Maybe the fact that I couldn't imagine a future meant that I didn't have one.

One thing was certain—I had no present.

14

COURT MARTIAL

In the name of God the beneficent and the merciful and his prophet Mohammad (peace be upon him) . . . So began my letter to the Minister of Information, His Eminence Hojjat-al-Eslam Rayshahri, a supposed confession, another "last chance." My interrogator was waiting anxiously to read it.

My interrogator asked me to write a few lines describing how sorry I am, and to request your forgiveness. I am not sure I understood him correctly. Honestly, I don't understand what kind of apology or forgiveness he is looking for. I have done nothing to apologize for, and do not need anyone's forgiveness but God's. If you give me a chance to speak at a fair trial, my thanks and appreciation will be with you always. I signed it, *Your obedient Yadollah Sharifirad.*

My interrogator took the letter away and left me alone.

I hadn't been in this room before. It was like a crypt, stucco-walled and equipped with an arsenal of torture tools, some of them I'd never seen before. Lashes and cables and tires and electrical batons that fit neatly in a case installed on the wall next to the entrance. There were screwdrivers, pincers, and knives, plus some objects whose purpose I could only guess at, all locked up on a shelf. Different lengths of rope and chain hung from a wall and the ceiling. It occurred to me that these very implements of torture, and perhaps this very same room, had seen torture at the hands of SAVAK. Thousands would have died in here, mainly members of Hezbollah, "God's party."

The interrogator returned, but not alone, and I knew that my tormentors' patience had run out. I don't have the words to accurately describe the ordeal they put me through. If I screamed for an hour, you might begin to get the picture. Think crucifixion, without the part where Christ pleads, "Father, forgive them, for they know not what they do." I swore if I ever met one of those animals on the street, I'd rip his heart out.

It took weeks for the terror to subside. Body and soul, I was raw and scarred and trembling. Every part of my body ached. Finally, though, I was back on my feet, and promising myself that if I was lucky enough to get out, I would leave Iran, somehow. Khomeini's perverted version of Islam was killing all that was human inside me, and I longed for the merciful God that my loving father had prayed to. I vowed, then and there, to turn my back on this revolution and its primitive gangs of believers. I would find a place where religion was a private matter, and where God did everything in his power to end all this blind and dangerous believing. God was powerful enough that he didn't depend on anyone's feeble little beliefs to prop him up.

Above all, God was trusting. He wanted us to see the truth for ourselves. Otherwise, why give us a heart and a brain and free will?

In the spring of 1989, not long after the Iranian New Year, I was taken to a hearing at Chahar-rahe-ghasr, one block from the armed forces headquarters. It was a court martial. The same old questions were pressed upon me, only this time by higher-ranking interrogators. When they were done, I was told that my family was waiting in the next room. Before I could be led out, the door pushed open and my younger son, Shahrokh, ran towards me. *"Baba, baba!"* he cried. Never mind my military escort, he jumped at me and hung on, his arms tight around my neck. That poor child, how else could he resolve the many months of painful confusion?

Later that day, I was moved to a larger cell occupied by another prisoner, an Iraqi who spoke no Farsi. Since I spoke no Arabic, we kept mostly to ourselves, but it was infinitely better than being alone. A few days later, we were joined by more inmates, an army Lieutenant and two colonels. They had been arrested for failing to properly defend the borders after a disastrous attack by forces of the mujahedeen (the Islamist modernist guerrilla group) based in Iraq. Instead of fighting to the death, these officers had retreated. Fearing execution, they were nervous wrecks. I gave them the benefit of my experience in that hell-hole, some how-to-survive advice. In a word, "accept"—everything. The constant sadness, the pain, the hopelessness. I kept them busy talking and exercising and reading the religious texts, and it gave me a new purpose.

My spirits were further lifted by almost daily deliveries to my cell, packages of food from my wife, via a guard. That one guard had somehow managed to maintain a shred of goodness inside him, and it restored my faith in humanity. Simple acts of kindness like that were the bottom line for any healthy, free-thinking spirit. During the month of Ramadan, a package of *lavash* bread arrived, still warm from the oven. And with it, some *Lighvan paneer*, cheese from the city of Lighvan, renowned for its cheese, and a variety of fruits. I tell you, Akram was seen as some kind of angel in our cell.

Unexpectedly—things only happened unexpectedly—I was taken back to the court martial, where the guards left me waiting in a basement room. I was under no illusion that I stood any chance of winning my case, or even arguing it. Having no lawyer to represent me, I had rehearsed my own defence, providing snappy and factual answers to the prosecutor's questions. Still waiting, I convinced a guard to provide me with paper and pencil so I could prepare a written argument. This amounted to nothing more than the answers they would have been familiar with already, and I had no way of knowing what other questions

I might be asked. Nevertheless, I prepared my response, a kind of life story, the truth of my life as it related to the charges against me:

In the name of God, the beneficent and the merciful, Your Honour, gentlemen of the court, I appeal to you to acknowledge my history as a courageous and dedicated soldier and pilot who has risked his life to defend our country. There isn't a patriot who loves this land more than I do. To be justly labelled a traitor would require that a person such as I had committed crimes against his country of major proportions. But these are tiny mistakes of which I am accused. Such small mistakes anyone could make at any time, and are not offences that should bring down cries of "Traitor!" or "Spy!" upon his head. Or "Fornicator!," as my interrogator has called me.

Gentlemen, I was born in a little village north of Tehran, a place called Nesa-Olya, Taleghan, through which runs the river Shahroud, the River of the King, and beside which stands the mountain which all of you known as Alborz, the King of the Mountains. My village had only thirty cottages and a population of no more than 150. These were people whom I loved as much as my own family. Eventually, I was required to move to Tehran for a better education. The big city was another world, yet it didn't change my love and respect for the proud country people. In Tehran, I couldn't help but notice the poor living amongst the rich, the beggars by the side of the road. They reminded me of how hard the peasant folk worked their fields or tended their flocks for such a meagre income. These struggling people, both in the city and in the country, have always had my sympathy, and I grew up with a burning desire to help them create better lives for themselves. It bothered me how difficult it appeared to be to change things, to narrow the gap between the rich and the poor. My education led me not into the field where I might have helped them directly, but into the Air Force Academy where I imagined that one day, after reaching the top of my profession, I would be in a position to bring my influence to bear on a program to improve the lot of these people. My plan seemed to be unfolding as I had hoped, with promotions that led to my becoming a captain. Then, the Revolution began and I heard the voice of the entire nation screaming for justice against the inequalities that the government had created in Iran. I was behind this revolution all the way. I especially loved the three main slogans shouted by the thousands of demonstrators: "Independence, Freedom, and Islamic Republic." But two of those three never came to pass. The reality of the Revolution never provided freedom and independence. Many of my friends were arrested and executed for their beliefs. What kind of freedom is that? Their families were not allowed to hold funerals for them, nor cry at their graves. You have to understand how much this broke my heart, to see wives and children searching my face for answers to explain why their fathers or husbands or children or brothers were killed. I had no answers. Yet, I spoke to them to ease their grief. Not because I was anti-Islam or anti-Revolution, but because these were simply more people I loved, because I am a lover of people, and all the more a lover of people who need comfort. I believed then and I believe now that executing our own people is not the best way to bring about the objectives of revolution. It is not the only solution to correcting mistakes, nor is it the best way to purge the nation of destructive elements within the revolutionary cause. And I am not the only one who thinks this way. In fact, gentlemen, tell me if I'm wrong, but I believe what I am preaching is in the spirit of the Koran. God's prophet spoke of mercy. And Imam Ali spoke about forgiveness.

When the war broke out, many pilots were saved from the firing squads only to be strapped into jets and ordered to take on dangerous missions in the fight against Saddam. I may have argued that this was unwise, that it was not to our advantage to send them off without preparation or training. How could these pilots concentrate? How could they perform after being physically destroyed in prison. Without exception, these brave men perished in battle.

If I spoke up in their names, it was because I was under the impression that in a revolution that pronounced "Freedom!," I was free to think and speak according to my God-given intelligence. Free to interact with anybody without regard for their beliefs. I was enthusiastic about our new freedoms, so not for a second did I worry about being prosecuted for my words or deeds.

As for my contact with foreigners—please remember that I was a military attaché. My relationship with the Argentinian chargé d'affaires was entirely social. Mine was simply a friendly visit in the spirit of, let's say, meeting an old school friend, and I did my best to show him a good time while he was a visitor to Iran. If he was an American agent working for the CIA, which I do not believe, then I can only say that I didn't know a thing about it. And if I misjudged him, then it was an honest mistake, and I am no less a patriot, and as such I am ready to answer for it.

Once, on a lecture tour of Tehran schools, I met the son of a pilot who had been executed for taking part in the attempted *coup d'état*. He began to cry at the memory of his father—perhaps I reminded him of his father—so I hugged him and cried with him. He reminded me of my own boys, and what they'd be like without me. Should I have hid my emotions? I don't think a rock could have kept its tears inside at such a moment. Yet, I feel persecuted for showing honest emotion. Does that mean I'm anti-Revolution, or against Islam? Because I cried for a child? If what I'm saying makes no sense to you, then my appeal to this court is pointless. Consider my words to be addressed to God, for only he can come to my rescue.

You want to know about my contact with the Americans. I met them mainly at our scheduled monthly gatherings of military attachés. Otherwise, we met at events to which all other diplomats were also invited. My conversations with the Americans were no different than with other diplomats. Did I have any reason to show animosity towards them? No. One of them in particular I rather liked. I enjoyed his company because, like me, he had been a fighter pilot. But did any of them quiz me about my country or approach me for the purposes of spying or such a thing? Absolutely not. Had they done so, that would have been the end of our relationship. On only one occasion did an American ask me about anything remotely strategic—it concerned the number of Afghan refugees in Iran. I directed him to that long-standing international military publication called *Jane's Weekly Magazine*, and after that he never pursued it any further with me.

If these actions of mine warrant punishment, so be it. But don't let it be said that I am a spy, because the thought of betraying my own country has never entered my head. I am still a hero of the war. And please, I want you to consider this—the reason a soldier finds the courage to carry out dangerous missions is due to an extraordinary love for his country.

If there is a question of my failing to spend money allocated to my office for the purposes of purchasing strategic information from abroad, it was because I didn't need it. My popularity within the diplomatic corps made it easy for me to access information without the need for money. Why spend when it wasn't necessary? Didn't we need all our resources to fight Saddam Hussein?

You are accusing me of being sexually promiscuous, and of possessing videos from the time of the Shah. I save this for last because it strikes me as humorous, and I mean no disrespect to the court, but isn't it natural and healthy for a young man to show an interest in girls singing and dancing? We're talking about a time when I was in school and still unmarried. How unfair to ask me to rationalize this perfectly natural stage of a boy's life. Consider my conduct as a married man if you want. I have little to say about the videotapes, except that we recorded them from the television about four years ago, but they are long forgotten, like last week's news.

I had these points jotted down and ready in my pocket, should I have needed them for reference in the face of questions from the prosecution. Around 4 p.m., I was escorted upstairs.

You couldn't call it a courtroom, just a judge sitting behind a regular office desk, and a colonel in civilian clothes acting as the prosecutor, and a young male secretary sitting on the other side of the judge. I was directed into a chair in front of them. Without any kind of ceremony, the prosecutor stated as fact that I'd had unauthorized contact with foreigners and had spied for the Americans against Iran and the Revolution. That was his case. That was it! I wasn't sure how to begin my own defence without a lawyer, so I started to talk about myself according to my notes, more or less, until the judge interrupted me.

"I'm not here to listen to you praise yourself for being a hero," he said. "If you want to speak, speak about the wrongs you have committed." He used the analogy of going to the doctor, where you describe what's wrong with you, not list every organ that's behaving itself.

"Your Honour," I said. "You know—and the whole nation knows—about my dedication to my country. After my crash in Iraq and my safe return, thanks to Kurdish rebels, nobody could believe I would be able to fly again, but I did. I flew out of the 4th Tactical Air Base, in Dezful, where I was made base commander's deputy in operations. I began flying again, even dangerous missions deep into Iraq. Why did I do it? Because I felt it was my responsibility. How could a few broken bones stop me from defending Iranian skies? With such an attitude, tell me, Your Honour, how could I have done something hurtful to this country? What more could I have done to dedicate myself to the cause? To prove my love for the country, religion, and revolution?

"As you know, it was thought that I was killed in action. My family lived through my funeral. Imagine how my wife felt about me going off to war after that. You can bet that she pleaded with me to be more careful. She cried every time I left home, and she held me hard, as if it was my very last time, but I still went. As for the accusations of the crimes I have committed, what can I say? I am not a lawyer, so I cannot defend myself in a professional manner. I only ask that you remember God and listen as he does, with his heart. If you still truly believe that I am lying, and that I have wronged this country, then, full in the knowledge that God, the higher judge, is watching these proceedings, please pass sentence upon me. My life depends on your decision."

I handed over my ragged notes to the judge, but he didn't look at them, and just passed them to his secretary. He seemed weary, and keen to get things over with, but he must have noticed the tears that had swollen my eyes, although he must have been accustomed to seeing defendants in much worse shape than me. But maybe none so talkative. I'd cragged on with my speech for about twenty minutes. I was escorted out of the room and out of the building and back to my cell.

After three days, still no verdict that I knew of, but I was moved to a larger cell occupied by four others. A few days later, I was transferred to the public prison located within the confines of Jamshidieh Military Base in northwest Tehran. The first night there, they shaved my head and beard.

I got along well with the other prisoners, about four hundred of them. It was a unique environment, all of us equal, our ranks obliterated, along with our wealth, education, and social status. Guilty or innocent, it made no difference to how we treated each other. We all helped each other to solve problems as they arose. Strange to say, but I experienced it as a kind of paradise compared with the solitary confinement.

Months passed easily now that I had access to books, and I was healthy enough to begin a physical-fitness regimen. One day, unannounced, I was taken to the visitors' room where Akram was waiting with my daughter held tightly in her arms. My wife was draped head to foot in a silky black chador, which only emphasized the beauty of her green eyes, like two unwashed emeralds shining on the face of the moon. For all the beauty of her face, she appeared neither happy nor sad. Not crying, not smiling, she exuded a love deeper than any superficial emotion could express, something far behind the eyes, perhaps at the level of the soul. It was almost too much, almost disturbing. I directed my attention to Mahrokh, who reached for me and hugged me and kissed me. After I regained my composure, I asked Akram if she had news of my verdict, since I'd never heard. Her first reaction was to divert her gaze to the ground. Not a good sign.

"They gave you ten years," she said.

I was beyond outrage. Nothing anyone could do about it. "Ten years is too long for you to suffer through waiting for me," I said. I knew I had to say what I couldn't believe I would ever say to my beloved wife. "You have to forget me so you can enjoy the rest of your life."

"Don't talk like that, Yadi."

"You have to divorce me," I told her.

"I won't," she said. "Stop talking like that. I love you."

"The kids will be better off if you remarry."

"Life without you is meaningless," she said. "I'm your wife and the mother of your children until I die. So, please, Yadi, stop talking to me like that. Or I will leave immediately."

We cried in each other's arms, with Mahrokh staring at us. When the guard told us our time was up, we only had time for a quick good-bye. But we looked at each other in a way that solidified our vows. The visit left me strong, but feeling no less guilty for what I'd put my family through.

I found out a few days later that my ten-year sentence was a conditional sentence, of which about nine years would be served in the community. Any of my actions or words that would be considered—by the authorities' standards—to be harmful to the Islamic Republic would land me right back in jail. As part of my conditional sentence I was also required to physically report, on a weekly basis, to the Office of the Court Martial.

So, less than a year later, I was released from jail and discharged from the air force. Finally, I could go home. Finally, I was free—well, for a few days at least—until I realized that freedom in Iran was just an illusion.

15

AKRAM'S STORY

———

It was an emotional farewell for me and my fellow prisoners, before I walked out of prison. We had bonded in a way that would be impossible in ordinary life. I'd become something of a leader within the inmate population, so they might have regretted the loss of someone who could empathize with them.

Once I was back on the street, I marvelled at the life we take for granted—cars, buses, people going about their business. Nothing had changed. Everything was wonderfully normal. I hailed a cab and directed the driver to take me home. On the street where I lived, it was like no one knew me after my one-year absence. Perhaps it was because I had no flying suit on, I guessed, or it was just an illusion. The cold reception didn't dampen my spirits as I knocked on my door. You can't imagine how shocked my family was to see me. They'd planned to pick me up at the prison, but not until later that day.

I'd never felt so lucky to be alive. And free and happy. Everything I had ever wanted was there around me, within reach, not least the sky, but particularly my precious home. No more "Hadji!" or "109!" Once again, I was "Yadi," my real name. What a joy!

I hadn't had the opportunity to quiz my wife about her arrest, and I wasn't sure it was the right time. Better to let things settle, I thought, and she'll volunteer to tell the story herself, just as she'd done after my miraculous return from Iraq. But this homecoming was a different story. A celebration had greeted me after my crash, a houseful of well-wishers, friends who wanted to stay and party into the night. This time not a soul dared to be seen socializing with an accused traitor, an anti-Revolutionist, a person branded as anti-Islam and an enemy of Aya-tollah Khomeini.

I remembered my return from Iraq, and the calming effect Akram's tale of woe had had on me. Her ordeal—believing I was dead—was a nightmare for her if it was true, but I was alive and the ordeal was over, I thought. Nevertheless, hearing about it was like listening to sad music. She'd confessed to having had premonitions well in advance of my fateful mission, her sleep disturbed by nightmares of my death. She hadn't been able to concentrate or eat or hide her anxiety from friends and neighbours who wondered why she seemed so distracted. She had been praying, not so much for me as for God to bring the Iran-Iraq War to an end. Reports of other pilots gone missing—almost a daily occurrence—convinced her that it was only a matter of time before she got the news that her husband had crashed or had been hit by a missile, or had simply failed to return.

"You don't know what an actor I became in front of you, Yadi," she had said. "But since I knew what responsibility you carried on your shoulders, I didn't want to distract you. Remember the day I asked you, 'If the war starts, and I ask you not to fly or call in sick, would you listen to me?' And you replied, 'No! And don't ever ask me that question again.' You explained how love of family is different than love of country, and that you couldn't sacrifice the nation in order to live another day with your family. Your statement sounded cruel, but it was the truth. After that, I never asked you again. But each time you left for the command post, I was worried sick until you returned again at night. If ever you were late, my heart would ache, and each moment that passed, I couldn't help imagining bad news—an unexpected phone call or a knock on the door—the fear would cause my heart to stop. You had advised me to keep my phone conversations short so that the phone was available for emergencies. But, in the days before your crash, I couldn't help myself, I was so nervous—all day I was on the phone to my mother, sisters, and brothers, and other relatives and friends. I was just trying to keep my mind off you. I often counted the planes taking off and then landing. If the numbers didn't correspond, I was terrified that it was you who hadn't returned.

"Do you remember the day before you disappeared, when I asked you to invite my cousin and her husband for lunch for the next day? It wasn't like you to agree so immediately, and without questioning. You even suggested we invite one or two of our family friends as well. After our agreement you said it was better for me to be busy preparing for guests than to be alone in the house. You encouraged me, lunch or dinner, it didn't matter, good idea. And what did I do? Instead of appreciating this change in you, all I did was get even crazier, like I had an idea, a premonition, like a bee buzzing in my head that something was going to happen. And in my mind's eye, I became that bee without its favourite flower. So, I craved your scent, your sweetness, all the more before I lost you.

"The night before you left on your last mission, I couldn't sleep. I was obsessing about all the possible ways you might encounter trouble. I fought a futile battle against following these thoughts, and got very depressed. It was the worst night of my life, although there would be many bad nights to follow. But, eventually, the day dawned, and you received a call from the command post. You put your flying suit out, shined your boots, and wrapped your red scarf around your neck. You looked very alert. You didn't want to talk with me or wake up the kids before you left. You just gave them a kiss while they slept, and before closing the door on them, you checked one last time to see if they were peeking out from under the covers. You only took a cup of tea that morning, never mind that I insisted you eat something. No, you were ready to go. Your eyes were full of love for me, I remember that so well. And the way you held me so tightly in your arms, I could hear your heart beating. I felt so safe there with you, and so reluctant to let the moment pass, I had thoughts of asking you to call your commander to postpone your mission for one more day. But such thoughts were childish and I let them pass. I don't know if you noticed, but after you kissed me goodbye, and as you were leaving, I held the door half open and kept watching you as you slowly vanished out of sight. I remained standing there when Shahram interrupted my reverie, asking for a glass of water. While I got Shahram what he wanted, I thought again about calling your commander and asking him to postpone the mission. But what kind of wife would do a thing like that? You would never have forgiven me.

"I remained in the kitchen, stunned, without thinking or doing anything, just waiting by the window until I heard the roaring sounds of jet engines, and then watched as three planes rose into the hazy sky. You were in the lead plane, I knew that, with your wingmen on either side, and once again I watched until the sky absorbed every last speck of you. By then I was crying. Before the kids noticed, I washed my face and tried to appear as normal as possible. I had no appetite for breakfast, or lunch, but then I recalled how encouraging you'd been about inviting my cousin, so I began thinking about what we'd all eat later.

"An hour after you took off, I was back searching the skies again, in the direction you most often appeared on your return flights. Twice I cut myself at the chopping board. Eventually, two planes landed, and my mood brightened, magically. The meal was ready and I was expecting your call from the base at any minute. Half an hour passed and you didn't call. I imagined that your debriefing was taking longer than usual, that's all. Or that you were having words with your commander, or that you decided to come right home without calling. Sometimes you liked to surprise me like that. I waited by the phone for another fifteen minutes before I began to feel anxious. Even our guests were late, so I was doubly restless. It would not have been improper for me to phone the command post, and I was just about to do that when I heard a rap on the door. Thinking that it was you trying to surprise me, I knocked over the telephone table in my rush to reach the door, but it was my cousin Batool and her husband, Faizi. I brought them in and sat them down, so it was definitely time to call you to say that our guests were here. I picked the phone off the floor and got Major Firouz Ahmaripour on the line. I asked him to find you and tell you that our lunch guests had arrived. He explained that you were busy, but that he would deliver the message, all polite and everything. Then he said goodbye and hung up.

"I busied myself, offering our guests cold drinks, but they preferred tea. I was returning from the kitchen with two glasses of hot tea when the telephone rang. This time I was absolutely sure it was you, but it was Colonel Farzaneh. Just the sound of his voice and my heart shattered, like a fine crystal glass, into a million pieces.

"'How are you, Mrs. Sharifi?' he asked. 'And the kids, how are they?' Before I could answer, he continued with, 'I'm sorry to tell you that Captain Sharifi was involved in a dogfight with Iraqi MiGs and had to eject. Our fighters are flying into the area right now with helicopters to search for him. It'll take a few hours to find him, so please sit tight, and try not to worry. When we get the news, we'll call you.'

"I don't know what I said, but he soon hung up. I'm not even sure what he said, exactly. After the part about you getting shot down and having to eject, I felt dizzy, and eventually the telephone receiver fell out of my hand, and I guess I must have passed out on the floor, because when I opened my eyes, my cousin was trying to help me get up, and Faizi was on the phone, listening to the news from the commander. They both looked scared, my cousin and her husband. They tried to reassure me, but they couldn't, could they? Later, more of our invited friends arrived, two couples, Mr. Rasoul Adeli and Mr. Mohammad Mohammadi with their wives Esmat and Asraf. They seemed to think that discussing the details of your flight, and all the mechanics involved in ejecting would somehow make me feel better. They started theorizing where you might be, somewhere near the Iran-Iraq border. They were sure you were safe, and they reminded me that helicopters were looking for you as we spoke. Our little family gathering, which was supposed to be such a happy afternoon, turned into something more like a funeral party.

"I spoke on the phone with one of you wingmen, Captain Abbasian, who'd heard you radioing just as you were intercepted by the MiGs. You'd said, 'Hey, boys! MiG! MiG!' Abbasian was sure that you were safe. He was most convincing, and this optimism made it a little easier to believe that you might have survived. I pretended, anyway. I tried to act cool, and kept busy with my guests, making them feel welcome, when, of course, they must have felt very awkward and probably were thinking what a stroke of bad luck to have been invited in here just when a catastrophe had occurred. I kept offering them food, but nobody was hungry. They only pretended to eat, as did I.

"After lunch, I couldn't do anything—I was so emotionally drained. My cousin cleaned up, and by 5 p.m., we'd received no further news. The search-and-rescue team was still out there looking for you, or so Colonel Farzaneh said. I started to believe he was lying, just to keep me calm, to prepare me for the worst. So, I appealed to Mr. Mohammadi and Mr. Adeli to take me to the command post.

"We met Colonel Farzaneh, who welcomed us warmly and directed us to a room full of maps covered with lines and dots of red and blue, none of which I understood. He showed me the exact location where you had ejected. It was Kurdish rebel country, he explained, full of people who are fighting against Saddam, just as we were. We shouldn't give up, he told me, because search helicopters were still in the air looking for my husband. Iraqi planes were also concentrated in the area, which seemed to give him extra hope that you were alive and yet not arrested by the enemy. At any rate, I was satisfied that everything was being done to find you. On top of that, they praised you for being one of the best pilots in the country, and for having had survival training for just this kind of incident, so that even if they didn't find you that night, there was still hope of finding you alive, later. All this perked me up a bit, for sure. Our guests were certainly more hopeful, and their optimism infected me somewhat, so we left there in a better frame of mind, a little less worried. Just to be even more sure, I asked Mohammadi and Adeli to help me find another of your wingmen, Lieutenant Ardestani. I wanted to compare his story with that of Captain Abbasian and Colonel Farzaneh.

"We found Lieutenant Ardestani at home, and when he saw us, I noticed that he seemed to be a little less sure of himself, even a little nervous. He asked us to come in, but we declined his offer because we were in a rush I asked him if he knew about your crash, and what he said we'd pretty much heard already, but the way he said it, his answers coming in short little clips, and his eyes darting to the floor, never looking at me directly, I felt he was being evasive, trying to hide the truth from me. So there I was again, feeling desperate. I thanked him and said good night.

"When I arrived home, I only had to open the door to see what kind of mood the kids were in—not my usual high-energy boys. That time of day, they'd normally be running around the house, playing and laughing and fighting. But they were behaving like strangers towards each other, sitting each by himself in some corner of the house, like orphans, or like pearls without their shells. The situation was too much for me, and I burst into tears, right there in front of my guests, who had remained while Adeli and Mohammadi took me to the command post. Shahram ran towards me, Shahrokh right behind him, trying to move his older brother so he could hug me, so they got hold of me from both sides, right there in the doorway and started to cry their eyes out. Nothing or nobody could make them stop. What was worse, they seemed to think that your disappearance was my fault, or at least that it was my responsibility to bring you back. I felt so powerless and hopeless. What a situation for our guests to be in, with all the ladies crying and their husbands valiantly trying to encourage me. But their sorrowful voices betrayed them.

"At around 6 p.m., my guests left. Back to their own jobs, their own homes and children. Except my cousin, who stayed and shared our sadness through that long night, which passed without a wink of sleep. My mind was bombarded with possibilities, including the idea that you might be dead. Until they had your burnt body as proof, I knew that your commander would play games with me, to prepare me for the worst. I could see it coming, all the patriotic language, how you'd martyred yourself for Iran and the Revolution. Then the words of Captain Abbasian and Lieutenant Ardestani would come to mind and once again I would be mildly encouraged that you might still be alive. Of course, if you were alive, you would have been captured. And the Iraqis knew all about you, if the rumours were true that Saddam Hussein had a list of pilots they especially wanted dead. You'd done so much damage to their war machine. You would be tortured, not just like a simple soldier, but in keeping with your stature and courage. They would kill you under such torture, no doubt about it, unless you confessed information they wanted, which, of course, you wouldn't, knowing you as I do. So it seemed like one way or another, you were dead. Unless you escaped. But then, it was the coldest part of winter, and the terrain, all the way from where you crashed, to the Iranian border, was mountainous, very rugged. You would have needed food, not just the few raisins and pistachio nuts that you always carried with you. And what about clothing? What would keep you warm in those freezing temperatures?

"My cousin tried to distract me, chattering continuously, asking questions, engaging me any way she could. Shahram pretended not to be listening, but anytime my voice started to tremble or my eyes got teary, he bent his head and cried quietly. This became too much for my cousin, who asked the kids to say good night and go to their bedrooms. But still, I could hear them awake, playing your favourite song, 'Khalabanlar' ('Pilots'), which you had recorded the previous evening. It was so sad to hear it without you there. This time, with no apologies, I retreated to our bedroom and for the first time, I cried like a baby. After that, I felt well enough to look in on the kids, but quietly so that I wouldn't disturb them. I heard the cassette player very low, and Shahrokh questioning his older brother. 'Why are you crying?' he asked. 'Because we don't have a dad anymore,' Shahram replied. 'Yes, we do, he's gone to Alak to bomb Saddam.' Shahram explained that it wasn't Alak, it was Iraq. He told his brother that one of his friends had a father who hadn't come back from the war. The family had to leave their military house after that because their father was no longer a soldier. He'd died in Iraq. This talk broke my heart.

"All I could see in my mind's eye was an unbroken wall, neverendingly long, with no possibility of looking beyond. My cousin, who had so far done a heroic job on me, couldn't hide her sorrow any longer, and started to cry with me. I felt a bit better after that.

"I brought the kids out to join us in the living room so that they wouldn't sink to far into hopelessness. They remained quiet, like two old men. It was the first time I'd ever seen them together without their being physical with each other, without playing, without having fun and raising hell and ignoring my warnings. They seemed to have vanished from childhood. It was like they'd realized their job now was to stay with me and look after me in your absence.

"Shahrokh was the only one to fall asleep that night, and only for about two hours. The rest of us stayed awake, but avoiding eye contact. We couldn't bear to be caught seen in such a state of sadness. When morning dawned, the telephone started ringing, one caller after another, friends, relatives, mere acquaintances who wanted to know what had happened to you. What could I say? I had nothing to tell them. Relatives showed up from cities near and far, wanting to share my pain. I appreciated it, despite running on empty, because the worst thing of all was to be alone. They actually picked up the mood by creating an atmosphere of pride in who you were, and what a patriot you were, and how dedicated you were to the war effort, and all that you'd accomplished. The house was full of respect and love for you. I couldn't have expected anything better, given the circumstances.

"Every day after that, we had visitors. Shahrokh took it upon himself to be your protector, prohibiting anyone from entering your study, or to touch your books or any of your personal things. At mealtimes, if anyone appeared to be about to sit in your chair, he would jump into the seat and say, 'You can't sit here—this is Daddy's chair. If you sit there, where will Daddy sit? Can't you understand?' This went for me, too—I couldn't go to your study or alter anything, either. He wouldn't even let me vacuum in there! Everything had to be just as it had been before you left. You can go see for yourself—your extra flight suit hanging there to dry. I bet it's dry by now! Your shirt is lying on the ironing table, the book you were reading that night is still open, face down, waiting for you. Would you believe that the children wouldn't even let me change the sheets on the bed. Every night at bedtime, they would be first to lie down on your side of the bed for a few minutes to enjoy the scent that they identified as yours. I admit it, I loved it too, plus, I had the whole night to enjoy that little bit of you that still lingered there. Yadi, thank God you're back."

This time, as I explained earlier, returning from prison brought not a single well-wisher. No relative, no friend, nobody. I was left to watch my wife prepare her dinner celebration. She had lots to tell me, I knew it, like the things that had happened to her after my arrest. It wouldn't be as poignant as the stories she told of her suffering after my crash, but I wanted to hear everything, whenever she felt ready to go into it.

Akram made a mountain of food, as usual, with all my favourite dishes. And there was so much of it that she wouldn't have to cook for a week, but it was my responsibility to finish everything. We sat around the table, strangely quiet, just feasting on each other. I had the image of us as five volleyball players, all trying to keep the ball of love in the air, not wanting it to touch the ground. Mahrokh, who was four years old then, kissed me unexpectedly, time and time again. She gave me a gift of a doll, one of her favourites. "Mahdokht" she called it. Of course, at bedtime, everyone wanted to sleep on our bed. The boys could be convinced to retreat to their own room, but not Mahrokh.

Three days passed without anyone asking me directly what had happened to me. I thought I would suit up and risk a visit to headquarters. My boss would be less emotional.

"We were all worried about you, Sharifi," he said. It was a warm greeting, which I appreciated. "We didn't expect to see you again."

He seemed truly glad to see me, and acknowledged me as an excellent officer and a good person, just a little careless on religious matters, he suggested. No doubt that was the reason for my arrest, my boss said. I didn't bother to comment, only thanked him for his concern. I proceeded to the Intelligence Service to procure my letter of discharge from the armed forces, along with two pages of instructions to help me navigate the bureaucratic maze to sign off and sign out on every last detail. I didn't want to overlook anything. I didn't want to be found in possession of anything that belonged to the army or air force. That was the last day I wore the uniform that I had so proudly worn for twenty-one years.

I took advantage of my visit to drop in on Brigadier General Sattari. He had been a friend of mine, not a pilot but a radar man, who had risen to the post of commander of the air force, probably due to his close relations with a few high-ranking clergy. I phoned his secretary to advise him that I would be showing up, and was put on hold for a few minutes, then told that the general was not in his office. It sounded like a lie. More likely, he didn't want to see me. I ran into his operations deputy, Colonel Ardestani, my wingman on that fateful mission, seven years ago. He had been promoted to the rank of Colonel because he was a faithful Muslim and the follower of Ayatollah Khamenei. He wasn't too happy to see me, either—probably because I had been his squadron commander at that time, and he might have experienced a little fallout from my arrest, himself. He might have been happier if I'd died in the crash. In hindsight, I could see that he must have thought I was too harsh on the Revolution, although he never mentioned it, not to me, at least. I asked him to say goodbye to any of my old friends that he should happen to run into.

That was it, that summer day in 1989, my last day as Colonel Sharifirad. From then on, I was "Mr." and starting a new life.

When I arrived home, Akram was furious with the whole system that had treated me so badly. She couldn't even look at me, she was that angry. The government and the entire hierarchy of the armed forces were nothing but cowards, she said. And she couldn't just stop there, so she started in on all that had happened to her since my arrest.

"It was about 11 a.m. when the doorbell rang. Someone introduced himself as a government drug controller. They'd received information that drugs were being hidden in our apartment, and so he was obliged to check it out. I let him in, since it was obviously a mistake that would be realized quickly. But then seven more officers followed him in, some with guns. First, they disconnected the phone. Then they opened everything, from the fridge, to the electrical-breaker cabinet, to boxes in our storage area. They kept at it for five hours, and of course they came away empty-handed. No drugs.

"The boys came back from school to see all these strange men in the house. Men and guns. Little Mahrokh sat on the chair, petrified. Your brother-in-law came over. He couldn't believe what was going on, but he kept quiet until the search was over, and they left saying they'd be back the next day. They took all our photos, family and military, everything. Oh, yes, and your small Sony radio and tape recorder and all our video cassettes. Documents too, all of it, and none of it returned. They told me that you'd gone to Bandar Abbas on a special mission, and would be back soon. They also took the suitcase that your friend, the Argentinian chargé d'affaires, left here for safekeeping while he travelled south to Isfahan and Shiraz. When you didn't come home on time, I called your co-worker, Colonel Mirkiani, and asked him if he knew anything about this. He didn't know anything. Night fell and still you didn't show up. I was terrified. What had happened to you?

"The next morning, two more men arrived, one of them a major in the air force. They continued the search, rechecking everything, but still they couldn't find anything that satisfied them. That's the last I saw of them, except for a call one day to ask me about the Argentinian chargé d'affaires. What could I say? I knew nothing about his trip to Iran. I knew nothing about your relations with diplomats in Pakistan. The Americans, I knew less than nothing about. I didn't know anything, although I wanted to say something that might help bring you back."

"So, they didn't arrest you?" I asked. "Or torture you, or put you in solitary confinement?"

"Nothing like that," she said. "They just pressured me to tell them about your dealings with the Americans, but as you know, there was nothing to say, since I was never interested in your government business."

"Then they lied to me!" I said. "So what else happened?"

"Every day I made an effort to speak to some government official about your arrest, but no one could do anything."

"Who did you talk to?" I asked.

"I met the adviser to President Rafsanjani. Mr. Mohajerani was his name. And Brigadier General Salimi, military adviser to the Ayatollah Khomeini, and Mr. Rahimi, the ex-ambassador of Iran in Pakistan, and personnel in your office, and in the court martial, although I don't remember their names."

"And no one helped you?" I asked.

"They tried to help, but they couldn't. They described your situation as very dangerous, so they had to tread lightly. They were scared to stick their noses where they might not be welcome. Someone in your office told me—it was just a guess, they said—that you might be in a special armed forces prison in Jamshidieh army base with the code name 336. When you called me from jail, I didn't know where you were. Then I was invited to visit you, then they cancelled it. After I got your letter from the hospital, and learned that you had been tortured, I had to see you and find out what had happened.

"One day, I went to the court martial to arrange an appointment to see one of the clergymen responsible for judging officers like you, but I got nowhere. In fact, they asked me to leave the building. Another judge noticed me, Hojjat-al-Islam Younesi. He wanted to know what I wanted, and I explained who you were and asked him why you had been arrested and why I had not been told where you were. He gave me some kind of fancy answer. I honestly could not believe it. He chastised me, first of all, for being so naive as to think you had done nothing wrong. You were an agent of the CIA—did you know that, Yadi?

Even your crash and the Kurds swooping in to help you—all that was an American plan. 'Go home,' he told me. 'I have no time for you.' I went home all right, broken-hearted and hopeless. What else could I have done?

"In all that time, I hadn't mentioned your arrest to many people. Not to your mother, not even to most of my relatives, either. It felt dishonourable to talk about it, since it was an affront to your dignity. I did discuss it with my brother and your brother-in-law, but even with them I felt embarrassed. Besides them, nobody was aware that you had been arrested." She stopped.

"Can we just forget about it?" Akram asked me. "Everything! Let's not talk about this anymore. Let's think only about the future, and about our new life. We both need new jobs. We have kids who have to eat. Crying about this injustice isn't going to help anything. Are you listening?"

"Yes, I'm listening," I said.

"Why don't you answer then?" she asked.

"I have no answers," I said. "The truth is, I don't know what I'm going to do. I don't know anything except flying."

Akram had nothing to say to that. On that day, we didn't have a clue about our next step.

16

THE ILLUSION OF NORMAL

Arrests continued to happen everywhere and for no reason. People were detained without charge, hung without trial, their deaths unannounced, simply disappeared without a trace. One friend, and only one, found the courage to pay me a visit in those first ten days after my release from prison. I really couldn't blame the others. They would have been afraid of being observed by the Intelligence Service.

Despite being cut off from my past life, I enjoyed every minute of freedom. Free to go out and look at the sky, free to feel the warmth of the sun on my face for as long as I wanted. The day had no structure, and no limit to the time I could spend with my family in the long evenings after dinner, just enjoying being together. When the house fell asleep, I often remained awake to look at my wife lying there with her eyes closed. She seemed so relaxed and worry free. I would go to the kids' rooms and watch them, such innocents. Back in bed, I would lie there, restless, afraid of the dark, and fearing nightmares, the minute I dozed off.

Financially, I was in big trouble. My bank accounts had been closed by the Intelligence Service, and remained confiscated. My only source of income was a fraction of my former salary. My lifelong savings had vanished. Akram had hidden some cash at home, but I didn't know how long we could survive on that. Finding government work was out of the question, so I had to consider how to go about becoming a businessman. I would need a loan, but the banks wouldn't look at me.

As for my kids, their hopes for any kind of further education were squelched. University, though a ways down the road for them, would be out of bounds, so on one hand I had my freedom, but on the other I was worried to death about our future. Neither did I trust the Intelligence Service to leave me alone. I was still very much in their sights, particularly once a week when I was required to sign in at the office of the court martial, and if for any reason I left Tehran, they had to be informed. So, in fact, I wasn't really free at all. My prison had only become larger. But I decided not to mention these restrictions to Akram, since it would only upset her. I decided instead to act as free as I could. I planned a short trip to the holy city of Mahshad.

Mahshad is the site of the tomb of Imam Reza, the eighth religious leader of the Shia Muslims, who lived in the ninth century. I told Akram that while in prison I'd vowed to make this pilgrimage, and she accepted that as a good enough reason to take a well-earned break from our boys, Shahram and Shahrokh, taking only little Mahrokh. For Akram and me, the trip was like a second honeymoon.

After quickly paying our respects at the tomb of Imam Reza, Akram made the most of the shopping opportunities. She's a woman who knows how to shop, and disregarding our financial trouble she proved it, purchasing jewellery and *firoozeh* (turquoise) with her small cash savings. Exhausted from being on her feet all day, she and Mahrokh returned to the hotel, while I felt the urge to spend more time with Imam Reza.

The story goes that Imam Reza died before he became caliph of the Muslims, poisoned by grapes given to him by his wife. She reasoned that if he died from the poison, what kind of caliph must he have been? History was much kinder to him, as Shia Muslims around the world realized they had lost a great leader, and to this day they flock to his grave to touch and kiss the tomb.

Many behave as if he's still with us, appealing to him to solve their problems. The mausoleum is equal or better to any palace, with thousands of gold and silver pieces adorning the walls, along with mirrors of different colours. A magnificent chandelier hangs in the central hall, under the central dome. You can strain your neck gawking at it, which is all you want to do, given the scale of it, as huge and bright as the sky. Everybody who enters is impressed, but I seemed to be the only one appreciating it in silence. There is not a standard practice in that place, all differ, from one room to another. Chattering away to God or to the soul of the Imam are more common, all of which sounds like a lot of groaning and crying. Illiterate peasants pay a handsome fee to the local clergy to pray for them. Not a bad business. Or you can buy candles and light them up, which apparently makes the spirit of the Imam happy.

I sat next to an old man who had his head cranked back as he prayed to the golden ceiling of the tomb. He held his hands in front of his face, palms open, praying loudly and mournfully in Arabic. Occasionally, he referred to his fingers, as if he was counting off a list of forgivenesses he was asking of God, or a plea to Imam Reza to absolve sins he had committed in his lifetime. Then he started praying for the safe return of his son, who was a prisoner of war in Iraq. His lamentations were like the cries of a hungry child, and I couldn't take it any longer and searched for a quieter spot.

People generally shuffled from place to place, lost in their serious thoughts, not a single person smiling. This was not a place you saw anyone enjoying themselves. Everyone had problems of some kind, all of them appealing to Imam Reza to fix their lives, since he had a reputation as a healer. Any incurable disease at all, he could handle. Barren women were said to have been made fertile as a result of his powers.

The grave itself sat within a beautifully carved protective latticework covered with gold and silver. You could see through to the sarcophagus, which was covered with a black-and-green cloth. But around this burial plot lay at least a million dollars in small bills, a single day's take from a never-ending stream of the faithful, most of them ragged poor. These pilgrims began pressing close against me, pushing and shoving from all sides, so I stepped back to watch how they tried to reach and touch the latticework. My excitement at being there, combined with the cacophony of mournful incantations, sent me into an altered state, somewhere between believing and denying the power of such exotic worship.

I couldn't come to terms with the contrast between the poverty of the people visiting the tomb and the blatant extravagance of the place. These people, who looked chronically hungry, seemed willing to leave what little they had on the tomb and on the glittering walls. I wondered why a man of God needed such a luxurious resting place. To my mind, it didn't properly reflect the humility with which he lived his life. Did he really need doors of gold? Even his famous old sword, hanging high on the wall, was framed in gold. This kind of religiosity had always been too complicated for my simple mind, so I performed my evening *namaaz* and left. Akram must have been wondering where I was.

As I made my way back to the hotel, I thought of Khomeini, and doubted very much that his tomb would ever become a tourist destination. I hadn't really known him until his return to Iran, in 1979, after fifteen years of exile in Iraq and France. Watching him on television, as he emerged from the plane at Mehrabad Airport, I was struck by how slow and old he appeared to be. But where was the love? I couldn't see it. Stepping down onto Iranian soil, Khomeini showed no emotion at all, which astounded me. No love of country, no appreciation for his homeland, not even the slightest gesture of appreciation to the thousands who greeted him. How do you compare the compassion of someone like Imam Reza to someone as self-centred as Khomeini? You can't.

Khomeini's homecoming speech took place in the Beheshteh Zahra Cemetery, where, for the most part, he talked about the poor, promising them his help. Otherwise, he focused on the Shah, blaming him for "destroying our country and expanding the graveyards." So, what had this "saviour" done for us. After ten years of rule, Khomeini had far more blood on his hands than the Shah had in thirty years. And that wasn't counting the casualties in Khomeini's ongoing war with Saddam Hussein. Just before my release from prison, five thousand members of the Mojahedin-e-Khalgh Party had been executed because, in Khomeini's eyes, they'd been unfaithful to his cause. Then he ordered their blood be sucked from their veins in order to replenish the national blood bank, which was at a low ebb, due to his stupid war. To protect my sanity, I had to dispel the thought from my mind. This man was an ayatollah? Hailed as a representative of God on earth? I don't think so! And I doubt God thought so, either.

I had become nervous and outraged, all sweaty and boiling over inside, just thinking of the injustice of the Ayatollah's regime. His end couldn't come too soon.

I arrived at the hotel and knocked on our room door. Before Akram could say a thing, Mahrokh ran into my arms, asking me where I'd been. I knew that I was in for a lecture, since it wasn't like Mahrokh to question my whereabouts. Like mother, like daughter, I thought. Sure enough, Akram had been worried about me. I explained that I'd been thinking.

"You think too much," she said. "You'll wind up in trouble again if you don't just act normal."

"Actually, I've been praying," I said. That made her even angrier. "I'm sorry, I can't help it," I said. "I'm worrying about everything these days. Especially about our future."

"Quit worrying," she said. "Everything is going to turn out all right."

She changed the subject, telling me about her daydreams while I'd been at the tomb of Imam Reza, about what a fortunate life we had, all things considered. We just had to forget about that one horrible year. Overall, we'd had a wonderful time together, with only one year of bad luck. We should resume our positive attitude, she said. We should expect good fortune to revisit us soon. Mahrokh fell asleep while we were chatting, so we abandoned plans to head for a restaurant. We had dinner in our room and made an early night of it.

I awoke the next morning to a golden glow filling the room. I went to the window, surprised to see the Golden Temple of Imam Reza so close, the reflected sunrise off the dome lighting up this new life of ours. We had breakfast in the room, then headed for the covered market, where Akram once again made the most of it. As I said earlier, she is in her element when she is shopping. Nothing distracts her, neither fatigue nor hunger nor existential problems. She forgets about everything, especially me, and I'm reduced to being her butler, following her around, one hand holding on to Mahrokh, the other hand lugging her many purchases.

After a few days in Mahshad, it was time to return to Tehran. On the plane, as my wife and daughter were sleeping, I recalled my first big trip outside the country when I was twenty-two years old. We were a group of five cadets heading for America for pilot training, overnighting in London on the way, in a hotel in the heart of the city. My buddies couldn't wait to hit the streets and introduce me to the nightlife. They must have thought I was weird, not wanting to join them, but I viewed it as a sin to stare at naked women. I would loosen up a bit once we arrived at Lakeland Air Force Base in San Antonio, Texas.

Four months I was there, taking an intensive English course, and during that time I met a girl in a clothing store. She was a real knockout, as Americans would say. I asked her out. I was with friends at the time, and she turned me down, but she promised to show us where the action was, a dance club called Chamisal. The place had a Mexican theme, noisy and full of teenagers. When the music started up, my buddies put the moves on her, monopolizing her on the dance floor while I sat back and watched. She must have taken pity on me, because she asked me to dance. After the first number, she didn't seem to want to quit, so we kept dancing. In fact, we stuck together the whole evening, to the annoyance of my friends who tried to cut in, as if I should share her. By the time they were ready to go, she was pretty drunk, so I called a cab to take her back to her place. My buddies had to admit defeat at that point—I'd outmanoeuvred them—but the night was over for me too, because she was in no condition to do anything but kiss me good night, give me her phone number and close the cab door in my face.

The next afternoon, I called her and made a real date. Her name was Leonore, that much I'd learned, and that she was a model working for a big clothing store. She showed up at a popular downtown restaurant wearing a red tank top and a pair of tight shorts that had the whole restaurant gawking at her. I wanted to ask her to be a little more discreet with the way she was flashing her long legs and leaning over the table, giving everybody a good look at her other assets, but I didn't have the English to say it properly. Back in Iran, she would have been arrested for leaving the house dressed like that. And I would have been locked away for being an accessory to the crime.

After that, we met up almost on a daily basis, and before long I couldn't live without her. If a day passed without seeing her, I had trouble sleeping, I missed her that much. I guess I'd fallen in love with her, and she seemed to have been equally attracted to me. For a few months, our relationship continued, although some people would have said it was pretty tame, since we kept our intimacy to kissing and hugging and holding hands, if you can believe that. As much as I loved her, I respected her, and didn't want to make advances that might offend her. After all, in Iran, girls aren't permitted to have sex outside of marriage. I was still thinking as a good Iranian.

After graduating from language school, I was assigned to Randolph Air Force Base, near San Antonio, to begin my pilot training. The day had been coming, I knew it. Now it would be difficult to continue seeing her, but after a week of being separated, she showed up at the base. We met at the bus stop outside the main gate of the base. This time, she was dressed more conservatively, but somehow still managed to look sexy. What a girl. We hugged like two long-lost lovers. She wouldn't let go of me. We wasted no time heading for my room at the base, and then once behind closed doors, we didn't waste a second. I hardly recognized myself, behaving like such an animal, but I couldn't get enough of her. Something about this woman, something similar to that girl in the village who smelled like God's perfumed rain, the one I "touched" for the first time. This force was mysterious and powerful and worth surrendering to, that's all I can say in my defence.

Leonore was the only girlfriend I had during my stay in Texas. Our relationship came to a sudden end when I received a call from her. She was at the airport on her way to meet a friend in North Carolina, who was in some kind of trouble. There was no time to catch up with her before she left, so there I was, not only suffering from a broken heart, but wondering why she'd vanished so unexpectedly. I never saw her again. There was the odd long-distance phone call, and then a letter explained it all:

My Dearest Yadi,
I still love you, and find you in my dreams. Thank you for always being such a gentleman. I apologize for not telling you this before, but I was married when we were together. My husband and I had separated, and so I felt free to see you, but now we are trying to work things out again. I'm sorry if I've hurt you, sorry also for myself, because I hadn't expected our love to grow so strong.

The seat-belt signs flashed on. The pilot announced his ETA at Mehrabad Airport in Tehran, and began his descent from 28,000 feet. Mahrokh woke up. Akram opened her eyes and glanced at me, critically, as if she'd been reading my mind. Was it possible? I felt flushed and closed my eyes to hide from any more scrutiny, and to return to the past.

At the Randolph AFB, I was trained on the T-41 and the T-37. My T-37 instructor was Captain Green, a very pleasant guy, but I managed to bring out the worst in him during a series of touch-and-go landings. Twice on final approach, I forgot to lower the landing gear. He slammed the top of the instrument panel.

My father Najiallah in 1967.
This is the last picture I have
of my father.

My mother Ozra in 1948.

Me as a 12-year-old in 1958.

Akram and me in 1972. This is our first picture together. We were married a few months later.

ABOVE: My family after my father passed away. L–R seated: Nasrin (my youngest sister), Akbar (my brother), Shahin (my middle sister); L–R standing: Akram (my wife), Ozra (my mother), Mahin (my oldest sister), and her second-born, Afshin.

OPPOSITE TOP: My birthplace Nesa Olia Taleghan.

OPPOSITE BOTTOM: With my F-5A fighter jet at the Williams Air Force base in Phoenix, Arizona (1972).

ABOVE: During the Iran-Iraq war: with my F5-E Tiger 2 fighter jet at the 4th
Tactical Air Force Base in Dezful, Iran (1981).

OPPOSITE: Air Cadet Yadi Sharifirad at Lackland Air Force Base, San Antonio,
Texas (1971).

ABOVE: This picture was taken in 1976 during an inspection of the 5th Tactical Air Force Base of Merzifun, Turkey. L–R: Brigadier General Ahmet Cesur (base commander), Major Bocak, Major General Cemal Engin (Turkish Air Force commander). I'm in the centre background.

OPPOSITE TOP: After returning from a successful mission during the Iran-Iraq war with a group of pilots and technicians at the 4th Tactical Air Force Base in Dezful, Iran (1981). I'm in the front row, sixth from left.

OPPOSITE BOTTOM: With a group of my classmates at the Williams Air Force Base in Phoenix, Arizona (1972). Sitting: Asgari. Standing L–R: unknown, Yadi Sharifirad, Bolghand, Modarress, Marasoli, Zolfaghari, Shoa-Azar.

ABOVE: 2nd tactical Air Force base, Tabriz, Iran (1980). My return from Iraq after my crash. In the foreground, Colonel Farzaneh (base commander) stands with me. Kok Mohammad can be seen in the background between us. The other men in the background are pilots.

OPPOSITE: 2nd Tactical Air Force base, Tabriz, Iran (1980). My return from Iraq after my crash. Shahram, left, and my wife, right, accompany me in a welcoming ceremony.

ABOVE: Tehran, Iran (1985). All Iranian military attachés were summoned to Iran for political briefing about the Iran-Iraq war and this group picture was taken after our meeting with the president of Iran, Ayatollah Ali Khamenei, now the supreme leader of Iran (in the first row with turban). I'm third from right in the second row, wearing a flying suit and white scarf.

OPPOSITE, TOP LEFT: Air Force headquarters, Tehran (1980). Welcoming ceremony by the Air Force vice commander. L–R: Kok Muhammad, Colonel Farzaneh, Shahram, Akram, and me.

TOP RIGHT: Islamabad, Pakistan (1987). Iranian Armed Forces day celebration. Me with Major General Shafiq from the Pakistan Army.

BOTTOM LEFT: Islamabad, Pakistan (1987). Iranian Armed Forces day celebration. Me with George Alejandro Livingston, Argentinean chargé d'affaires in Pakistan.

BOTTOM RIGHT: Bursa, Turkey (1994). L–R: Sami Gunduz, me, Maksüt Demir and his wife, Emel, Gokcen, Mrs. Gunduz.

TOP LEFT: Dubai, UAE (2005). My brother and me seeing one another after 11 years.

TOP RIGHT: Dubai Airport, UAE (2005). My younger son, Shahrokh, sees his aunts (my sisters) and cousins again after 13 years. L–R: my niece Maryam, my older sister Mahin, my son Shahrokh, and my niece Sahar.

BOTTOM LEFT: Istanbul, Turkey (2009). Maksüt Demir and Ahmet Ergonen, two good friends of mine.

OPPOSITE, BOTTOM RIGHT: Vancouver Airport, Canada (1994). My arrival in Canada after almost three years of separation from my wife and children. I'm holding my daughter Mahrokh, and Akram is beside me.

ABOVE: Vancouver Airport, Canada (1994). L–R: Akram, my younger son Shahrokh, my daughter Mahrokh, me, and my older son Shahram.

My children, L–R: Shahrokh, Mahrokh, and Shahram (2009).

"A monkey could fly better than you!" he shouted.

I didn't appreciate his criticism, although I probably deserved it. When we had landed and were taxiing in, he started laughing and telling me that he had been joking with me. I didn't believe him—I think he was trying to shake me up, and who could blame him? If I ever landed without wheels, that would have been the end of loverboy.

I moved on to Vance AFB, in Enid, Oklahoma, and began flying the T-38, graduating at the end of November 1971. From there, it was on to the Fairchild AFB for the survival course, and finally to Williams AFB, in Phoenix, Arizona, to complete the training in Freedom Fighters, the old F-5. By springtime 1972, I was a fully fledged fighter pilot, and it was time to return to Iran.

Three months after my return to Iran, I was married to the beautiful Akram, and less than a year later, I became a father to our first son, Shahram. We were stationed at the 3rd Tactical Air Base in the city of Hamedan in western Iran, where winter temperatures plunged to 45 below. But when you're in love, and your whole life is going better than you've ever hoped, what's a little nip in the air? We enjoyed every moment, including trying to start the car when it was a frozen block of metal and grease.

From Hamedan, I was transferred to the 2nd Tactical Air Base, in Tabriz. While stationed there, I was dispatched as an exchange officer to Turkey, part of the CENTO (Central Treaty Organization), a mutual defence alliance between Great Britain, the United States, Iran, Pakistan, and Turkey. For a year, I flew with Turkish air force pilots out of Merzifon near the Black Sea. I made many good friends, some I would later call on to save my life. We didn't return to Iran until December 1977, and a year later, in May 1978, we were blessed with another son, Shahrokh.

Less than a year later, in February 1979, Khomeini's Revolution routed the Shah from power, and suddenly fear became a powerful part of our lives as thousands were executed by firing squad or hung in the streets. Many of these pilots, Shah loyalists, were close to me personally or professionally. It was at that point when I crashed in Iraq. I met the Ayatollah Khomeini for the second time when I was based with my squadron at the 4th Tactical Air Base, in Dezful.

In 1983, I was assigned to Pakistan as a first military attaché after the Islamic Revolution, and for three years I was privileged to live the diplomatic life. Our daughter, Mahrokh, was born in June 1986, making Akram and I the happiest couple alive. It would be hard to imagine a more satisfying existence. I could have contact with any top political figures in the country regarding my job. Once I took advantage of my diplomatic status and complained of a personal matter to one of President Khamenei's advisers during their visit to Pakistan. I had been unjustly treated by a producer who paid me nothing for the film rights to my book. I was even tempted to say something to our president in our short official meeting, but I restrained myself in the face of his appreciation for my many achievements in the war, and also as a military attaché.

My duties as military attaché in Pakistan terminated in October 1986, when I returned to Tehran and began working at Joint Armed Forces headquarters. My arrest, torture, prosecution, and discharge from the armed forces followed in that order.

"You were dreaming," Akram said, cutting into my reverie.

"No, I don't think so," I said.

"You had a little smile on your face," she said. "And then a frown. Something was going on in your head."

"I thought you were asleep," I said.

"I was for a while—but I was really just thinking."

"About what?" I asked.

"How we're going to spend the rest of our lives in a country that's become a prison for us."

"Any ideas?" I asked.

We were interrupted by the pilot's landing announcement. The thought was left suspended in midair, a question that we would have to deal with very soon.

As the plane landed, I had a view over the Mehrabad Air Force Base, and the fighter jets parked along the runway. It was regrettable that I would no longer be at the controls of those great machines. But seeing my boys again made up for any degree of self-pity I was feeling. I took the family out to a pizza place near the Shah's old palace, where Akram and I watched our children play in the park in front of the restaurant. She told me that an idea was growing inside her, to become a hairdresser and aesthetician. She wanted my opinion whether or not to register for the course. We both agreed that the courses could be a good way to keep her busy and get her mind off things. So, she did, and she took her studies seriously, and loved them.

As for me, I landed a job in a carpet store in Karimkhan Avenue. The owner, Mr. Esfandiary, didn't bring up the subject of my salary, perhaps because he was waiting to see how good I was at selling rugs. But at month's end, without any concern for how badly I'd done, he matched my air force salary. It felt good to have gained a friend, someone who respected me and allowed me to come and go as I wished, without worrying about how much he should deduct from my pay. What a relief to be paid regularly and without fail. Eventually, I experimented with buying and selling carpets on my own, and started making more money than I'd ever made in the air force.

Akram didn't take long to graduate, and began working in a beauty salon on Pasdaran Avenue. This was much preferred to her previous profession as a nurse's aide. At the same time, I began teaching basic English to students in the Ministry of Oil, and to some high-ranking people in the Ministry of Mines and Metals. The only thing wrong with this otherwise rejuvenated life of ours was the weekly visits to the court martial office to sign in. Shady individuals often followed us, keeping us on edge and preventing me from integrating fully back into life in Tehran. In fact, it kept my family in a constant state of fear, and I began to feel as vulnerable as that rabbit living on the hill behind my village. I felt the shadow growing larger around me.

"We can't continue living like criminals," Akram said.

"I know," I said.

"What about Canada?" she said.

What about it? A land of cowboys and dogsleds and ice. Lots of ice.

"Never mind," she said, "you won't like the cold."

"I'll learn to love it," I said.

17

A PLAN

Akram's older brother had nothing but good things to say about Canada after living there for fifteen years. I knew very little about it, except that it was part of the old British empire, and the second biggest country in the world; we knew that from school. Known for ice hockey and full of Aboriginals called Indians. Montreal had been the site of the World's Fair in 1967. And going further back, the Canadian prime minister had won the Nobel Prize for coming up with a peace plan during the Suez Canal crisis, sometime in the late 1950s. While I served in Pakistan, a Canadian acquaintance told me about the time Canada invaded the United States and burned down the White House. That occurred about two hundred years ago. I didn't think that was very nice, but I was curious to know the story behind it. Other than that, I knew nothing. Perhaps there wasn't much more to know. Canada seemed refreshingly simple and pure, just like cowboys and snow.

Akram couldn't imagine how we could even think of leaving while under twenty-four-hour surveillance. We needed a plan I told her, but one so secret that not even our own brothers and sisters would suspect anything. She gave me one of her loving looks, but a bit distant, as if she was taking stock of my life, and it wasn't a pretty sight. Like looking at an eagle with a broken wing—kind of pathetic. It forced me to come up with a plan, right there, on the spot. They would have to exit first, my wife and the kids. If I was arrested again, at least they would be free.

As for me, I would have to wait for my freedom. I would know it when I saw it again, when I disembarked from some flight ending somewhere in the free world. I would know it with my whole being. Who can forget what breathing free air is like? My feet would know the feel of an easy stride down the corridors of an airport free of armed soldiers. My eyes would recognize the happy gait of free people hurrying through customs towards their wives and sons and daughters who were waiting for them. If freedom could be defined in simple words, I would blurt it out and be done with it. But freedom's more than a list of synonyms for liberty and independence. It's not as fixed as a word or a commodity. It's a story. And we know what can happen in a story when the hero loses his focus—there's no more story. Freedom-loving people are enthusiastic for life in all its contradictions, and they keep their precious freedom alive by constant kindness on the one hand, and vigilance on the other. It's a fragile thing that can be lost when we take it for granted, trust me.

We left on another trip, the whole family, driving north to the Caspian Sea. It was early March 1990. We weren't quite ready to make our escape, but I needed another break from probing eyes. On the way back to Tehran, I had the urge to make a detour to see my mother in Karaj City. On our trip, we'd bought her a gift of smoked herring. We were surprised to find her not at home. My sisters, who lived only a few blocks away, didn't know where she was, either. We organized a search, from hospitals to police stations to the morgue, of all places.

"She wasn't sick, to my knowledge," my older sister, Mahin, said.

"At least she never complained to us," my other sister, Nasrin, said. "Although she was thinking of visiting Mahshad."

We inquired at travel agencies and then at hotels in the holy cities of Qom and Mahshad, but we found no clue as to my mother's whereabouts. She had vanished.

I couldn't avoid the thought that she might be dead. I checked everything in her house. All her things were arranged nicely in just the right spots. A few apples and oranges, some candy, a plate of pistachios on the table. Was she expecting some guests? Who? The worst sight was her closet full of clothes, waiting silently to be picked out and worn again by no one but her. The most disturbing sign was the few unwashed dishes in the sink, which told me that she hadn't gone far.

Some days later, while I was teaching in the oil ministry, my brother-in-law Khodaverdi showed up with a possible lead. There was an unnamed corpse in the coroner's office in Tehran. Her age and description and date of death were suspiciously familiar. We rushed there immediately and were soon standing above a corpse covered with a white sheet stained with dried blood. The tag read, "Unknown woman, about 60–65 years old, died in a car accident." I lifted the sheet from her face—it was my mother. Grey and still. I was numb, speechless. I could only stare at her there on the bare floor, her kind face, her half-closed eyes and half-open lips. My mother dead, I couldn't believe it.

On the evening of March 8, just after sunset, she had been struck by a minibus while crossing to the Ekbatan housing complex. She'd been heading to my older sister's to pay them a New Year's visit, but she never made it. She died right there, on the spot, with no identification on her. Such a short trip, she must have thought that she didn't need it. With the help of relatives and friends, we moved her body to Behesht-e Zahra Cemetery for the funeral, and then took her coffin to Taleghan, our ancestral village, where she was buried at the foot of the hills, where I used to watch eagles fly, when I was a child.

Two days later, we returned to Tehran, and began to get serious about our escape plans. First, Akram needed to acquire a visa to Canada. I investigated the process, all the time trying to keep my grief locked away inside me. When the Canadian embassy in Tehran turned her down, I was surprised how much this upset her. In a fit of revenge, she made a plan to visit friends in Turkey, with the idea of reapplying at the Canadian embassy in Ankara. Well, she got a rude shock at

Tehran's Mehrabad Airport. They wouldn't let her leave the country. I'd never seen her so upset. She cried all the way home in the car, absolutely desperate. What could I do but promise her that it would sort itself out? I just needed a little more time.

I procured a letter from the court martial office that allowed my wife and two youngest children to travel abroad, but Shahram, who was approaching military age, was barred from leaving the country. As for me, it goes without saying that I was going nowhere. So, with Mahrokh in her arms, Akram left for Turkey, where they had a wonderful time with friends we'd met in 1976, during our year with the pilot-exchange program between Iran and Turkey. Maksüt Demir and Colonel (later made general) Ahmet Ergönen and their families treated them as kin. But on the matter of the visa for Canada, once again she came up empty-handed, and returned home feeling more hopeless than ever about her life in Iran. Something had to be done. Something desperate and final. We knew we had to escape.

We decided that Akram would leave first with the younger children, Shahrokh and Mahrokh. Shahram and I would follow later. It would be a difficult mission to plan and a dangerous one to execute, but what choice did we have? To stay meant living under a kind of house arrest for the foreseeable future. My departure seemed particularly dangerous, since I had those weekly reports to sign. Not to mention the goon squads following me around. To leave Tehran, even for a day, meant obtaining special permission. Nevertheless, on August 27, 1991, we put the first phase of our plan into action. My wife and the kids packed to leave home forever.

Having barely slept, and with the suitcases sitting next to the door, Akram tried to bolster herself with one last glass of tea. Shahram had said his farewells before he left for school, and it was a good thing, because the situation was emotional enough without his tears complicating matters. As usual, Shahrokh and Mahrokh were chasing each other around the house. When it came time to go, Akram had only to wrap some meals and place them in the freezer. She'd cooked a few days' supply so that Shahram and I wouldn't have to immediately make a mess in the kitchen.

"That's why I love you so much," I said.

"Is that it?" she said. "Just for my cooking?"

We both smiled. I pulled her into a hug. "You're the reason I stay alive," I whispered.

I loaded the suitcases into the trunk of the car, and returned for one last check of the house, then locked the door behind me. The midday traffic was horrendous, giving us plenty of time to review our plan before we reached the airport. I'd hired an agent named Mohammad to facilitate and expedite their departure from the airport and provide them some kind of acceptable travel documents from Singapore to Canada. His legitimacy had been confirmed by a friend of mine whose family had been sent to Canada by Mohammad not long ago. Upon spotting him in the terminal building, we were to ignore him. Akram and the kids would check their bags and obtain their boarding cards in the usual manner, just by standing in line with everyone else.

"Stay cool," I reminded Akram. "Mohammad knows what he's doing. He's very experienced at this."

"He better be," Akram said. "Otherwise we're out $25,000. Did you pay him the whole amount in advance?"

"Yes," I said.

"Why?"

"Because he had to pay off his people. His agents, people in security."

"And you believed him?"

"What choice did I have?"

Akram didn't answer.

We found Mohammad holding down a position in one of the lineups. So far, so good. We didn't acknowledge him, just stepped into his lineup, according to the plan. We watched him check in ahead of us, assessing the agent behind the counter. Although she wore a shawl, I could tell by the way her loose colourful scarf carelessly covered her hair that she was the type who would have preferred not to. When our turn came, she signalled us to open the suitcases.

"Any gold?" she asked. "Diamonds? Rare gems or jewellery?" She continued to inspect the suitcases.

"Only wedding rings and a gold chain and pendant," Akram answered.

"Foreign exchange?" she asked. "How much are you taking out of the country?"

"A thousand dollars," Akram replied.

"You're only allowed five hundred," the woman said. She winked and asked me to close the suitcases. Akram gave me a searching look. I winked at her, shut the suitcases, and set them on the scales.

"Thank you, madam," Akram said with a smile as she reached for the three boarding passes to Singapore.

So far, everything had worked well. We had over an hour to say our long goodbyes. Akram always enjoyed eating in expensive places, so upstairs we went to a restaurant that had once been a special treat for us. But that was before the Revolution. They'd eliminated all signs of Western decadence: no bar or alcohol, no exotic pictures on the walls, no waitresses—only waiters in suits, but no ties. Nevertheless, we enjoyed our last lunch together, keeping smiles on our faces, careful not to show any sign of sadness, tension, or trepidation. We had to assume that we were being watched. Our parting had to have all the appearances of a short trip.

Leaving the restaurant, we headed for the departure lounge downstairs, me carrying Mahrokh while Shahrokh held his mother's hand, and all of us unusually quiet. I wanted to scream my defiance at this country for forcing us through this secret procedure, just to live as a family in freedom. But I couldn't say a word, couldn't let my eyes get too moist, just had to keep smiling.

"Daddy, you can put me down, if you're tired," Mahrokh said.

"No, honey, I'm not tired at all," I said. I asked her to sing a song, one in particular I liked, but she was shy with all these strangers around. "Then sing it softly in my ear," I said.

I could feel her sweet warm breath on my neck.

"Fellow traveller, don't go alone;
Take me with you.
If you go,
I will be alone."

Big mistake to ask her to sing. Big mistake! Was I crazy, or what? To camouflage my overwhelming sadness, I faked a smile, but that only sent a shower of tears down my face.

"Why are you crying, Daddy?" she asked.

"Oh, it was just an accident," I said. "It was supposed to be a laugh, but I pushed the wrong button by mistake."

"No, Daddy," she said. "You didn't push any buttons!"

This gave us both a good reason to laugh, and got me out of my predicament. Now, it was my turn to sing a song for Mahrokh.

"The one about a kiss!" she said.

I whispered softly in her ear:

"O girl!
The beautiful one,
Kiss me for one last time,
For I am going towards my fate.
The past has passed me by,
I seek my destiny today;
Kiss me for one last time."

She kissed me, of course. And we continued our terminal promenade with Shahrokh holding me tightly around the waist. He had a cute habit of leaning his head against my abdomen. I told him it was dangerous to push too hard against my stomach after such a big lunch. He laughed and pushed harder.

What a light and intimate hour we spent, too soon gone. Akram and I embraced each other, but to be sure I didn't say something and ruin everything, she planted a kiss on my lips, then said a few words before turning and heading towards the departure gate. Shahrokh hugged me hard around the waist. I was surprised at his strength, as if he'd been working out, but he was far too young for that. I bent down to kiss him, but he retaliated with a barrage of kisses all over my face, perhaps to avoid having to make eye contact with me, and to avoid having to say goodbye. Then he turned and followed his mother. Mahrokh, who had been hanging on to my leg, jumped into my arms and gave me the most loving kiss she could muster.

"Aren't you coming with us, Daddy?" she asked.

"No, darling," I said, setting her down. "I'm going to come later."

"Why?" she asked.

"Because I don't have a ticket. Go!"

I watched them pass through the security check, and farther towards the departure gate until they vanished from sight. And still I leaned against the glass barrier, my forehead touching the window, trying to hide any tears that might roll down my face. Mahrokh startled me, seeing her again, running towards me. Had she forgotten something? Her doll, perhaps? She didn't have it with her. From the other side of the glass she showed me her boarding card, as if that's what I needed to come with her. I waved her off as Akram showed up to collect her, shouting, "Let's go! The plane is leaving, hurry up!" Mahrokh had her lips to the glass, so I crouched down until I was almost sitting on the floor to kiss her back, through the pane, until Akram grabbed her hand and pulled her away, not daring to look at me. But I could see that she was starting to cry, too. So, as it turned out, we were quite a spectacle, making just the sort of scene we absolutely wanted to avoid, with total strangers watching us, some getting emotional right along with us. Akram risked one final look at me as she led Mahrokh away, one last wave before she disappeared through security, one last time.

I ran upstairs to an observation window to wait for the jetliner to close its doors and begin taxiing down the runway. I'd never felt such sadness, watching my family disappear. I should be rational about it, I thought, since ours wasn't the first family to send their kids abroad, some for an education, some to escape military service, some to escape death at the hands of Khomeini executioners. Standing there waiting for twenty minutes, I couldn't help remembering the most famous flight to freedom from Mehrabad Airport, when the last king of Iran, Mohammad Reza Shah Pahlavi, fled the country on January 16, 1979. Officially, it was for a few weeks' rest overseas, but he must have known he wasn't coming back. He'd lost the confidence of the people; even lost the battle before Khomeini set foot back in Iran, and that was it, the end of 2500 years of monarchy in Persia. We were hopeful that he'd return, but that was wishful thinking; deluded thinking, in fact, the way Iranians have lived for so many years, hoping that the ayatollahs would abandon their reign of terror over ordinary citizens. I remember the Shah's private plane shrinking in the distance, becoming just another flake of snow in the wind that swirled around the airport on that day so long ago.

The roar of the plane taking off brought me back to reality. I cast a little prayer God's way to help me find the strength to live with a heart so bruised with grief, once for my family and again for the Shah. You know, he couldn't find a country in which to die. Morocco, the Bahamas, Mexico, Panama, even the United States wouldn't allow him to land, so it was finally back to Egypt, the only country that offered him shelter. None of the foreign heads of state—people who had known the Shah for over a quarter of a century—offered a helping hand. Not even President Carter, whose visit to Iran on New Year's Eve, 1977, was indelibly inscribed in our collective memory—he who raised his glass of champagne to the Shah and proclaimed Iran "an island of stability." But where was this admiration when Khomeini claimed moral authority over Iran, even from exile in France? Carter urged the Shah to leave the country for the sake of human rights! For Iranians, Carter is, arguably, the most despised of all the U.S. presidents. (Well, maybe the second most.) A religious man himself, he should have been able to empathize with those whose rights were stolen. In so many ways we lost our right to live as happy families—by arrest, execution, murder, or simply terror, splitting families, destroying them by forcing them to flee. So many last voyages of loved ones who never returned home. Imagine all the loneliness.

Words from the Koran reverberated through the lounge. I wanted to get out of there. Descending the staircase towards the main exit, I felt dwarfed by slogans prominent on the walls of the lounge: "Death to American Imperialists!" And death to "Israeli Zionists" and "Russian Communists." Also, quotations from Khomeini's "Party of God," the Hezbollah: "Men who wear ties are American lackeys." "Veiling is a woman's protection." "My sister, guard your veil, my brother, guard your eyes." A poster depicted a woman with her head covered by a black chador. I felt especially sorry for women struggling with this regime, for the humiliation and oppression they experienced at the onset of the Revolution, their dress code radically altered, no more styles from Europe, no more makeup, no more appearances in public with men who are not their father, brother, or husband, their legal marriage age lowered from eighteen to nine, stoning once again the proper punishment for crimes of adultery and prostitution. Right out of the seventh century.

I noticed a woman from the "morality police" looking for female passengers improperly covered up, or wearing makeup. I watched her grab a young woman by the arm and yell, "Cover your hair properly! Do you disrespect Islamic law? I will take you to the *komiteh*!" she said, referring to the Islamic police. Nobody wants an encounter with the Islamic morality squad, trust me.

I hurried out of there to the parking lot, grateful that at least my family would not have to experience this kind of terror anymore. Back in the car, I could smell Akram's perfume. I had the most vivid memory of how Shahrokh always made me laugh. That boy meant more to me than the moon means to the sky at night.

Shahram had not returned from school by the time I arrived home. The emptiness of the house startled me. I would have to become accustomed to it, and it wasn't going to be easy. Mahrokh's favourite doll, Mahdokht, lay on her bed. I picked her up, but she just kept looking at the ceiling, imagine that. I left her alone and entered Shahrokh's bedroom. What a mess—walnut shells strewn everywhere, sunflower seeds and chocolate all over the place, clothes shoved under the bed. The rest of the house was clean and organized, almost as if we were expecting guests. I couldn't wait around for Shahram, since I was due to teach at the oil ministry. I set the table for him and drove to work.

My thirty-two students, all young adults, were waiting for me. I dreaded the spotlight, dreaded even having to speak, that's how close I was to breaking down. They noticed something wrong, and one of them risked asking me. I told them the first part of the story, nothing about our plan and their final destination. It was a temporary short trip—and legal—to Singapore and back. I said it was very difficult to say goodbye to the kids travelling abroad, and apologized for having such a tender heart, but they didn't mind. Someone suggested that we cancel the class. They would explain it to the school's director. I accepted their compassionate offer.

After my students left, I remained alone in the room to compose myself; I mean, to toughen myself up. Emotions are okay, they're natural, but they shouldn't take over. If every emotional breeze blew me over, how would I survive a stiff wind? It wouldn't be a pretty sight. I took a few deep breaths to bolster myself against the outside world.

When I arrived home, Shahram was reorganizing his room. He was handling the family's absence better than I was. The phone rang. I knew it was Akram even before I answered. They had arrived in Singapore with everyone in good spirits, all things considered.

"It's a beautiful city," she said. "I wish one day you and I can visit it together."

"Anywhere together," I said.

She asked me how I was doing, and I lied, "Fine, fine, fine." You just never knew who might have been listening in. I convinced Akram that I was taking care of Shahram and that we'd manage okay.

For the next few days, Shahram acted like my sheepdog, keeping me away from restaurants and tea houses that had been our family favourites. I occasionally snuck off by myself for a hint of that life that no longer existed. Before Akram left, she had professional photos taken of herself and the kids. One of them, I had framed. I hung it on the wall at the foot of my bed so that she would be the last thing I saw before closing my eyes at night and the first thing I saw in the morning.

My students in the two ministries kept me busy. Occasionally, I'd spend an afternoon with Mr. Esfandiary in the carpet shop, chatting with the many new friends I'd made among his clientele. My mealtimes became little more than necessary pit stops, my cooking proving either too salty or too bland. At bedtime, Akram and I usually spoke by phone. She had been required to linger in Singapore for three weeks while organizing her onward journey to Canada, via Japan. Soon, Akram called from Tokyo to tell me she had lost Mahrokh's ticket. Worse yet, she didn't have the necessary documents to obtain another one, resulting in her deportation to Indonesia.

That next week in Singapore, when she phoned, Akram sounded frightened and exhausted. She wasn't sure she had the stamina to find another route to Vancouver. But she did, via New Zealand and Honolulu. She landed in the province of British Columbia, on Canada's west coast, on September 28, 1991. She was interviewed at the airport by immigration officers and was granted the refugee status with two kids.

Shahram's escape wouldn't be as simple as bribing ticket agents. I had to seriously consider the risks involved in sending him out the back door. It was startling and sad to hear that many Iranians were forced to leave their homeland by the path less travelled.

18

SHAHRAM

Akram's first call from Singapore had been intentionally brief and unexciting, so as not to alert anyone who might be listening in. We only wanted to hear each other's voices. I had briefed Akram before her departure that at this point the telephone was not an appropriate means of communication. During my years of service as a diplomat, I had learned that it was easy for telephones to be tapped. Also, we wanted anyone who might be listening in to believe that Akram had left Iran of her own volition, and I had nothing to do with it. The reason for this was that my conditional sentence did not give me any room to do something that could be labelled by the government as a "mistake," which would then give them the ammunition to incarcerate and torture me all over again. However, at no point was I ever sure if anyone was listening to our phone conversations; but I had to be careful rather than careless.

When he hung up, Shahram broke into tears.

I had been impressed with the quality of Shahram's grief. As he said goodbye to his mother, brother, and sister, his were not the arbitrary tears of a child, but the specific pain of a man already missing something near and dear to his heart.

"Are you okay?" I asked.

"I miss Mom so much," he said. "And Mahrokh, too."

"Not Shahrokh?" I kidded.

"Yeah—him too."

I gave him a hug and told him it was okay to talk about it. In fact, I'd been the gloomiest one; I was the one who'd been moping around the house. "Every day I come home to this empty house, it tears my heart up," I confessed. Shahram seemed relieved to hear it.

"When I would come home from school," he said, "and I'd buzz to get in, Mahrokh's little baby voice would answer me over the intercom. She was the one who always let me in and welcomed me home by running to meet me at the door."

"She's going to tear up some young man's heart someday," I said. "Not too soon though, I hope. Not for a long time."

"As soon as she would open the door," Shahram continued, "I could smell dinner cooking. Do you remember? Now, I have to use keys to get in."

"And the house is empty," I said.

"I still expect all those smells," he said. "Mom's cooking. What I wouldn't give for that right now. And I still expect Mahrokh to come running."

"Well, there's a bright side to their being gone," I said. "Shahrokh's bed is always made!"

"Even that makes me sad," Shahram said. "I can't believe that the pain hasn't eased up. I'm sorry, Dad, I can't help it."

His sincere suffering made me realize what a man he was already. He would grow up to be a real man, there was no doubt about it. I just had to get him out of Iran.

"We'll just have to tough it out," I said. "But I promise you, every day that passes is a day closer to your joining them. We just need to have patience." I told Shahram that he could spend the night in my room, if it would make him feel better, and he took me up on the offer, on one condition.

"Promise me, Dad, that you won't mistake me for Mom in the middle of the night."

We laughed, and it felt good to be able to laugh with my son as if he were a man.

Shahram was under strict orders from me not to mention a word of this family intrigue to any family or friends. Talking about their vacation or short trip to Singapore was okay if necessary; otherwise, absolutely nothing. It wasn't an easy thing to ask of anyone, but especially a youth who would soon be leaving all his family and friends behind forever. Not one word could he mention to any of them, because the associated risks could potentially cost us our lives. He understood. Eventually, after a few months of research and planning, I told Shahram how he was going to make his exit.

I'd found a smuggler named Agha-Nouri, a soft-spoken man, tall, with white skin, who wore thick glasses, and was almost bald. He had a good reputation among his kind. The deal we struck was worth US$15,000, money I had acquired from selling my car and borrowing from a friend. For that fee, Shahram would be escorted overland to Turkey. There would be three payments of five thousand dollars each, one just prior to departure, the second to be split among the guides taking Shahram over the border, and a third payment once Shahram had crossed safely into Turkey. At that point, he would phone me. Of course, Shahram and I would have our code language to confirm that he had actually arrived safely, and where exactly he was.

A few days after first contacting Nouri, I met him at his stationery shop. This time, he was accompanied by another smuggler, a Turkish Kurd named Bigler. Bigler was tall, heavy-set, olive-skinned, with a thick black moustache. He dressed well and spoke Farsi with a Turkish accent. Bigler explained that he didn't personally accompany his clients over the mountains, but that he nevertheless could ensure Shahram's safety once he was in Turkish territory. It was decided that in a week's time, I would drive Shahram and Nouri to Tabriz, a city in northwestern Iran, where I would hand Shahram over to Bigler and his men.

One week, that's all we had left together. He wouldn't know about his departure, I decided, until the day before. Best to avoid bungling the escape plan that way. It was agony not being able to share with him my trepidation—I felt almost panic—wondering if we'd ever see each other again.

On the evening of December 15, 1991, I told Shahram that these were his last few hours at home. He had difficulty coming to grips with his imminent departure—that all his belongings had to be left behind, from his favourite soccer shoes to the collection of Spider-Man comics, which he would have protected with his life. Everything had to stay. He could take only his warmest clothes, and for extra energy a few nuts, plus a small flask of water. And one set of street clothes for his arrival in Turkey. I gave him some Iranian money to keep in his waist wallet in case of emergency.

Nouri and a friend of his, Hassan, showed up at the house after dark and waited while Shahram zipped himself into his green army jacket and picked up his backpack. Before leaving, he took one more long look around the home he would never see again.

"Goodbye, house," he said.

It was a cruel way to force a boy to say goodbye to his childhood memories, and I was paying for it, stifling the tears I knew were in his heart.

Nouri had parked his car a discreet distance away because we were leaving in Shahram's BMW, a recent gift from me upon his earning his driver's licence. The night seemed particularly eerie, despite the music tapes that Shahram was playing. I heard nothing but my own conflicting thoughts about this mission: Shahram's escape versus the possibility that I might never see him again.

We travelled as far as Ghazvin, about 100 kilometres, filled up with gas and continued westward towards Tabriz, another 500 icy kilometres to the northwest. We seemed to be the only ones crazy enough to be travelling in such dangerous conditions at night. Our brakes were useless on some icy patches. You needed to gear down to keep control, but on one treacherous bend, I hit the brakes, which made the car spin like a horse trying to throw its rider. A couple of 360 degree turns later, we came to rest in a snowbank.

"*Ya Imam Zaman!*" Nouri cried. It was a common exclamation in such circumstances, calling on the twelfth Imam.

Everyone was okay, but there we were, half-buried. We got out to inspect the damage—nothing serious, until we noticed that two tires were flat. Who carried more than one spare? Then we discovered that the heater had conked out, which allowed the windows to quickly frost up. We dug around the tires so they could be removed, but the lug nuts wouldn't budge. Shahram was the last of us to apply his muscle to the job, and to our surprise he loosened them all. I took it as a good omen, that he could take care of himself. You can see how my mind was looking for assurance any way it could.

We changed one tire, then waited for some kind of saviour to show up and help us with the second. Mercifully, the first vehicle we flagged down stopped. It was a truck transporting building supplies, which was going the other direction, back towards Ghazvin. We offered to pay the driver and his passenger if they'd help us out. It was a major sacrifice of their time to take Nouri and Hassan into town and wait until the tire was repaired and chains were purchased, then drive them back. After all that, they would have to tow us back onto the road. This took no small amount of bargaining skills, but they accepted, and off they want, leaving Shahram and me with the car. We put on as many clothes as we could, and didn't talk much except for the occasional "Are you all right?" or "Are you warm enough?"

Two hours later, they returned with a new tire. While Shahram took charge of replacing it, we heard how the tire man, woken from his sleep, agreed to open his shop only after a bribe of double the price of the tire. Once the truck driver had towed us back onto the road, we installed the chains and resumed our journey.

Proceeding at a much slower pace, I estimated that we'd arrive in Tabriz four hours behind schedule. Would Bigler wait for us? That precipitated other worries, such as the possibility of Shahram's being arrested. For weeks, the thought had haunted me until my deepest organs felt bruised. I was impatient to see this plan put into action, but I was also suspicious about it.

Shahram must have felt my anxiety, because he ejected the tape of Persian ballads, which tend to be on the sad side, and replaced it with Chris de Burgh, his favourite singer at the time. I thought "Lady in Red" would cheer me up, but it expressed the same kind of pain that was tormenting me. (That song became cemented in my memory, and still brings tears to my eyes when I hear it.) I would have found something to weep about in "Jingle Bells," which shows what a wreck I was. Taking relief from driving, I pretended to sleep in the back seat beside Nouri, but I was aware of the new day dawning.

A grey light reflected off a world covered in fresh snow. Nothing but white wherever you looked. We passed through the city of Zanjan, after which the road improved and our speed picked up. At about two o'clock in the afternoon we arrived in Tabriz.

We made straight for our meeting place, a small tea house next to the main bus station. Bigler had instructed us to order a drink when we got there, then wait for him. When he and his men arrived and got seated with their cups of tea, one of them would exit to buy a bus ticket next door. Shahram was supposed to follow him out and wait behind him in the lineup, making no effort at communicating with him.

Shahram would purchase a ticket for a village in the most north-western part of Iran, near the Turkish border. Then he'd get on the bus, sticking as close as possible to his secret companion. Bigler had made it very clear that under no circumstances should Shahram and I show any emotion upon parting. No long goodbye, and especially no tears. None at all. Shahram was supposed to shake our hands, bidding us a conventional goodbye, as if he was simply off to visit a family member for a few days. He wasn't wearing anything fashionable, nothing that would have hinted at "Tehran," just simple clothes that were a little bit dirtier than he would have normally been comfortable in. That was the plan.

I had only taken my first sip of tea when Bigler arrived with two other men and sat at a table nearby. I avoided looking at Shahram. There was no way I wanted him to know what was going on inside me. One loving glance between us and I would have blown our cover. My only job at this point was to present a strong and confident face, to encourage him, but the truth was, I wanted to scream. Thank God, Shahram was avoiding eye contact with me, too.

According to the plan, Shahram returned with his ticket and shook our hands, giving us that pleasant smile of his, and a quick hug. I could tell he wanted to say something, but his throat must have been dry and tight, like mine. Watching him walk out of there was like a slow death for me. Any parent would understand, but a thousand words, a thousand libraries, couldn't help prepare you. I found myself getting to my feet—it wasn't planned, it wasn't conscious at all—I just needed to embrace my son one more time. Without thinking or considering the consequences, I went after him.

He was walking towards the buses in that unique way he had of walking, swinging slightly side to side. I was smart enough not to run, but I felt I couldn't shout his name, and not just because my throat was clogged, but because I knew I'd burst into tears. Well, I shouted anyway. He turned, not surprised to see me, I could tell. He started back towards me, each step faster than the last, until we met and melted together, crying as discreetly as we could, our tears mixing together on our cheeks. So much for my stalwart example. To hell with it! I kissed his sad face, trying to fill my lungs with his scent, hoping to trap it there and have it with me forever. Suddenly, a poem by Mehdi Soheili came to mind:

My flower, don't you cry.
In the reflection of your teardrops,
I can see my own sadness.
For your tears know,
I have an ocean of sadness.

Neither of us could say goodbye, not even after we let go of each other, and once again I had to endure watching my son walk away. He stopped on the steps of the minibus, as if he'd changed his mind about going, and turned around to give me his last wave, then disappeared inside. The windows were grimy, just like the rest of the bus station, just like the rest of this country, so I didn't stand a chance of catching one last glimpse of him. The bus idled for a few minutes, then moved out of the depot. I saw the palm of a hand pressed against the pane, and whether or not it was my son's, it was good enough for me, and I raised a hand in a blind farewell.

I had no more tears left, but what was that dizziness? A heart attack felt like a real possibility. Nouri and Hassan had to help me to the car, even wanted to take me to the hospital.

"What good would that do?" I said. "No medicine can cure what I have."

"Bigler is furious with you," they said. "He left."

"Sorry," I said. Of course, I wasn't sorry at all. I wouldn't have exchanged that last hug for the world.

Someone mentioned food, but the concept of eating seemed surreal. We found a restaurant serving traditional Persian dishes, where I tried unsuccessfully to swallow a few morsels. I couldn't see clearly, couldn't hear well; it was almost as if I was having an out-of-body experience. We left the restaurant and found an auto shop where we installed a new battery and windshield wipers. After that, we faced the long haul back to Tehran. With Hassan at the wheel, I huddled under a blanket in the back seat and let the tears flow unchecked, my misery camouflaged by the radio.

We arrived in Tehran in the small hours of a Sunday morning. Nouri and Hassan took me home first and stayed with me for a while, but what I needed more than their compassion was time alone to digest what had just happened. I sat in the living room and rehashed the last thirty hours, replayed it over and over again, interrupting myself every few minutes, wondering, "Where is he? Is he safe?" Going into Shahram's bedroom was a big mistake. A pile of his clothes sat neatly on a chair. I was to mail them to Turkey upon his arrival, but the sight of them was too much, and later, in the shower, I discovered what it's like to cry totally and without shame.

Five days passed without a word from Shahram. Nouri kept assuring me that the plan would be successful, but how could I believe anything without hearing from Shahram myself? My desperation was made worse because neither of us had told anyone, not even family members, so no one was asking. This only made me feel more isolated. While I was blaming myself for this state of affairs, the phone rang.

"Mr. Sharifirad?" It was a female voice.

"Who's calling?" I asked.

"Niloofar, a friend of Shahram's."

I told her that Shahram had gone on a short vacation to Shomal, a popular resort on the Caspian Sea. I had no idea when he'd be back.

"I'll phone back next week," she said.

"Perfect, you do that," I said, wondering how long I could pull that off.

Naturally, I had been hanging around the house more than usual, waiting for his call, any call, if not from Shahram, himself, then from Nouri, who might have had a number where Shahram could be reached. On the seventh day, the call came, from Nouri. He had a number. I hung up and dialed the old rotary phone with trembling hands. A busy signal, damn! This wasn't the old Yadi, cursing and snapping and letting every little thing get on his nerves. I kept dialing until I got a ring, and finally an answer, a Turkish woman asking who was calling. In broken Turkish, I cobbled together a request to speak to my son. Those few seconds waiting seemed like hours.

"*Salam, Baba,*" he said.

Thank God. I could breathe again.

"How's the weather?" I asked.

"It's good, yeah, it's good," he said. "A few clouds on the way, but otherwise the weather is pretty good."

I was dying to say what I wanted, because our plan was to stick to our code. So far, he'd let me know he was okay, he was in good shape. What a relief.

"Do you want to go skiing with me later this week?" I said.

"Can't, Dad, sorry," he said, confirming that he was in Turkey. Bigger relief.

Our short conversation continued, fake and ridiculous, and still I didn't want to say goodbye. But when I did, it was with some assurance that the worst part of my son's journey to Canada was behind him. I called Nouri, asking him to drop by, and he showed up within the hour to pick up his final five thousand dollars, according to our agreement. He hung around to have tea, and left with a smile on his face.

Shahram's friends kept calling, some of them sounding suspicious, but what could I do but to continue lying? His closest friends dropped by to say hello. One day, Niloofar and her brother's fiancée showed up. They were convinced that he'd disappeared, as so many had in the previous dozen years. There wasn't a person in Tehran who didn't know someone who had been arrested on false charges, and they were sure I was covering it up. I must have been terrible at pretending; I could see that they could see it in my eyes. They deserved to know his fate. So I caved in.

"You'll never see him again," I said. Try saying that without crying.

Do I feel embarrassed for admitting all these tears? Sure. But what a relief it was to share this sadness with people who loved him.

Shahram was transported to Istanbul, Turkey's largest city, but a month and a half later he was still there. Bigler had predicted a ten-day stopover, so the delay was cause for concern. At first, Shahram had been lodged in a hotel by Bigler's organization, but had subsequently been transferred to a house with other Iranians, more of Bigler clients smuggled into Turkey. Although Shahram and I spoke regularly by phone, I was constantly after Bigler and Nouri for updates, and I guess my manners were deteriorating, because Bigler started to reject my calls. Eventually, though, he phoned with news that Shahram was booked on a flight to the Netherlands, within hours. I called Shahram, and he was excited. I told him to purchase a calling card so he could phone me the minute he landed in Holland. I didn't let on, but I was apprehensive about all the scrutiny he would face before reaching Canada. I was scared.

Sixteen hours later, by which time Shahram should have landed in Amsterdam, I waited for a call, but none came. I phoned both Bigler and Nouri, but neither of them picked up. I was getting tired of feeling so desperate. Nouri finally phoned. Where was Shahram? I demanded to know, but he knew nothing. Yelling at him wouldn't help, but that didn't stop me. He tried to calm me down, but I couldn't think for a second why I should be calm. Seventy-two hours passed. I left a threatening message on Bigler's answering service, promising to make his life a living hell if he didn't phone me with news of my son. I had powerful friends in Turkey, I warned him, who could ruin him. Okay, I was getting crazy, and nobody liked it less than I, but twenty-four hours, that's all I gave him—get in touch with me, or else!

Bigler called not long before my deadline, with bad news. Shahram had been deported from the Netherlands for insufficient documentation. He was heading back to Turkey. Bigler said he would call later, when Shahram was back in his hands. Once again, I warned him to keep his promise.

That night, Shahram called, still talking in code, but from the tone of his voice, I could tell he was very disturbed by events. He referred to "problems," but was hopeful that things would iron themselves out in the next few days. Our code was driving me crazy, so I broke into English, with all the risks that entailed.

"What happened in Holland?" I asked.

Bigler must have been standing next to him, because he didn't answer, only told me that he was okay and that he had to go. Before he hung up, I got Bigler on the line.

"If Shahram needs any special help," I said, "you've got to let me know. Under no circumstances can he be shipped back to Iran. I have friends in the Turkish Air Force. They can help us if he is in danger."

"That won't be necessary," Bigler assured me. "Everything's going to be fixed within the next few days."

Over the next eight days, I kept in touch with Bigler from the relative security of a pay phone. In that time, I spoke only twice with Shahram. He was being held in what they called the "foreigners' prison," while Bigler procured him another passport. Then, a late-night call from Shahram, from a phone outside the prison. Bigler had paid off a guard so that Shahram could phone me with the bad news. It seemed like the end of the line, since Bigler had run out of contacts or magic or whatever it was he counted on to do his job. The next likely step was Shahram's deportation to Iran, and naturally he was terribly upset.

"Don't lose faith, son," I said. "I promise you that nothing's going to happen to you. Just promise to keep me informed, any way you can."

After we said goodbye, I had no choice but to play my trump card. My Turkish friends, Ahmet Ergönen and Maksüt Demir. I called them immediately.

These old friends were now high-ranking officers, Ergönen in the Turkish Air Force and Demir in Turkish Airlines. The one I called first was Colonel Ergönen, but no one picked up, not even an answering machine! Next, I called Maksüt, who lived right there in Istanbul. I reached his answering service and left a long message explaining the crisis. I asked him to contact me as soon as possible. After that, I called my wife in Vancouver.

Akram knew nothing of Shahram's departure from Iran, and although he had phoned his mother from Turkey, he hadn't disclosed his whereabouts. He wanted to surprise her by showing up at her door. Well, forget that, now I had a lot of explaining to do, on a phone line that could have been tapped. I pretended that Shahram had acted impulsively on his own. Of course, Akram was not tickled with this news, not even about the intention to surprise her. I got an earful, mainly for not letting her know earlier. When she calmed down, I asked her to contact an immigration lawyer, and anyone else who might help Shahram avoid deportation. Later that day, the phone rang.

"Dad! I'm free!" I wasn't expecting Shahram, certainly not in a joyous mood. "Maksüt freed me!" He settled down enough to tell me the story of the last twelve days. "Dad, that Holland story was pure baloney, I never even left Istanbul."

"What!"

To my horror, he hadn't even made it into the airport terminal before he was arrested. Undercover police had become suspicious, watching him waiting in the airport parking lot with one of Bigler's men. They got stopped for questioning, and were detained for having irregular documents. It looked as if deportation was a sure thing until Maksüt stepped in.

"What did he do?" I said.

"He put up a bond," Shahram said, "to get me out of jail. He could lose his house, maybe even his job."

"Sounds like Maksüt," I said. "Basically, he put his life on the table for us."

Maksüt's heroics bought time to arrange the appropriate paperwork through the United Nations and the Canadian embassy. From that point, Bigler was out of the picture and Maksüt took over as Shahram's angel of mercy, and by February 25, the way was paved for Shahram to join his mother, brother, and sister in Canada. We thanked Maksüt and his family with phone calls, letters, and gifts, and still I felt our gratitude was insufficient.

After those agonizing few months, naturally I felt immense relief. Freedom existed, if not for me, at least for my family. Nothing could hurt them any longer. They would carry the Sharifrad name into the future. I savoured the victory for a day or two until it was time for me to start thinking like a caged animal again. I had another journey to organize. God give me patience, I prayed. My escape would require the patience of a saint, that's for sure. But I had to quit dreaming of revenge. Saints don't lie awake at night dreaming of revenge. I had to calm down. I had to become normal again. Whatever "normal" was.

19

LIFE ON A SHORT LEASH

My own escape plan had already been brewing at the back of my mind. Since Shahram's departure I was more suspicious and afraid of being watched. Any car driving by or a person walking behind me for long periods of time were considered as if they were following me. The first step was to establish the appearance of a normal existence. More than ever, I had to appear to be going nowhere. If I went somewhere, I would return on schedule. Every day off was an opportunity to establish a routine—go and come back. Disappear and return. Eventually, I would visit border towns to research the possibilities of escape, but first I would invent a reputation for myself as someone who always returned home from these short excursions.

I used these outings to read about Canada—books and magazines that gave me historical, geographical, or social facts about that country, Vancouver in particular. I read about Grouse Mountain, rising 4000 feet directly behind the city, where you could ski, and where people rode up and down in a gondola car, a hundred people at a time. In the summer, you could hike up the mountain through an evergreen forest to enjoy the panoramic view of the city, the ocean, and the mountains to the north, which was some of the most rugged country in the world.

You could wander off and be lost forever. In fact, bears sometimes wandered into people's yards at the edge of the town. I saw pictures of Lions Gate Bridge, which looked similar to the Golden Gate Bridge in San Francisco.

I read about Stanley Park, almost a thousand forested acres, making it the third largest urban park in North America. It was adjacent to downtown and almost totally surrounded by water. For thousands of years, I learned, the peninsula was a favourite place for native tribes along the west coast. It had become a military reserve that eventually burned down in 1886. I could picture people walking through the park, enjoying its Rose Garden, and running and cycling around the 10-kilometre seawall, which ended at English Bay, a beach that attracts millions of visitors every year because of its spectacular sunsets.

At nine every evening, I read, a cannon went off. It wasn't a sign of war, but of peace. You could hear it all over the city, a boom that resounded for miles to warn fishermen to stop fishing. In North Vancouver, there's a suspension bridge over the Capilano River, which must have been near my family's new home. If the information was correct, it was the world's longest and highest suspension footbridge.

I learned some other things about Canada. The biggest mall in the world, for instance, the West Edmonton Mall, was built by four Iranian brothers named Ghermezian. East of British Columbia, the provinces extend all the way to Newfoundland on the far east coast, 5000 kilometres away. I read about the old generations of Eskimos up north, called Inuit, meaning "eaters of raw fish." I found it interesting that the Eskimos had developed the custom of wife swapping, or temporary spouse exchange with their visitors. It was meant to be an act of hospitality, but I can tell you that if they were living under the law of the Ayatollah Khomeini, there wouldn't be a single Eskimo alive. They would all be stoned to death for adultery.

I always called my wife upon returning from my little trips. She sounded happy most of the time, but the kids were a growing concern. Shahram was always late coming home at night, always out with his friends, and Shahrokh would sometimes take her car without permission. And of course, I could tell from her voice that she needed me. Never, though, did she make the mistake of asking when I was leaving. She would talk about her job in a hair salon, and about her refresher courses for nursing aides. Shahram was doing well in college, but Shahrokh often had made himself unpopular with the school principal, who was always phoning Akram with complaints about his behaviour. He might have been a brat at school, but he was his little sister's chief protector and babysitter, which was a big relief. Still, the bad news always upset me, and I lost patience waiting for the right moment to make my break. If I hadn't needed to sell the house, I might have packed my bag after hanging up the phone.

I decided to sell the house right away, just get it over with so I could settle down to another routine. It was our dream home, but all our dreams were dust by that time. Anyway, the place was much too large for me. A smaller apartment in the same district would do fine. Gradually, I sold off excess furniture, but when it came time to kiss my library goodbye, well, that was more difficult. Two thousand volumes! Collecting and reading them had been my lifetime's passion. But what was I going to do—pack them on my back? I had no choice.

I knew intelligence agents had been watching me. I had to see myself objectively, through their eyes. "There's Sharifi selling his house and paying off his debts. There he is starting an import-export business, and making pretty good money, too, from sporting goods from Korea and clothing from Turkey. He's still teaching at two ministries and putting in shifts at the carpet shop. He's a busy guy, that Sharifi."

Life fell into a pleasant routine of business during the week and socializing on the weekend. Mainly, I'd visit friends for singing, and dancing to live music. It often didn't feel like Iran, since this kind of entertainment had been forbidden. But we did as we pleased behind closed doors. Women dressed as they had in the time of the Shah, even more liberally, in fact. And of course the veil was nowhere to be seen. If the *komiteh* raided us, we would have been in serious trouble. But our frustration was growing; there was a limit to what we would tolerate, so these parties were minor victories in the underground resistance against the regime. Eventually, I risked my life, tried to live freely and fearlessly. I examined my situation from the eye of the intelligence service and decided it was my turn to throw a party, to reciprocate for all the times I'd been a guest.

I invited musicians, and more guests than I could fit into my apartment. The younger ones had to stand, which was okay with them because they preferred to dance anyway. And dance they did, rocking the place until the building shook, stopping only to feast on the best catered food in town. The only safeguard against detection was one person standing guard, in case suspicious individuals were seen approaching. Halfway through the evening the phone rang. I could hardly hear the voice at the other end, so I took the phone into the bedroom and closed the door. The gentleman apologized for interrupting my party, still not having introduced himself.

"Who is this?" I said.

"Mohseni," he said, "from the Intelligence Office, armed forces headquarters."

"What I can do for you at this time of night," I asked in my most sober and polite voice. "Is it important?"

"It is, in fact," he said. "But I don't want to disappoint your guests by forcing you to leave them. Let's meet at 8 a.m. at the Office of Formalities on Pasdaran Avenue. Do you know where that is?"

"Of course," I said. I'd hosted a foreign delegation there when Colonel Beigi headed that organization.

"Tomorrow, then," Mohseni said.

"And the reason for the meeting?" I said.

"You'll hear about it tomorrow," he said, and hung up.

The evening was ruined.

The next morning I got out of bed already exhausted, and hungover and more depressed than usual.

It was only a ten-minute drive from my apartment to the front gates of the Office of Formalities. Two soldiers stood guard in the lobby. I inquired about the office of Mr. Mohseni, and was shown to his door, which swung open even as I reached for the doorknob. I was facing a man in his early thirties, with a three-day growth of beard.

"Colonel Sharifirad, I am Mohseni."

No handshake, he just showed me inside to an expensively appointed lounge area furnished with magnificent carpets and collectibles. He pointed me into a leather chair and sat opposite, where he pulled documents from his briefcase.

"Okay, Colonel. Do you know why you're here?"

"No," I said. "And for the record, Mr. Mohseni, I'm not longer a colonel."

"Title is not important," he said. "Mister or colonel doesn't change anything. The reason I called you here concerns the departure of your family. They are in Canada, yes?"

"That's right," I said.

"Including your eldest son, Shahram. How did you manage to get him out of the country?"

I had a feeling that the truth would be the shortest distance between me and tomorrow's breakfast. "I had him smuggled out," I said.

"By the CIA?"

"No, a local smuggler. I don't now any CIA agents, by the way."

"Any embassy help you out?"

"As I said, I hired a common smuggler. They managed fine."

"And how did you find a smuggler?" Mohseni said. "Who introduced him to you?"

"It was my wife, as a matter of fact."

"Your wife? And how would she happen to be acquainted with smugglers?"

"Iranians living in Canada recommended him. They gave us his name, and assured us that he could be trusted."

"Okay, what's his name, and where does he live?"

I knew they'd find out sooner or later, possibly by torture if I resisted. "Nouri," I said. "I can't guarantee you that that's his real name. He has a stationery store on Tehran Nou Avenue."

"Did he take your son to Turkey?"

"No. He had an agent do that by the name of Bigler."

"Is this the truth or are you playing games, and wasting my time?"

"I'm telling you the truth," I said.

"Don't you know that your son is forbidden to leave Iran?"

"Of course," I said.

"He is due to be drafted into the armed forces. Due to serve the country. You knew that."

"Of course."

"I believe this constitutes a crime on your part. You've broken the rules of your court martial. Did you know that?"

"I didn't know that helping my son to save his life was a crime," I replied.

"Save his life?" Mohseni replied. "Save him from what?"

"From what?" I said. "Are you serious?" I was heading for trouble if I kept it up, so I started to invent a story. "From becoming depressed," I said. "I was worried for my son's sanity. I was afraid to leave him at home. I couldn't go anywhere without him tagging along. He was afraid of being kidnapped. It's crazy, I know, but you can imagine how that tied me down, being a single parent, and how it affected my teaching, and my business."

"Are you sure the person your wife talked to in Canada wasn't an American agent?" Mohseni said.

"How can I be sure of anything so far away? But I don't think so. I have no reason to think so."

"Are you going to ask your wife to return?" Mohseni asked. "What if we promise you complete freedom here? Total security?"

"I don't think she'll listen to anything I have to say anymore," I said. "If she cared about me, she wouldn't have left me in the first place."

He examined some documents. "It's odd you should say that, Colonel. Our records show that she was a loving wife. A very dutiful and loving wife who worked hard for your release while you were in prison. She went after the authorities to have you pardoned. Doesn't sound like she doesn't care."

"That was then," I said. "When she thought things might work out. That I'd be restored to my military position. She knew me as a pilot who was paid respect. But that all vanished, didn't it? Everything changed, and she with it. Changed her mind about me, that's for sure. Went and joined another community of Iranians in Canada."

"You're telling me that she left on her own?"

"That's what I'm telling you."

"You're telling me her leaving wasn't carefully planned, and that you had nothing to do with it? Please, Colonel Sharifi."

"I'm telling you, we never discussed it. Why should we? We'd just bought a new house—check your file. We had two cars, our children were attending the best school in town. Why should we think of giving that up to risk living in a country where we'd be foreigners, probably second-class citizens?"

"Because the CIA asked you to do exactly that," Mohseni explained.

"That's just silly," I said. "It doesn't make any sense!"

It was a strange conversation, totally disconnected from reality, what with me lying and him being absurd.

"We knew all about it," Mohseni continued. "That's why we had you on such a long leash, even letting your son go. So we could follow you and make a list of all your contacts, all the people in this smuggling organization. Not surprising, most of your contacts are anti-Revolution and anti-Islamic."

"You're accusing me of being a CIA agent and anti-Islamic?" I said.

I could feel my temperature rising, and not from having spun that fantastic lie, but from being trapped in the same old endless dialogue. I'd have to stand on my war record again, dredge it all up and throw it at them. I was as patriotic as any man. And if they wanted to talk about faith—what else would make a man strap himself into the cockpit of an airplane, risking his life to combat the real enemy? My actions were on record for everyone to see, so if that didn't prove my patriotism, what could I do to convince them? Nothing.

"Whatever you've been told to do with me," I said, "you better go right ahead and do it."

Another man entered, and Mohseni stood respectfully and didn't sit again until the man made a gesture for him to do so. He must have been listening to our conversation, because he didn't even examine the interrogation report before telling Mohseni to quit wasting his time. "Your answers are garbage," he shouted at me.

"Good for the garbage heap," Mohseni repeated. "Yes, sir."

His boss glared at me with repulsion, as if I smelled like a dead dog. I had the feeling he wanted to kick me in the face, because he was trembling slightly. "You think I'm a fool?"

"I don't even know you, sir."

"Well, I know you—squadron commander in Tabriz and base commander deputy in operations in Dezful," he snarled.

"Correct."

"You loved to talk, briefing your wingmen for a full hour, for a half-hour flight. And you expect me to believe that you didn't plan your family's departure? You think I'm a fool?" he repeated.

"My wife made the arrangements," I said. "She made a preliminary trip to Turkey with my daughter. Next, she went to Singapore but never returned. What could I do?"

"And you tell us that you didn't know about your eldest son's departure, either."

"I've explained that already," I said. "I accept part of the responsibility for it."

"Your problem, Sharifi, is that you don't believe in Islam," he continued. "You worship your so-called patriotism. Don't you know that's prohibited by Islam as well? Muslims worship only God. Your country can be loved but not worshipped."

"Religion and country, I love them both the same," I said. "Is there something wrong with that? Love is my religion, not words. I'm fed up with words, but that's all I hear from you people."

"You love Islam? I don't think so, Sharifi. Or you wouldn't have sent your family to America. What is America? Our greatest enemy. The greatest enemy of Islam. Look at the Muslims in Palestine, persecuted by Israel. And who is behind Israel? I don't understand why they freed you. What have you to say, Colonel?"

I was out of words, emptied of explanations, tired of trying to make a case for deeds and actions that were logical, reasonable, and sane. The problem was that Iran was no longer any of those things.

"I have here two orders," he said, brandishing some sheets of paper. "One for your release and one for your arrest."

More games, always trying to make us beg for mercy. He told me to stay where I was while he left to do a little fact checking about Nouri. "You're in for a worse experience than last time," he warned me.

I was in the hands of a group who called themselves Moghallede Imam Khomeini, the followers of Khomeini, who'd had me under surveillance. They must have remained convinced that I was involved in espionage, and that once free, I would lead them to my agents and associates. The soldier guarding me brought me a badly needed cup of tea, complete with a respectful little click of the heels. The gesture reminded me of the old days, but as I drank the tea my future looked extremely bleak again. They might be purging the final remaining American-trained pilots who served in the Shah's armed forces. It was a miracle that a few of us had survived this long.

I thought back to the early days of the revolutionary government, and how they'd ordered military commanders to single out the pilots who were especially loyal to the old regime, and to keep a close eye on them. Khomeini smelled a potential coup and he was right—the Nojeh military coup of 1980—but it failed spectacularly to bring down the government of Abolhassan Banisadr and the Ayatollah Khomeini. Many pilots were executed, many more thrown in prison, while the rest, regardless of their role in the action, lost any chance of promotion. In fact, they were downgraded, even forced to retire. The lack of experienced commanders meant that low-ranking officers who were loyal to the Revolution were promoted well above their level of competence. Untested men became lieutenant colonels and majors, and were given command of tactical air bases.

At the beginning of the war, before the Revolutionary Army had time to train a new breed of fighting men, the pilots of the old regime had to defend the borders against Iraq, especially at cities like Ahvaz, the capital of Khozestan province. Imagine risking your life on the battlefront to fight for a country that was waiting to stab you in the back. We fought, anyway, defending against the invaders. At the same time, in the most ironic of situations, we pilots realized that we owed our personal survival to the threat posed by our enemy. The more successful Iraq forces were, the longer we were saved from our own regime. It doesn't get any more twisted than that. And the purging and killing hadn't stopped after all those years. Paranoia and murder had become an addiction of the ayatollahs. Only recently, in 1992, the regime had executed two more friends of mine, one an F-5 pilot, the other, one of the best R-F4 pilots in the war. They'd been accused of spying for the CIA.

My situation looked dire. I couldn't survive another prison tour. As far as I was concerned to be executed by firing squad would be more desirable than another round of torture.

It was past midnight when I heard the guards at the main gate changing their shift. My guard had left at 9 p.m. and had not returned. I was exhausted from worrying, my mind spinning with random useless thoughts. I became more depressed by the hour, until late in the night, Mohseni entered the room. He stood in front of me holding his briefcase, looking tired and upset.

"Okay, Colonel, we're done."

"What do you mean?" I asked.

"I mean we're done," he said, placing a document in front of me. "My job is over." He threw me a pen.

My heart was pounding. "What's this?" I said.

"Read it. You'll find out."

It was difficult to concentrate, my glance darting around the page for the part where I'd read my death sentence. But, no, it was nothing more than conditions for my ongoing parole. More restrictions against travel and more frequent check-ins. And a promise to bring my family back to Iran, but otherwise nothing to worry about. It wasn't a death sentence at all. I signed it quickly, my hand shaking. I even shook Mohseni's hand, that's how much I couldn't wait to get out of there.

Back home, as desperately tired as I was, I started immediately working on my escape plan. My freedom wouldn't last long, I was sure of it. I would always be the CIA agent they wanted me to be. A finely calculated plan is what I needed, but my head wouldn't co-operate. I had to get some sleep.

20

DERVISHES

I returned to my routine of teaching and visiting my business associates, not forgetting for a moment the possibility of being tailed. On my first return visit to Mohseni's office, one of his co-workers invited me to work with him. His name was Khaleghi, and he wanted me to help him profile the activities of the Pakistani military attaché in Iran.

"Okay," I said. He seemed delighted. "But first you have to give me an order in writing," I added. I smelled a plot to catch me associating with foreigners.

The delight faded from his face. He must have thought he was dealing with an idiot. When we met again a few days later, Khaleghi told me they didn't want to bother with written permission.

"I'm not doing anything without a formal requisition from your boss," I said. I wasn't going to be falsely accused again.

My fears of entrapment were confirmed a few days later when I heard from Nouri, the smuggler. He came on to me with an offer to escape the country. The venture was inexpensive and foolproof, altogether too good to be true. And he kept talking about my family, like they were bait. As much as I missed them, I was disciplined enough not to talk about my wife and kids with anyone I didn't know. I couldn't mention them without sounding as if I was dying of thirst.

"Thanks, anyway," I said. "But, you know, I'm really enjoying my life in Tehran right now." I could hardly believe those words were coming out of my mouth. I told Nouri that I would apply for a passport, and that my departure would be legal, or not at all.

Poor Nouri, he seemed as if he was trying to get out of a trap. He'd obviously become a stooge for the Intelligence Service, as a condition of his own freedom, no doubt.

Then Mohseni invited me out for lunch at the Homa Hotel on Bijan Street near Vanak Square. He had a proposal: bring my family back to Iran or have the Intelligence Office on my case for the rest of my life. He assured me they had surveillance methods that I was entirely unaware of.

"I'll think about it," I said.

I guess I thought about it too long, because soon I was fired from my teaching job at the oil ministry. There was no way of being sure if Mohseni was behind the firing, but I was suspicious. Meanwhile, my job with the Ministry of Mines and Metals proceeded without a problem, but at the point of scheduling me for the next semester, I resigned. First, I didn't want further entanglement with the government, but more important, I had to be free of any kind of schedule so I could more easily execute my escape plan.

The key was to establish another recurring pattern: leave home, come back. Short trips to different parts of the country, return, leave again, and again return. Create a pattern that would make me predictable. Perhaps if the pattern of my activities was boring enough, I might fall off the Intelligence Service radar. Wishful thinking. At the same time, I applied for a passport. Sure, obtaining one at this point was hopeless, even ridiculous, but maybe applying for one lent me legitimacy, the appearance of being in no rush to leave. I had to take things slowly and build a reputation of reliability.

Late in July 1993, a friend of mine, Mohimani, invited me to join him on a trip to Bakhtaran, a provincial capital in the western section of Iranian Kurdistan. He owed me some money, and felt he could get his hands on the proceeds of a land sale being transacted by one of his associates, and pay me back. Together with a friend of his, Mohsen, we packed into my little Renault and left Tehran early in the morning. It was hot, a real summer's day. Even with the windows open, the car was a sauna before we reached the city limits.

"Perhaps another day would be better," I said.

"Be patient," Mohimani said.

Once we were on the highway we cooled off, and once past the toll booth we got up some speed and felt better. From Tehran to Qazvin, the route was easy going on a three-lane divided highway that traversed a vast plain. Not much to recommend it, if you're a tourist. After three hours, and my passengers fast asleep, we approached the 3rd Tactical Air Force Base outside the city of Hamedan where I had been assigned after my return from the United States in 1972 It was during my stay there that I married Akram, and where Shahram was born. This was the notorious Nojeh Base, the home of the leading groups of the fighter pilots and the headquarters of the operations against the Islamic regime and the staging ground for the unsuccessful *coup d'état* in the early days of the Islamic Revolution. My thoughts were still on that tragic chapter of Iranian history as we entered Hamedan.

I woke Mohimani to share pleasant memories of how Akram and I used to picnic in the region. I spoke of kebabs and fresh bread with basil on the side, and of great restaurants, particularly Boali Hotel and the parties held in their dance club. I pointed out a single minaret marking the tomb of the father of Avicenna, arguably the world's most renowned philosopher, but there was no stopping. This was no pleasure trip. We kept on going through Asadabad Pass, then down to Kangavar, where we stopped for a well-earned break at a tea house. Half an hour later we were on our way again, not stopping until we arrived at our hotel in Bakhtaran. The service was terrible, and the furniture old and seedy. What a dump!

We took an hour's rest, then drove around the city, stopping at the foot of Bistoon Mountain. The rocks are covered with writings and drawings, reminders from centuries past of a fable that any Iranian could tell you:

A young warrior named Farhad was in love with Shirin, whose name meant "sweet." Forbidden to see each other, they were forced to communicate their love using various signs. Every night, Farhad struck the rock with his adze, a signal that proved he was still alive, as much as it was a sign of his love. If Shirin failed to hear Farhad's love beats, she couldn't sleep. The writings represented Shirin's pining for her lover, back when love and human emotion was fodder for poets.

Tonight no sound of the adze can be heard from the Bistoon.
Maybe Farhad is dreaming about Shirin,
Or maybe Farhad has fallen off to a sweet sleep.

I woke early due to Mohiman's fearful snoring. At the end of the corridor was a public shower. As I said, this wasn't a real hotel at all, not even a restaurant for our breakfast. We picked up Mohimani's associate, a man named Ghobadian, whose family owned a lot of real estate in the Bakhtaran region. We headed for the nearby town of Marivaan, but my fellow travellers were taking forever to get around to talking business.

"Relax, Sharifi," Mohimani said. "We'll show you something you won't soon forget."

We passed through countryside that was a feast for the eyes: hills and valleys, rocky in parts, other areas rich with fertile loam. Some crops, mostly wheat, were still green, while others were turning yellow ripe, the clusters of grain so heavy that the stalks swayed in response to the slightest breeze. The sight mesmerized me, the slow heaving and rising of ripe wheat and barley, like an ocean swell. The way the stalks bowed and straightened reminded me of the Japanese style of paying respect. They say it's an acknowledgement of the God that resides within us. Scenes like these are God's gift to those who have eyes to see, and I thought, how could the people who farmed the land not be awed by such natural works of art? They were touched by such miracles, of course, which was why I loved the peasants who tilled the soil, these patient men and women with weathered faces and sickles in hand. We stopped so that I could savour the scene.

An old man approached us. He offered us water and bread and cheese, what he had with him. His face was brown and creased like a walnut shell and his smile reminded me of the Kurdish warriors in Iraq who had risked their lives for me. I had a little daydream, right there, of being as tough and adaptable as they were, somehow surviving every kind of hardship. Politics and borders appeared to mean nothing to these people. What a way to live truly free.

On the way to Marivaan, we saw dead tanks and trucks and military vehicles of all kinds. It boggled the mind, trying to guess the number of dead, the number of souls who were forced to sacrifice themselves in order to satisfy the hunger for power of Saddam and Khomeini.

Once in Marivaan, Ghobadian directed us to the house of a friend, who invited us in. We sat on rough carpets of gypsy origin. I must have looked uncomfortable leaning against the wall, because a young man offered me two large pillows. Our host's wife, in Kurdish dress, spread a plastic sheet in front of us and brought us each a bowl of *aabgoosht*. Along with the broth were dishes of mashed peas, potato, meat, plus rows of sliced onions and other fresh vegetables on the side.

"*Befarmayid*," she said. "Here you are! Make yourselves at home."

Tremendous meal! Then a short nap, after which Ghobadian took us to a small mosque in the city centre. Before entering, we were required to perform simple ablutions at an artesian well, which had its source in the mountain just outside the town. We washed our hands, mouth, face, arms, and toes before proceeding inside, where twenty-two men seated in a circle were waiting for us, their heads covered with scarves or turbans of different colours. These were the *deravish* (dervishes), the members of the Muslim religious brotherhood who vow poverty and austerity but different from whirling Sufi dervishes from Turkey. Ghobadian informed me that these were the most respected group of *deravish* in Marivaan. *Darvish* was the singular, I was told, and *deravish* the plural. As we arrived, they stood up to welcome us, placing their hands on their chests and then bowing low, almost to their knees. I followed their lead, and bowed my head. Then we all sat down, our backs to the wall.

Fifteen minutes passed in total silence. Then the master nodded in our direction—must have been asking our permission to begin the ceremony, because twelve *deravish* stood. In a circle, with their eyes closed and hands linked, they began moving slowly in a circle, and chanting repetitively, *"Ho! Ho! Ho!"* The men who remained seated beat tambourines, louder with each round of the circle. Also, the dancers hooted louder and their bowing became more exaggerated, and you could see them sweating. They doffed their head scarves, revealing their magnificent dark hair. It was easy to imagine that they'd never had a haircut in their lives. This hair was tossed up and around like the tails of wild horses stampeding in a sacred circle. The tambourines grew even louder, while the chant changed to include the name of Ali. *"Ali, Ali, Ali, Ali, Ho-ho, Ali, Ali, Ali . . . !"* The performance gave me a serious case of goosebumps.

Ghobadian leaned into my ear. "They like Ali as their God."

Ali was Prophet Mohammad's son-in-law, the fourth caliph of Islam, and first imam of the Shiite Muslims. I was so moved by this reverential performance that I began swaying, myself, driven by the sound of the tambourines, and entering a pleasant state of disbelief. By that I mean I suspended my belief about everything else I'd known up to this point. I had to, especially when one *darvish* started swallowing broken glass! Another one was eating stones, while another held hot coals, and yet another pierced his cheek with a spear and withdrew it out the other cheek.

They were surely in a trance, an ecstasy of some kind, an altered state, which so affected me my eyes filled with tears. I was unfamiliar with the emotion that gripped me. I must have looked horrified, because the master made a hand gesture that initiated the end of the ceremony. Slowly, the tambourines calmed down, then the *deravish*, themselves. As they came to a stop, their sweating faces resumed a normal colour, but otherwise they didn't resemble the men who had begun the performance. They were beacons of bliss and light and relaxation.

One *darvish* placed a large plastic sheet in the middle of the floor, while others brought food and invited us to move close and eat with them. It was apparently their custom to wait until we began eating before they tucked in themselves. Everyone on earth goes before them, that's part of their practice. It must have made for a simple and peaceful life, never worrying about tomorrow, unless it's for someone else. You can't imagine the relief—to feel happy and proud of my own country again—to meet people who had found a way to live free, regardless of where they lived. It was as if some long-forgotten part of my heart was playing out in front of me. I could hardly thank them enough.

I spent the night being attacked by mosquitoes at the house of Ghobadian's friend. The assault was unrelenting, from the moment my head hit the pillow, until I arose in the morning. What a relief to finally get up and begin the journey back to Bakhtaran, where my friends finally got down to business. Ghobadian had some property for sale, but he explained that the market had cooled off, so the whole trip proved to be something of a wild goose chase. Perhaps that's why they'd given me the *darvish* experience—so the trip wasn't a dead loss. They'd succeeded. I was still on a high. What's more, their intentions had been pure. They were good and reliable men. What more could I ask for?

Ghobadian remained in Bakhtaran to continue trying to unload some real estate, while Mohsen returned to Tehran, and Mohimani and I headed towards the Turkish border, in the far northwest corner of Iran. I was suspicious but not certain that I was being watched or followed by the Intelligence Service. I took all the precautionary measures I knew and took one more step towards my plan. I wanted to meet a smuggler in the town of Maako. Hossein was his name. I told him to start making arrangements for my escape through the mountains into Turkey.

21

TOURIST LIKE ME

I sold my apartment in Tehran and moved to a house in Niavaran Street, not far from Khomeini's residence. It was an old house with more space than I needed, even had a swimming pool in the front yard, but the backyard was what sold me; it featured a grove of walnut trees. Perfect cover for me to come and go unnoticed.

That summer of 1993 was so humid, I was sweating even before the sun had risen. I woke one morning with a dizzy headache, but I had booked another trip, already paid for it, this one south to Isfahan and Shiraz. My journeys were getting longer, aimed at building a file of evidence that showed I could be trusted to return. I shaved, took a shower, and warmed my belly with a large mug of red tea, fortified with two extra-strength aspirin. I wasn't hungry, but I ate, anyway; a loaf of *lavash* bread with white cheese and a boiled egg. I'd packed the previous evening, so all I had to do was leave the house, but almost through the gate, it hit me: I'd forgotten to phone Intelligence. Now I was running late. I dialed Mohseni's number and it rang until the answering machine cut in. I explained that I was joining a bus tour to Isfahan and Shiraz, and hung up.

It was a twenty-minute cab ride to the travel office on Motahari Avenue. It was crammed with chattering people, mostly women, which didn't help my headache. When we boarded, I was careful to take a seat beside a young man, because I was basically picking my neighbour for the next few days. Our soft-spoken driver introduced himself as Ali, and welcomed us on board. He was young and overweight but a happy sort of fellow with short hair, red cheeks, and white teeth. His co-driver, Morad, was a nervous type with small eyes, or maybe it was just the quickness of his movements that produced that effect.

As the bus started to move, Ali shouted, *"Salavat!"*

We all shouted, "Peace be upon Prophet Mohammad!"

Any journey from Tehran starts slowly. It takes approximately forty-five minutes to reach the highway. Once there, we picked up speed, and were well and truly on our way to the holy city of Qom, and farther south. "Four hundred and eighty-three kilometres to the city of Isfahan!" Ali announced.

Some passengers were already asleep despite the non-stop chatter. Only a few, like myself, were content to sit in silence and watch the passing panorama. Morad kept the passengers in the front seats entertained with his impersonations, which left them laughing so hard that others, behind them, wanted in on the joke. Morad began singing, taking off a popular singer, Mohammad Reza Shajarian. It wasn't supposed to be funny, but we laughed so hard that he began laughing himself and couldn't finish the song. I recognized the song as a poem from Hafez—*"Every place is the house of love, the synagogue as much as the mosque . . ."*

Then, a middle-aged lady with a bright voice started up, after which a man joined in and branched off on a song of his own. Then, a string of jokes from a gentleman at the back of the bus made us laugh some more. By the time we reached Qom, we had bonded as a family of fellow travellers, sharing even the snacks we'd brought with us; pistachios by the bushel had made the rounds of the bus, along with tea and cakes and sandwiches with bottled water. By the time we were through Qom, we had settled down to listen to one of Ali's tapes, the songs of

Leila Forouhar, an Iranian singer and actress making a career for herself in Los Angeles. A young woman rose to her feet without a *roosari* (head scarf), and began dancing in the aisle. But if we approached a town or passed a police station, Ali or Morad would sound a warning, and the ladies would sit down and cover up and our little caravan of fun would take a sober break.

By 3:30 p.m. we made it to Isfahan, one of the country's largest cities, and appropriately called *Isfahan Nesfe Jahan*, meaning "Isfahan is half the world." There's no other city in Iran to compare it with, perhaps no other city in the world. Every year, visitors pour into this historic city, its streets packed with shops doing a roaring business in high-quality arts and crafts. Woven items, mosaics, engravings, carpets, miniatures, and copper works are amongst the most popular purchases in Isfahan.

Hotel Abbasi was our destination, and a fine hotel it was, expensive by recent standards, harking back to the time of the Shah. But as we checked in I became suspicious of the bellhop, a young man who delivered our suitcases to our rooms. Something about his look—I'd become very familiar with that kind of look—eyes in which you couldn't see a flicker of compassion. I thanked him, tipped him, and let him go. I had to join my fellow travellers in the lobby.

After snacking our way across Iran, nobody was hungry. But there was great enthusiasm for shopping and sightseeing. We separated into four groups and disappeared into different quarters of the city. Mine was a group of five, including a recently married couple—Ramien and Lili—and two of their friends. We took a taxi to Chehar Bagh, a neighbourhood of garden streets and a busy boulevard lined with plane trees. It was more like a park than a downtown area, but it didn't lack shops. And that's where we were headed, like moths to a flame.

The businessmen of Isfahan are a breed unto themselves. Renowned for their cunning and intelligence, nobody's better at attracting customers and closing a deal. They can see a purchase coming a mile away, and seduce the most sophisticated buyer. But these merchants are also friendly, charming, and tactful, with a great sense of humour. Even their accent is unique in Iran, a soft intonation with a prolongation of the voice at the end. There wasn't one of us who expected to come out the winner in our dealings with them. Touch something in a shop, and your feet might as well be locked in a bear trap. Ask the price of anything, and consider yourself hooked on their lure. If offered tea or a little treat, like *gaz*, white Iranian candy, don't be fooled into thinking it's free. By no means mistake these salesmen as gratuitously generous, not at all, because without a doubt the cost will be added to the selling price, a price you can be assured you will be paying before he's finished with you; a price that's bound to be three or four times higher than the item is worth, no matter how hard you bargain. It shouldn't surprise anyone to learn that Isfahanis themselves are famous for being stingy. Not a penny do they spend without first considering all the excellent reasons for not spending it.

I bought an inlaid jewellery box for my wife, and then a miniature polo scene painted on camel bone. I offered the man a quarter of the price he was asking for, and he accepted, but then I changed my mind. He gave me an even greater discount and pretended to be quite the loser in this transaction. So, I agreed to pay him the money, and he wrapped up the purchases carefully and handed them to me, saying, "Enjoy them, my friend, but you know, you didn't win the game." And he started laughing. His sense of humour was irresistible. I mean, we were all laughing. "I'm kidding," he said. "I was just pulling your leg. Thank you for your business and I hope to see you again."

We strolled on to other shops. The newly married Ramien and Lili wanted to buy a handmade copper plate. When a price was agreed upon, and Ramien went to pay, the merchant suddenly became unwilling to accept his money. "Please take it," he said. "Pay me next time." Ramien insisted on paying, and two or three times the shop owner insisted in the same manner until finally accepting payment. This was just a custom called *taarof*, a traditional back-and-forth game of chit-chat that has no real meaning. If my friends had actually taken the merchant at face value, and left the shop without paying, he would have come after the customer and extracted the money from him. I'd been to Isfahan before with my wife and seen how *taarof* worked. I'd seen merchants play this game before, and still it exhausted me. I asked my group if they'd consider moving on to visit Miedane Naghshe Jahan, the Square of the Mirrors of the World. My companions agreed.

A three-storey structure overlooked the square, with a second-floor balcony from which King Abbas once observed military parades and watched polo games. That was four hundred years ago, during the Safavid dynasty (1501–1722). This was his capital before Isfahan became the Safavid capital. The square now featured a rectangular pool with fountains around and within it. The splashing display of water makes this a real gathering point for the city. The Mosque of Sheikh-Lout-Follah lay on the east side, a structure famous for its turquoise dome of mosaic and Koranic verses, and for its delicate architectural detailing and two minarets that seem to touch the sky.

Along the streets that surround the central pool are many antique shops crammed with both paying customers and tourists alike. One of the shopkeepers told us that, of all shahs in Persian history, King Abbas was the most popular. If the ex-Shah had behaved like Abbas, he could have remained king until he died of natural causes. During the time of Shah Abbas, anyone could file a complaint for being treated cruelly. The Shah, himself, used to wander anonymously throughout his city, often at night, disguised as a commoner. He would stop in the bazaar and listen to the mood of the people, paying special attention to their complaints, then take it upon himself to correct any injustice or corruption, especially if the problem was due to his government or the machinations of his relatives. I couldn't help comparing King Abbas to our current leaders, the clerics, and their many corruptions and cruelties, and the wealth they'd stolen from the Iranian people and secreted into their private overseas accounts. I abandoned those thoughts for the moment, as my little party moved on.

The largest bazaar in Isfahan was located on the north side of the square, a vast covered marketplace that we entered through an arched gateway. Tunnel-shaped alleys were well lit with lamps. There were so many shops, it would have taken a full day to visit them all, each store festooned with goods hanging from the ceiling and spilling onto the street. It was too much for an already tired shopper to take in. Many stores were lit by a single bulb, which made the lighting unusually intimate, sometimes glowing through the lacy carved detail in copper lanterns. Half an hour in the bazaar and we were ready for tea.

As we entered a small tea shop, a woman customer quickly covered more of her forehead with her chador. On the wall, I noticed portraits of Khomeini, Khamenei, and Rafsanjani peering down on us. Since Isfahanis are very religious people, we had to behave ourselves and follow tradition. We drank our tea without a lot of critical chatter, then left the shop to wait for a taxi.

While we were waiting, we decided on our next destination: Isfahan's most famous bridge. Si-o-Seh Pol and its thirty-three arches spans the Zayandeh Roud and connects two parts of the city. We couldn't find a taxi to accommodate all of us, so we broke into two parties. Ramien and I took the first taxi, while his wife and the two others planned to catch the next one. The back seat was occupied by three passengers so Ramien and I struggled to fit into one seat, my friend half on the handbrake and the driver groping under his leg to change gears. We had a good laugh during the short ride.

One can't help but stand in awe of Si-o-Seh Pol, really, one of the old masterpieces against which today's architecture looks uninspired. We watched families picnicking on the grassy banks of the river, and youngsters pedalling boats on the river and shouting and laughing. Some of the girls reminded me of my daughter, Mahrokh. How I missed her and the boys! When the other half of our group arrived, we sat on a bench with a good view of the bridge. I counted fourteen arcades in two levels, and two pavilions on either end. The entire bridge was illuminated by spotlights, which reflected on the river, making a spectacular sight, and reminding me of happier times. A short while later, we rose from our bench and walked on until we stopped at another tea house.

This place was packed, and while we waited for seats, some young men invited us to join them. They were smoking *ghalyan*, the water pipe, and called the waiter and ordered tea for us, and another pipe. What a joyful place it was. These new friends of ours were full of jokes particular to Isfahanis, which made us laugh and laugh. In the midst of all that fun I found myself missing my family, who weren't there to share the gaiety. Then, when two men entered the tea house, I sobered up, totally. It was a reaction born of all my experience with members of the Intelligence Service. They certainly looked ominous, and if their intention was to remind me that I was being watched, it worked. They couldn't find a seat, however, so they were more or less forced to leave.

My friends drank their tea, sucked on the pipe, and passed the tube along to the next person and finally to me. I held the nozzle in my hand and gave a puff, and then sucked in the smoke from the nozzle. I enjoyed the peaceful sound of the burbling water in the glass container. Ramien explained how smoking the water pipe made one relax, while cigarettes made one edgy and impatient. Being a non-smoker, I found it hard to believe that one type of tobacco consumption was different from any other. This was also Lili's first time with the water pipe, and she became so dizzy we had to usher her out for fresh air, and still she didn't perk up, so we returned to the hotel.

The next day, I visited the palace of the Shah Abbas, then returned to the bazaar for more window-shopping. That night, my friends and I went to a high-class restaurant where our budgets restricted us to low-class pizza, but we had a memorable time. The waiters weren't snobbish, and the bill wasn't unreasonable. We were back at our hotel by 11 p.m. for a good night's sleep before our onward journey in the morning.

"Did you have a good time in Isfahan?" Ali, the bus driver, shouted, watching us through the rear-view mirror and revving the engine.

"Yes!" we replied in unison.

"Are you ready to head out for Shiraz? If so, let's hear a big *Salavat!* to Prophet Mohammad and to his relatives, to ensure our safe journey." We responded, "Peace be upon Prophet Mohammad and his relatives." He put the bus in gear.

It didn't take us long to hit the highway. Most of the passengers closed their eyes and started to nap. Even Morad looked tired from our Isfahan tour. Ramien sat next to me.

"I scored some homemade vodka last night," he said. "What do you think of that?" It was clear he wanted to pop the cork right there and then.

"Better take it easy," I said. I was having enough fun without risking getting caught drunk and being whipped or lashed.

Ali turned on some music to liven things up, but no one was ready to party. Near the city of Abadeh, we pulled over for a police check. Ali had to personally check in at the office, but soon returned with his time sheets in his hands. We gave him a cheer for his good driving, and his good nature and gentle manner. He replied with a joke, which finally put us back in party mode. Morad took over with a few more jokes and finally a song, this time a serious attempt to be musical. On our way to Shiraz we stopped at Persepolis seventy kilometres northeast. Home of Cyrus the Great. My true Mecca.

22

BIRD IN A CAGE

We stepped off the bus at Persepolis and walked towards the few surviving stone pillars amidst the ancient ruins. Cyrus the Great (559–529 B.C.) had ruled from this palace. He'd never claimed to be a prophet, but he probably shone more light on more people's lives than many so-called religious figures. The Iranian clergy had tried to demolish this site in the summer of 1980, but the locals had organized themselves to prevent it, and somehow succeeded, thank God. For Iranians who are proud of their ancient history, there is no more important site than Persepolis, the home of the first "Emperor of the World." Strolling through the ruins, you have to use your imagination to reconstruct the past. I could easily transplant myself back 2500 years—walking from the bedrooms to the living rooms, to the grand hall, and finally to the kitchen where only a few stones on the ground gave evidence of the function of that place. I visualized Cyrus ruling the world from his jewelled throne, dispensing justice and planning his military strategy, in which he himself would lead his troops into battle. It's hard to believe there was once a time when ruler and ruled enjoyed such a mutual sense of respect.

Cyrus's grave was at the base of a hill, nearby. Nothing was inscribed on it, no statements detailing his accomplishments, nor any exaggerated expressions of the greatness of the man, just a humble arrangement of stones atop the six-tiered stone tomb. Cyrus had been lying there relatively undisturbed for 2500 years, due perhaps to its being such a humble resting place. No gold here, and no mullahs selling their services. I recalled Cyrus's advice for all those he anticipated might come here to pay their respects, and I shared it with my fellow travellers standing around the grave. "'Look at my grave,'" I quoted, "'and think of this king of Asia and the world, of whom nothing remains but dust. So do not envy me.'"

No one spoke. No one wanted to break the spell that is the hallmark of this sacred place.

I'd read many authors trying to explain why Cyrus the Great was so great. He was a fine commander and an excellent human being, but he was more than that. Although he conquered much territory, he never followed his victories with destruction. In fact, his soldiers were forbidden to pillage and rape. Nor were they to attack any tomb or holy site. Innocent civilians were allowed to continue living as free citizens. Cyrus was the first to put a code of human rights into practice, a copy of which is on display at the United Nations. Cyrus was a Zoroastrian, a follower of the great Iranian prophet Zartosht, who lived six centuries before Christ, and whose religion was based on three principles: pure thought, pure words, and pure actions.

Back in 1971, the former Shah celebrated 2500 years of Iranian civilization under benevolent monarchs, right here in this spot. He invited heads of states from all over the world to the event. In his speech, the Shah assured Cyrus, "You may rest now, for I am awake and standing vigil." But the Shah didn't live long after that, nor was he able to hand the torch to his son. Worse yet, he wouldn't have his final wish fulfilled: to be buried next to Cyrus the Great. He died in exile in Egypt.

We left Persepolis in silence, alone with our thoughts, reminded how short and fragile life is and how fast things can change. I recalled an old saying: Don't depend on your looks, for they may disappear with a fever, and never depend on your wealth, which can vanish in a day.

Past the town of Marvdasht we stopped at another police checkpoint, and then proceeded to Shiraz, entering the city through the Koran Gate. After checking in at the Hotel Homa and leaving our bags in our rooms, we separated into our own groups again. My little Isfahan group voted for another day of shopping, and I stuck with them despite being anxious to visit the tombs of the two most popular poets in Iran—Hafez and Saadi. The next day we made a pilgrimage to their graves.

Both Hafez and Saadi were ancient citizens of Shiraz. Hafez (1350–1390) was the mystic, while Saadi (1184–1233) was more the sage, one who offered insights into the experience of life. The tomb of Hafez was mobbed by pilgrims praying for his blessings. The grave itself was covered with black marble carved with his poems. We stood in silent respect, some of us trying to read every inscribed word, some of us with our eyes closed. I retreated to the garden that surrounded the tomb and talked to an old man who was holding a birdcage, and, yes, inside was a small bird. Attached to the outside of the cage was a box that held some folded papers.

"Are you selling the cage or the bird?" I asked.

"Neither," he said. "The paper! Whichever one my little bird picks out for you."

"How much?"

"That depends," he said, "on your generosity."

I gave him a donation, which he pocketed without counting, then snapped his fingers twice. The bird perked up and pecked at the bits of paper, picking up one in its beak and directing it towards me.

"Close your eyes," the man said. "And clear your mind and heart. Then open the paper, and read it."

I did as I was told. On the paper were lines from one of Hafez's poems:

Saki, the dawn is breaking:
Fill up the glass with wine.
Heaven's wheel no delay is making—
Haste, haste, while the day is thine!

I wasn't in such a celebratory mood, and wondered if perhaps the bird wasn't a bit too drunk on Hafez's divine wisdom. But never mind, the nice thing about a fortune is that you can read into it what you want. Forget the wine for now, but there was no doubt about the haste, about my growing urgency to get out of Iran. Thank you, Hafez, I thought.

"Thank you, old man," I said.

My group had vanished, but we had a contingency plan for "lost sheep." They would continue by cab to Saadi's tomb, which is what I did. The site was so crowded that the chance of finding my companions was slim, so I spent an hour admiring the dome over the tomb, all glass and studded with blue tiles, the interior walls adorned even more so with mosaics set at odd angles. I squeezed away from the crowd so that I could take in the larger picture, the crush of pilgrims, and the poetry that surrounded us on the walls. One of my favourite pieces went something like this:

We are all one, all from one heart.
As the body feels pain from any one of its injured parts,
So do we all feel the pain of any one of us.
If the misery of others leaves you indifferent,
and with no feelings of sorrow,
you cannot be called a human being.

My attention was drawn to a man pressing close to the gilded cage that covered Saadi's coffin. He gripped the bars, letting his forehead fall forward against the cage, his eyes closed, whispering prayers. It struck me as an act full of grace. He lifted his head, and began to sing loudly, "*Human beings are like body parts, created from the same essence...*" It was the same poem that had caught my eye. Beside him, two women—they must have been his wives or daughters—I couldn't tell because their chadors covered most parts of their faces—gripped the cloth in their teeth and wrung it with their hands. Saadi was right, I could feel their pain. When the man stood and moved on, the women moved with him. They were such a loyal little batch of believers that I recalled all the pain that my family had shared, and how, as the poet Hafez said, it was time to make haste, to bring an end to so much suffering.

Without finding my friends, I checked our itinerary for the next stop. Paradise Garden was a palace used by Mohammad Reza Shah Pahlavi when he and his family were in Shiraz, but it had been converted to a museum. I couldn't spot my group there either, so I wandered around, feasting my eyes on the fine furniture, gambling tables, and golden dishes. A tour guide was preaching the evils of the Shah, about his lavish lifestyle in the face of poverty all over Iran, even with millions dying of starvation. Too tired to chase down my group, I returned to the hotel for a cup of tea, then retreated to my room where I fell into a deep sleep.

I awoke to a knock on the door. My fellow travellers, I thought, and opened the door to see two men in dark suits and trimmed beards.

"Can I help you?" I said, my heart sinking.

"Are you Colonel Sharifirad?"

"I was a colonel," I said. The same old script. I had the strongest urge to strangle them. "What have I done this time?" I demanded. I could feel myself on the verge of getting dangerously reckless.

"We know nothing about it," the older one said. "We have orders, that's all. To return you to Tehran. Immediately."

They wouldn't let me leave word for my group. They would take care of that, just as they'd already explained my departure to hotel reception. It took forty minutes to reach the 6th Tactical Air Base outside Shiraz. I was familiar with it from my many visits as a fighter pilot. The men led me to a second-floor room furnished with a bed similar to the one on which I'd been tortured. This one was covered by a grey blanket, and on the bedside table sat the predictable books, the Koran and a copy of Khomeini's *Resaleh*. And a prayer mat. The men departed, leaving a private in charge, who asked me if I wanted a cup of tea. I wanted only to be left alone to conjure up vengeance upon these criminals who continued to ruin my life. Not surprisingly, I couldn't sleep.

In the morning, yesterday's well-groomed goons showed up to escort me to the ramp where I'd parked my jet many times. I was ushered into a C-130 cargo flight to Tehran. I recognized the pilot, once a friend of mine, but he pretended not to know me. I'd practised sympathy for these people who were only trying to protect their reputations, but in a rush of anger I realized that I did blame them. Betraying a friendship is inexcusable, especially when they knew I was falsely accused. The flight took over two hours.

From Mehrabad Air Base we drove towards the city. When I was handed a blindfold and told to put it on, I felt as though I'd circled back to the beginning of the most horrible chapter of my life. Sure enough, I was then made invisible to the world, resting my head in the lap of the older man beside me. I wanted to do anything but repeat this grim routine, but I had no choice. The many left and right turns confused me so that I'd lost my sense of direction by the time we came to a stop. Same procedure: led into a building, into a room, where I was left to sit in a chair for nine hours. Exhaustion and fury tainted all my thoughts until I had but one—to attack and kill the first person who entered the room, before he killed me. By the time someone did show up, a deeper wisdom took over, although I felt no need to be polite.

"Salaam, brother," he said.

Not likely, you son of a . . .

"You can take off your blindfold, Colonel."

He was short and fat, a redhead in a dirty army uniform without any sign of rank. He was pathetic. He sat behind the desk and began the interrogation, more stupid, idiotic, nonsequential questions that I had to answer on paper. Finally, he wanted to know why I hadn't reported to Mr. Mohseni before I left for Isfahan and Shiraz.

"I left him a phone message," I said.

"He didn't get a message," he said. "And why for five days prior to your leaving did you fail to check in and sign the book in the court martial office?"

"That's not true," I said. "I've always reported punctually. What's your next question?"

He had questions about my trip to Shiraz, like why had I separated from the group? He accused me of purposely ditching them. "We know you are planning to escape," he said. "From the port of Booshehr."

"You know more than I do," I said, barely managing to be polite.

"Your trip to Shiraz was a clever cover for your escape."

"That hadn't even crossed my mind," I said, starting to boil. "If I was planning to escape, why am I applying for a passport? Why have I waited for almost three years, already?"

"A pretty little trick," he replied.

"A pretty stupid trick," I retorted, "living under this kind of pressure for almost three years." I didn't know if I could keep the lid on. I couldn't bear to have my life ruined another day. "An animal shouldn't have to live like this!" I shouted. He seemed stunned, kind of blown back. "I hate this life! I hate all of you! If you want to kill me, go ahead! Whoever's threatened by my being alive, bring them in here and finish me off! Or else leave me alone!"

He stared at me: he obviously didn't know what to do next, so he took my papers and left the room. Two hours later he returned with Mr. Mohseni and someone clearly their superior. Between the two of them, they came up with a feeble excuse for their Shiraz agent's "erroneous reporting," but he wasn't backing down about my phone message.

"You forgot to leave your name, Colonel. So, this is a mutual mistake, I believe. You are free to go."

I left that unknown room behind—blindfolded—the unknown room in the unknown building in a country that I understood less and less with each day that passed. They knew what I was up to, but what they didn't know was how long I would play this game until I got it right.

23

THANK YOU, MR. BOOR-BOOR

I had a friend, Yazdan, whose eldest son, Amir, from his divorced wife, had struck it rich by winning the hand of the most beautiful girl in a small town in the northern province of Mazandaran, and I was invited to the wedding in 1993. The plan was for me to drive Yazdan to the wedding, along with his wife, daughter, and younger son. The groom lived in Ghaem Shahr, a region of lush jungle and gardens of oranges, lemons, grapefruits, and tangerines. On the first night we stayed at the home of Amir's brother-in-law, Yousef, where some of the wedding festivities were taking place. The house was packed upstairs and down, front yard and back. Typically, there was lunch and dinner and snacks, plenty for everyone. Meanwhile, the bride was having her own party in her own town nearby where she lived with her parents. On the evening of the second day, Amir's close friends and relatives piled into cars and headed for the bride's village. What a pretty polite, and shy girl she was. Her house was simple, with just two rooms, which were jammed with guests. At the first sight of the groom's party arriving, they burst into cheers. The women started up their screeching, tapping the sides of their mouths as they wailed happily This led to dancing, which led to the party spilling outside, leaving the groom and his family and friends to remain inside as the honoured guests.

While we were sitting around devouring tea, cakes, and the usual pistachios, dates, and fruits, a clergyman entered. He was short and fat and wore a white turban and black coat. He toted the Koran under his left arm, while in his right hand he clutched his loose robe. Some stood and bowed, others shuffled aside to make space for this man who had come to conclude the marriage contract, according to Islamic religious law.

The clergyman sat in front of the bride and groom, who sat in silence, staring respectfully at the floor. Directly in front of them, lay a square white cloth on which sat a mirror and a copy of the Koran, along with sweets and flowers. Two girls held up a fine silk veil, like an umbrella, over the couple, while another pair of women, in an act of symbolic good luck and happiness, rubbed two large chunks of sugar together, so that the grains collected in the net over the couple's heads. The clergyman began reciting Arabic phases, which I didn't understand, and I imagined no one else did either. He accompanied this incantation with meaningful looks at the bride's father. There was much bowing towards the clergyman. The father of the bride, especially, executed a special bow by placing his right hand on his chest as he bowed. The clergyman continued with more verses from the holy book, then directed a question to the bride.

"Do you take this man to be your lawfully wedded husband?" Something to that effect.

She didn't answer, but twice more the question was put, and at the third demand she answered, "Yes." Everyone cheered, and the women started up again with their mouth-tapping yells to express their delight, while the clergyman congratulated the brand-new husband and wife. Then he took his book and departed. Of course, the mother of the bride started to cry, which pretty much opened the floodgates. Every women in the room was crying. It was the same old story as far as I could tell: Mom was happy to see her daughter married, but wasn't so sure about her choice, and about the groom's ability to look after her daughter properly.

After the ceremony, the bride and groom climbed into a white car decorated with flowers and draped with colourful strips of cloth, and began the journey back to the groom's house in Gaen Shahr. Other vehicles joined the procession, honking non-stop until they arrived at Amir's house, where the ceremony would continue in privacy.

I stayed with Amir's family for two more days, one of them spent hiking in the jungles of Mazandaran province with Amir's two brothers-in-law and his young stepbrother, Ali. The second day, Yazdan and I visited relatives in neighbouring villages, where I met another clergyman, Hadji Alizadeh. I was interested to hear that he had connections with the Justice Department in Tehran. It was his wife, it turned out, who was related to someone in government. Actually, he had two wives, the second one being an attractive girl with whom he spent most of his time. It's a custom I'd never support in public, but privately I was thinking, who can blame him? Anyway, after talking him up, he felt confident that he could expedite my passport application. I handed him some money so he wouldn't forget his promise.

Not long after we had returned to Tehran, Hadji Alizadeh came around to see me. For more money. He'd pursued my case with the court martial authorities, he said, and they'd responded favourably. My hopes rose, then fell steadily over the weeks as nothing happened. Hearing nothing more from him, I figured I'd been taken advantage of, yet again. I decided to tackle the passport problem head-on.

I arranged a meeting with Mr. Boor-boor, the head of the executive department at the court martial office. At his office, the young soldier behind the desk told me to take a seat, where I watched an unarmed guard usher people in and out of Boor-boor's office. After waiting for what seemed half a day, my turn arrived. I wasn't expecting him to be so young, barely thirty! He hadn't shaved for a few days, which was a common look among agents of the regime. He looked more like a beggar than a government official!

"Well, what are you waiting for?" he snapped, even before I'd had a chance to sit down. I expected to be invited into a chair but he kept his nose in a file. "Say what you came here to say."

"I'm here about my passport application," I said.

"I'd like to give you one!" he shouted. "I wish you'd go! Why the authorities stop you dissidents from leaving Iran, I don't know. You're nothing but agents of foreign infidels! You should all go, if you ask me. You're all useless, in fact, you're a burden, a curse! A problem for everyone!" I wanted to agree with him, but he wasn't finished yet. "You smuggled your wife and kids out of the country, so why do you need a passport? Why don't you just leave illegally, too? Tell me! Why are you wasting my time? You're wasting my time! Do you hear me? Go!"

I stood there, filling with rage in the face of this madman. All my efforts to do things by the book—it was never going to pay off. More than two years I'd wasted, thinking I might work the system. Well, that was done with, thank you Mr. Boor-boor for making it all so clear to me. I didn't bother to restate my case, just got out of there before I said anything belligerent, hurried to my car and drove off. When I calmed down, I realized that the only way I was ever going to see my family again was to leave Iran illegally, just as Boor-boor had said, and sooner than later. I promised myself that when I made my escape, I'd write him and thank him for settling my mind. Hadn't he almost given me permission? He'd said, "Go! Do it!"

"Thank you, Mr. Boor-boor!"

I was heading home on automatic pilot, you might say, until it occurred to me that there was no one there waiting for me. No supper on the stove, no one caring if I showed up late or ever. Nothing was left to do but escape, leave Iran behind, the country I loved and had defended with my life. I wanted to leave immediately, or tomorrow, perhaps the day after tomorrow, at the latest. It was time to say my final goodbyes.

I sped out of town, northward towards the village of my birth, Nesa-Olya in Taleghan. When I arrived, the sun was setting, so I headed straight for the graveyard.

24

"I AM LEAVING"

I had to pay my respects to my deceased parents one last time. But I felt uneasy in the growing dusk, looking for my mother's grave. Like a foreboding, like I didn't feel comfortable in my own skin. I knelt down, still frightened, but of what? I wiped the debris off her grave-stone and with my closed eyes I traced the inscription of her name, reading it with my fingers so that I might feel her presence more strongly. I spoke to her, silently at first, telling her with no small degree of shame that I was leaving Iran.

"I am sorry, Mother. You will never feel my hands cleaning your grave again, never feel my tears wash your gravestone. I have come to say goodbye." I swear I could feel her hands playing with my hair, try-ing to calm me down.

"I'm alone," I continued. "Even friends and family are keeping their distance, for fear of reprisals. Nobody wants their life ruined, like the government has ruined mine—stolen my peace, my sleep, stolen my happiness, entirely. Being separated from my wife and kids has almost killed me. God has given me strength to somehow endure it, but my will and patience are spent. I can't take it anymore. I feel like a stranger in my own country. All I did was defend Iran with my life, and all I get in return is punishment. Where is the justice in that? You were always there for me, Mother, always the best listener, always loved me no matter what, and I took strength from that. Well, now I need it as never before, for what's ahead of me. I need your blessings and your prayers. I love you, Mother—I am sorry that I won't be able to visit you here again, but you are with me in my heart and in my thoughts, always. Goodbye, beloved Mother."

I opened my eyes, stood up, and made my way to another older cemetery where my father was buried. He was such a kind, patient, and virtuous man. Although he was poorly educated, to me he was the best teacher. He taught me how one is supposed to love his family. He taught me how to forgive, how to be a better person, how to be a man. He would always be the hero in my life. Standing beside him, I was afraid of nothing. In hard times, he continued to stand tall, like a mountain. And if I let him down, just one of his looks was my worst nightmare, even though that angry expression couldn't hide the ocean of love that lived there. Never was I afraid of him. I couldn't help the tears. He never approved of crying, but that night I had never been more broken-hearted.

"I'm sorry, Father," I said.

He believed that if you wanted something, you had to fight for it with all your might, and if you won, fine; but if you lost, you had to accept the results. Accept! You could not call it defeat, as long as you knew in your heart that you'd put everything into the effort. My thoughts rushed to the effort I'd need to escape Iran, and with that it was time to say goodbye, but memories began rushing through me like a film at high speed.

"Goodbye, Father. You won't be seeing me here again. Please don't be waiting for me, because I won't be back. My footsteps will never again wake you from your long sleep, but you're in my thoughts, always. And in my heart, just as Mother is. Please don't worry about me, because I'm not a child anymore. You taught me how to be a man, and you taught me well. If it weren't for you, I might not have survived these dark days. Sleep tight, Father, and I'll send you prayers in the breeze that blows the dust from your stone. Or in the rain that washes it, or the snow that blankets you. I'll ask the stars to sing for you, so that you fall asleep again after I leave. I love you, Father. I love you."

I moved away towards my village, to where I used to live, in almost total darkness. The houses were all the same, made from clods of clay, their entrances lit with a single lamp hanging on the walls. It was silent, like the village of the dead. Nothing was left of our place, the house I was born and raised in, nothing but a heap of soil, still eroding with every rainstorm. There was the old walnut tree, its canopy of leaves like an awning over our house. I recognized the branches, the ones I saw from my bedroom window, and remembered how they would bend with the weight of snow, and how I used to rescue the tree by shaking it off. On hot summer days I would climb the tree with no fear of falling, obsessed with reaching the top. The experience compared with flying, taking off with no other thought but a successful mission, never a thought of crashing. Once in the cockpit, I was a child on the rooftop, playing with a balloon, never realizing he was in danger of falling.

I had to make a guess where the door had been. I stood there for old time's sake, and suddenly I was a teenager again, in love for the first time. What an innocent love that was. I swear I could smell her as I did that night, just that one night, that's all we had together. My first and only one-night stand. My parents had left for one of those weddings that lasts three or four days. Outside, it was raining, and I heard a knock at the door. She was standing there, a peasant girl, pretty much my age, whom I knew but vaguely. She was soaked and shivering and asking to get out of the storm, so I invited her in, of course. Her scent intoxicated me. The impact of it was immediate. What was it? Earthy and sweet, like the first fall of spring rain on dry soil. Only sweeter. Petals of the wild rose, I don't know, to this day I don't know. She stayed close to the oil heater while I picked out some dry clothes. I'd never invaded my mother's wardrobe before. When I returned a few minutes later, she was struggling with her wet dress. She couldn't untie it. It was a primitive garment, knotted at the front between her breasts, so I asked her if she needed some help, pretending I didn't have a clue about these things, which was true. Anyway, yes, she said, she'd like some help, but I couldn't untie the thing either. So, I ripped it apart!

What was that? I was appalled at myself, but I swear I was under the influence of that scent, if not pure lust. Any way you look at it, it was a clumsy ploy to touch her breasts. What an idiot I felt! She turned away and sat all doubled up to protect her modesty.

"Sorry," I said. "It was an accident." I was sounding more moronic by the minute.

I vanished while she changed into my mother's clothes, but the memory of her continued to overpower me, and that smell of hers— I'd never smelled it before, not on a person. It was no bottled fragrance, I was positive about that; you couldn't capture such a wild essence. It was natural, like she'd been out all day in the fields collecting the sun in her hair and Mother Nature's oils on her skin, and then the rain must have vaporized it, I had no other explanation.

When I returned to the room, she was standing there in my mother's blue floral dress, her head down and her eyes fixed to the floor. Her body gave that dress a whole new look, and with her black hair falling over her shoulders and the room filled with her intoxicating scent, well, I was fighting to control myself, and it lasted until she asked me to kiss her. That was all we needed.

Hooting owls brought me back to reality, but another memory just as quickly took over: hearing those owls as a child at bedtime, with my mother at my bedside, singing lullabies. My imprisonment had a devastating effect on her health. She cursed those who tortured me, and often cried about the injustice, she said. Then, her sudden disappearance, and death.

My eyes had grown used to the darkness, so I made my way like a wildcat towards one of my favourite childhood haunts, high up, behind the village, Lo-a-sar. I could see only a trace of light reflecting off the river, but the sound of the water was crystal clear in the dead of night. On a sunny day you could see the river twisting and turning westward until it disappeared behind distant hills. You could see mountains in all directions, and shepherds with their herds like troupes of dancers performing on the slopes.

I'd brought Akram here, her first time in Taleghan, to show her the view. I picked a wildflower and gave it to her, along with some pretty effective sweet talk. I couldn't help myself—maybe it was that scent again. The flower was pink, not red, and actually didn't have any smell at all, but I explained to her why it was perfect: because it was wild and free, just like her. "I give you this flower," I said, "to wear next to your heart, so you can feel my love for you."

Then she kissed me on the lips, but immediately became embarrassed. I lifted her chin and saw that her green eyes were full of tears.

"You always know how to put a smile on my face," she said with her sweet Turkish accent, and then placed another kiss on my lips. "I thank God for crossing our paths together," she said. I began picking more flowers, but she said, "No, Yadi. Let them live. I will give you as many kisses as there are flowers in this valley."

I looked around—thousands of flowers everywhere! And we must have had the same thought; there are not enough hours in the day for anyone to keep that promise.

"I'll spend my whole life keeping my promise," she said, wrapping her arms around my neck and placing another kiss on my lips. So, you can see what kind of magic was in that place.

Abandoning my memories of Akram for the moment, I made my way back through the village. Dogs began barking as if I was a ghost, and kept it up until I reached the old wooden pedestrian bridge that connected the village to the main road. I took one last look behind me, my last goodbye to my birthplace and all my childhood memories. Goodbye forever.

I arrived back in Tehran just as the new day was dawning.

When I awoke, it was past noon. I sprung out of bed. Everything had an urgency about it, especially matters of business. The money in my main account was still frozen, so I needed to track down customers who owed me money. Cash now, please and thank you. Or as soon as humanly possible. Some settled on the spot, while others wrote post-dated cheques. Of course, I owed money as well, and wanted to clear my debts and settle my accounts and tie up as many loose ends as possible in two days. Anxious about how suspicious this might look, I invented a story about re-entering the rug business. At the same time, I was careful to avoid being followed. My travels through the city became intentionally complicated. I took taxis instead of my own car, and arranged my meetings in crowded public places where I could more easily get lost. Those were two insanely busy days. My last appointment was with the Money Exchange where I bought American dollars with my rial.

Before returning home I stopped at the home of my brother, Akbar, and left him with all the postdated cheques. I felt I was being watched all the time. I could see myself through their eyes, a man obsessing about business, frantically hurrying from one meeting to another; it wasn't like me at all. In my file, Intelligence must have described me as someone who balanced work with exercise, so I headed for the hills for a few hours' hiking at nearby Kolak-chal peak, but once home again, I closed the blinds and began packing.

Before the day was over, I would be gone, everything left as it lay, even my car sitting in the driveway. No more goodbyes, no more sentimentality. I touched nothing, just dropped everything and got the hell out. I cannot even write about this leaving, it was such a non-event. Friends of mine lived in the city centre, and that's where I headed.

I had the urge to keep going, to leave town and head north, but felt that I might have been watched if I had done so. If Intelligence got suspicious, perhaps even arrested me, they couldn't accuse me of attempting to leave the city. None of this could I explain to my friends, of course, so I convinced them that I was simply desperate to be among friends, absolutely fed up with living alone. It troubled me to deceive such loyal people, but I had no choice. They were aware that I had plans to join my family in Canada, but they thought I was doing it legally. It was the furthest thing from their minds that I would try to escape, and I did nothing to disillusion them. I stayed there for three days.

On the third day, I visited a few of my wife's favourite places, including Imam Zadeh Saleh's shrine at which she used to pray for me when I was in jail. Later, I phoned Akram. She had troubling news: both Shahrokh and Shahram had had operations. Shahrokh broke his elbow while wrestling, and Shahram had a long-standing knee problem. Another worry to add to my woes. I had news for her too, but how could I come right out and say it?

"I'm going on another trip," I told her. I paused intentionally, wanting her to think something was peculiar. "I'll contact you as soon as I return."

"Where are you going?" she said. "Who are you visiting?"

"Maksüt," I said.

I prayed that she'd figure out my meaning. Maksüt was our Turkish friend. She didn't ask questions, but I sensed her nervousness, so I brought the chat to a close. The last thing I needed was one of us getting emotional.

Within an hour, I said goodbye to my friend and his family, explaining that I was "spreading myself around," as they say, and heading to the home of another friend. As I opened the front door to go, their daughter Sogand called me from the top of the stairs asking me when I'd be back again.

"Next Thursday!"

I couldn't look at her, couldn't look back as I left. She would have seen the lie on my face. Or perhaps I didn't look because I knew that I would never see those fine people again. I hated the deceit, but it was necessary. I couldn't afford to plant even the smallest seed of suspicion.

As I blended into the crowds on the streets, a poem came to mind. One short stanza by Forough Farrokh-zad. It didn't want to go away. It wanted to be heard, like a message:

I am leaving,
But after I leave, please don't say that I wasn't loyal.
There was no other way for me, but to escape.

A love burning inside me, with no future,
Was dying a slow death from all the injustice.

I am leaving,
To wash with my tears, the burning spot where you placed your
    kiss,
I am leaving so that I stay alive forever in this poem.
I am leaving, not telling the truth,
And keeping my pride with me, since I will never see you again.

I took a cab to the house of my father's cousin, Amoo Mohammad. Nobody answered my knock, so I continued on to another friend, another Mohammad, whose wife, Flour, welcomed me in. They had three daughters who had always treated me like an uncle, and of course I had to spin the same sad story, that I was desperately alone in the world. Well, I wasn't lying. After we shared a refreshment, I went to visit my older sister, Mahin, who lived not far away.

She was alone with her twenty-two-year-old son, who had schizophrenia. Despite her brave smile, you could see how she carried that weight through the world. I gave her my usual big hug and she kissed me as no one else ever did, one for each cheek, and a third on my forehead. As she laid out a table, she asked me about Akram and the kids. I told her I was short of time, that I had just dropped by to see how she was doing. Neither could I look at her directly, because her sadness was more than I could bear, not to mention my guilt at leaving and how it might add to her burdens. Then, of course, there was also my grief at missing her already. Seeing the difficulty I was having with Mahin, I changed my mind about visiting my other two sisters. I called my brother and asked him to pick me up. It was hard not to cry as Mahin and I hugged goodbye. I so much wanted to look into her eyes, but I couldn't risk giving myself away. So I hurried to Akbar's car, perhaps a little too abruptly.

Akbar and I picked up a mutual friend on the way to a meeting I'd arranged for 7 p.m. It concerned a loan, a significant amount of money I'd given an acquaintance so he could expand his business, the understanding being that I would be repaid a year later. The year had lapsed and he hadn't shown any good faith in paying up. Whenever I asked him about it, all I received were feeble excuses and more promises for payment next week or the next month, but I never got satisfaction. This meeting was no better, even armed as I was with my brother and a friend. After two hours of negotiating, the fellow wrote me some suspicious-looking postdated cheques, which I gave to my brother when we left.

Akbar dropped me off at the home of Mohammad and Flour. I didn't know how to say goodbye to Akbar, either, and I held to my plan to keep him in the dark, not because I didn't trust him, but for his own safety. If, for any reason, I was caught and arrested trying to escape, he wouldn't know anything. Intelligence officers could harass him, but he'd be so obviously stunned that they'd believe him, or so I hoped. Of course, no one knew better than I that those bastards didn't need a confession to hang someone. They picked and chose from their own long list of crimes. Nevertheless, I opted not to tell my brother or anyone else, for that matter. No one knew, and that was the way I was going to keep it.

As I opened the car door to get out, he made his usual move to jump out and run around and open the door for his older brother, but I grabbed his arm and told him it wasn't necessary. His look surprised me—or maybe mine surprised him. This wasn't our usual goodbye, and we both knew it. I opened my arms to him and we fell into an embrace like two magnets. He knew I was leaving, he sensed it, and of course neither of us said a word, but our faces were soaked. I pulled away and got out, wiping my face, astonished that leaving a brother could be as difficult as saying farewell to a sister.

Mohammad was waiting for me inside, happy to have me as a guest, but wondering what had kept me and if I was okay. Flour showed me to my seat around the dinner table, which was full of my favourite dishes. I asked Mohammad why he hadn't made me *kabab koobideh*. It was a joke, since he knew that I loved his kebabs.

"Finish everything on the table, Yadi, and if you're not full, I'll whip some up for you." We all laughed.

After dinner, I was tired and anxious to get a good night's sleep, although I couldn't explain why. I needed to make an early start, that's all I had to say for them to prepare my bed and leave me to sleep. In the morning, after breakfast, I said goodbye to Flour, and she sprinkled some water behind me in a symbolic gesture of "safe trip and a quick return." Mohammad gave me a ride. After dropping off one daughter at school, he drove me to Azadi Square, the transportation hub in Tehran. He stopped in a no-parking zone, so we didn't have much time to say goodbye. When we shook hands, we studied each other, and much like Akbar, I think he had me pretty well figured out.

"Be careful," he said. That was it; he just opened his arms like a brother and let me give him one last hug.

"Better move your car," I said, "before you get a ticket."

I stepped back, waved to him, and turned towards the taxi stand across Azadi Square. Azadi meant "freedom," and I would have chuckled if I hadn't been so tense.

The square, which was really a circle, swarmed with peddlers and their wheeled carts, shouting to advertise fruits, vegetables, sandwiches, trinkets, books, you name it. I was dead focused on getting to the west side of the square without being noticed. There was the usual lineup of vehicles with their drivers shouting out their various destinations around the country. I approached a driver who appeared to have two paying passengers already secured in the back seat of his old Chevy Malibu, but he needed three more before he'd leave for Tabriz.

"I'm in a hurry," I said. "I'll pay for three seats. Let's go."

He acted as if he'd never heard such a thing, so I showed him the money. He was short and hunched with beady eyes, but the only quality I was looking for was alertness, and he seemed to pass that test. He opened the front door for me, deposited my bag in the trunk, and jumped behind the wheel where he friskily revved the engine. Before taking off, however, a young man rapped on the window.

"May I join you?" he shouted. He was in his early twenties with a short beard and a small pack over his shoulder.

"No," I said

"Sure!" the driver said. He took the fare from the new passenger and handed it to me. "Save your money," he said.

Money I didn't need, but a sense of security I couldn't get enough of. Now, I wasn't sure I had any at all.

"In the name of God, the merciful, and the beneficent!" the driver proclaimed, revving the engine while this unwelcome passenger settled himself between the two men in the back seat.

It was 9 a.m. on December 18, 1993. A cold sunny day. We hit the road.

25

GOODBYE TEHRAN

Our driver circled Azadi Square, mumbling in Turkish and swearing at drivers who didn't heed traffic signs, and generally at anyone who possessed only a fraction of the driving skills he had. Reaching the highway, we stopped at the toll booth before finally hitting the open road heading west.

We were a silent bunch, which was fine with me. I asked our driver to turn on the radio, but he resisted, claiming that the airwaves were full of garbage. Instead, he played a tape and sang along, not badly, either. It was a Turkish love song that moved him to such raptures that his eyes would close out of imagined love. I was relieved when he snapped out of his reverie to curse another driver for passing him. The back seat was asleep, and then I noticed our driver having trouble keeping his own eyes open.

"Why don't you pull over and take a break," I said.

He looked at me as if I was accusing him of something. "Maybe later," he muttered.

"You looked like you were falling asleep," I said.

"No, no! It's the light," he said. "It's hard on the eyes. So I shut them, see? To give them a break. Not to worry, mister, I know this road like the back of my hand. You'll get to Tabriz, okay? Relax."

Once through the city of Zanjan, the driver pulled off the road at a restaurant. Tea was all I needed, and I drank it with two sugar cubes, as usual, but the cafeteria clatter irritated me, so I drank up and waited outside. When the driver appeared, he was missing that third character. We waited a few minutes, then the driver went looking for him. They came out, arguing. The guy wanted to make another phone call home to his parents, and just about coming to blows about it. The heavier of the two men sided with the driver, and that settled it. But back on the road, the driver was obviously still agitated, because his driving was erratic.

"You trying to kill us?" I said. "Slow down."

The back seat backed me up on that one. No one was in a rush.

"Can't you see that car behind me?" the driver shouted. "He's trying to overtake us."

"So? Let him," I said.

"Are you joking with me, mister?" he said.

We let him know, all of us, that we wanted him to slow down.

"Listen, I drive this road twice a day," he said. "Never has one of those cheap little Paykans ever overtaken me. A Paykan pass a Chevy? Not a chance! It's the principle of the thing."

"What kind of principle is that?" I said. "You're risking our lives, and that's against *my* principles!"

"This is an American car!" he said. "Even if it was on the garbage heap, it's worth more than a brand-new Paykan!"

He put the pedal to the floor and left that cheap little Paykan in the dust. I could tell from the chuckling in the back seat that they'd come around to the driver's way of thinking. Suddenly, the car got all chatty. The two friends in the back had known each other for a long time, and lived in Tabriz, while the mystery man claimed he was a medical student attending university in Tabriz. He was returning from a week's vacation in Tehran, or so he said. I didn't entirely trust his story. He wanted to know what I did for a living, so I explained that I was a businessman heading to Maako to pick up some imported goods.

"Hey, I'm from Maako," he said.

"No kidding," I said. And that's all I said. I couldn't believe my luck.

By 5:30 p.m., we were entering Tabriz, all of us tired and hungry at the end of our journey together. We parted company, but I remained paranoid that I might still be a blip on Intelligence's radar screen.

Tabriz was one of my favourite cities. Akram was born and raised there, and Shahrokh too, born while I was posted there with the 2nd Tactical Air Base. It was from that base that I took off on the mission from which I never returned, the one that made me a "living martyr." I knew every street, shop, restaurant, and point of interest, like Shahgholi, located on the east side of the city, and Golestan Park, more central, and closer to the west side of the city, the Blue Mosque, the Clock Square, and the Big Bazaar.

I was looking forward to checking out the latest developments in the city, and to dropping in on the family friends where I was hoping to spend the night. As always, they opened their home to me, even though a visit at this time of year should have raised suspicion. When the purpose of my visit came up in conversation, I changed the subject. It was another round of goodbyes the next morning, and I wasn't getting any better at it. Their son, Ali, offered to give me a lift to the bus station in Gajel Square, where two years earlier I'd had my traumatic farewell with Shahram. On the way, Ali told me how he'd recently returned from America, where he'd been working as an engineer. He wanted to help his father settle gracefully into retirement, and then take over the family business.

Leaving Ali, I headed for the car-for-hire stand, where I quickly struck a deal to pay for all five seats. The driver was a pleasant fellow, dark skinned with salt-and-pepper hair and a large nose and moustache. He spoke Turkish, as most people did in Tabriz. I could manage in Turkish, but I wanted to conceal my accent from him until we were out of town. Best that he didn't know I wasn't from that area.

On the way out of town, heading northwest, we had to pass my old air base. I couldn't take my eyes off it. I told the driver to slow down. The gate was the same, and the fork in the road, one leading to the residential blocks and the other to the flight line, everything the same, but older and grimier. I had the strongest urge to stop for a while and wallow in the grave of all my memories, but I resisted. I savoured the sight of the control tower and runway, and the ramp on which eighteen F-5E Tiger II fighters were parked in a row.

On the far side of the field sat my old squadron departments. There were the transport trucks and helicopters where I was given my hero's welcome in 1980. Memories flooded back, like an old addiction, so I told the driver to speed up. The security guards at the main gate were looking my way. Was I paranoid? You bet I was. But if ever there was a time to be watching over my shoulder, this was it.

The rocking motion of the car on the uneven road soon made me sleepy, but I wanted to stay awake to take it all in: the mountains, hills, and plains in that far northwest corner of Iran, all so familiar and benign in these final hours of my life in this country. Before noon we were there.

Maako is a small city, sitting so snugly at the base of a cliff, the mountain seems to hang over the town. I asked to be dropped at the junction of the road that leads to the Turkish border. It was a short walk from there to the central market and the tiny electronics shop run by Hossein and his six older brothers, where I'd met him before. I found him keeping warm by the oil heater, and he invited me in. He looked as I remembered him, strong, tall, and healthy with a permanent grin on his face.

"You might have to stay here tonight," he said.

"Why?"

"Your guide, he is not back yet. Tomorrow for sure."

Apparently, the guide hadn't yet returned from his last trip to the Turkish border. Not a good omen, I thought.

Hossein introduced me to his older brother, Vazeir, who worked behind a small desk at the back. He stood up and shook my hand. He was about forty, big, beet cheeked, muscular and moustached, but with short hair. Both of them spoke Farsi with Turkish accents, and were real gentlemen. But they couldn't make their best guide appear out of thin air. They'd put a call out for him.

Hossein fetched me a glass of tea while I gazed at the meagre wares on their shelves—two radios, a tape recorder, eleven rice cookers and pressure cookers, two heaters, four 18-inch television sets, and one 27-inch, and a few cartons not yet opened. Not a roaring success, this business, I thought. Not the kind of business that would support two successful-looking men. They obviously had some under-the-table operation going on, especially of the kind I was in the market for.

The three of us chatted and drank tea until it was time for lunch, when we headed off to a restaurant in the busy market. I remember the meal to this day: hot *sangak* bread, and minced lamb kabab with raw onion and fresh vegetables on the side. I was dismayed to learn that the nearest washroom was at the nearby mosque where people queued in a single lineup for two restrooms.

Back at the shop, I had nothing to do but wait while the brothers went about their business. Vazeir spoke continuously on the phone, mysterious phone calls in Turkish to people I could only imagine. Hossein tended customers who dropped in, a suspicious collection of characters, all of them. Eventually, Vazeir heard from my guide—he would be late returning from his last mission, which meant I would have to stay the night at their house. They were very apologetic.

Theirs was a well-furnished house, luxurious, in fact, with expensive rugs handmade in Tabriz. We sat down, the three of us, at a table big enough for twelve, and tucked into two barbecued chickens on a white oval platter, the birds smothered with pomegranate and walnut sauce, and rice with saffron sprinkled on it, and more appetizers and dessert items. While we ate, Vazeir and Hossein outlined their revised plan.

I would stay two days in Maako, which surprised me, but for the plan to succeed the risks would have to be mitigated, which was their business, and of course I left it all in their hands. They were the experts. As they were talking, Vazeir's young son and daughter played a game of peeping into the room and disappearing, then laughing hysterically. Hossein put a stop to it, and returned with an apology and an explanation. The kids wanted to say hello, but were too shy. Neither of them wanted to be the first. I suggested letting the children sort it out for themselves, so we made a game of it ourselves, seeing who was the bravest.

Eventually, I felt comfortable enough with Hossein to ask him why he hadn't become a doctor or engineer or teacher, something he liked. Even raising cattle would be safer than running these risks. He had once applied to the university, he said, but was rejected, so he became a small-town teacher, barely making ends meet. To bolster his income, he worked weekends ferrying people back and forth between Maako and Tabriz in his old rattletrap Paykan. As for farming, Hossein described a tragic situation.

"Have you seen any cattle?" he asked me.

"As a matter of fact, no," I said.

"The farms are abandoned," he said.

"Why?"

"Think about it. Farms need the younger generation, but where are they? Gone. Sacrificed to the war. Their parents can't farm productively, so they live off their small pensions."

The government awarded pensions to families upon the deaths of their sons, brothers, fathers, and husbands.

"This is a sad country," I said.

"You're right," he said.

Thinking back to the time of the Shah, I couldn't recall exactly how well the average citizen fared under his leadership, but my father and brothers had certainly been able to make a decent living without resorting to illegal activities. Now, only a few elite bureaucrats were actually enjoying the fruits of their labour in Iran, while the great majority worked long days just to put food on the table.

"Furthermore," Hossein said, "the journey you are about to take is well worn by the feet of educated people like yourself. Doctors, engineers, politicians, officers in the armed forces, they've all passed through here." He'd forgotten to mention the non-believers in Shia Islam, especially the Baha'i and the Jews. So many people forced to escape their homeland for the chance to live freely again.

"Some successfully, some not," Hossein admitted.

He didn't have to tell me. I knew that people were getting shot as they made their way over the mountains, gunned down by border guards before they could taste that precious freedom. Some got lost up there in the cold. You could easily die of starvation on the journey to freedom.

"I've known a lot of smugglers," Hossein said, "and I've never heard of one hired to escort the working class out of the country."

His point was this: in a volatile political environment, it was better to be a neighbourhood grocer than a big-time scientist, soldier, or erudite politician. The higher up you are, the more vulnerable to a change in the political winds. New rulers tended to be paranoid about old allegiances, and much too willing to exterminate supporters of the previous regime. Perhaps all government agents had a tragic end built into their life stories.

"No, education is not for me," Hossein said.

Vazeir reminded us that we had much to do tomorrow.

Hossein and I shared a room with two beds made up with handmade woollen blankets, each with an oversized red pillow. I didn't sleep well for worrying about my plans. Until my guide showed up, my departure couldn't be finalized.

We passed the next day in the shop drinking tea and waiting, as we had the previous day. By evening, the guide hadn't yet returned from Turkey, so back we went to Vazeir's house, but by then I must have been showing my impatience, because Hossein put forth an alternative plan. If my guide didn't show up the next day, he promised that he would hire another one, someone he knew to be the best in the business, but also the most expensive. Hossein spoke of him in a tone of voice that made the man sound like some kind of legend.

"He's never failed," he said. "He can find his way through the no man's land blindfolded. He'll penetrate the border, if he has to burrow through rat tunnels."

"Okay, Hossein," I said. "I get the picture."

His assurance did much to settle me down, however.

That was December 21, 1993, the longest night of the year. Iranians call it Sha-be-Chelleh, the winter solstice, and it's a night they like to celebrate by eating sweets, nuts, and fruits, especially watermelon, in the belief that it will protect them from the heat of the coming summer. I was invited by the brothers to join their families in the celebration.

The next morning, I wandered around the city with only one important item on my agenda. The post office. I mailed off documents, my driver's licence, and a few photographs. I would keep nothing but U.S. dollars to pay my smuggler, and the addresses and phone numbers of friends in Istanbul, which I had sewn into a seam of my jacket lapel. I walked out of the post office as a man with no identity. Midafternoon, Hossein drove me to Vazeir's house, where his brother was waiting.

"Are you ready?"

"I am," I said.

Vazeir smiled. "I know you are, it's a stupid question."

We had a good laugh, just the tension reliever I needed.

Daylight was already starting to fade when I was shown into the back seat of a crew cab, a pickup truck with an extra row of seats. We were soon out of Maako but moving slowly on a road that was narrow and icy. Hossein fought hard to keep the truck on the road, and eventually we got stuck in deep snow. Vazeir and I pushed us clear, and once the truck was moving, Hossein didn't want to stop and risk getting stuck again. We ran to catch up, all the way to the top of a rise where the road turned into its final switchback before heading downhill.

We encountered two foot soldiers patrolling the road. They waved us down. Their winter gear made them look huge, all draped with a white slicker for camouflage. Of course, they had rifles slung over their shoulders. I could hardly breathe.

"Our father lives up ahead, in Aaghgol village," Vazeir told me.

The soldiers recognized Hossein and his brother, even before the vehicle came to a stop, then waved again, a friendly hello, and directed us onward. I heaved a sigh, but at the same time I was upset for panicking prematurely. Vazeir could see how tense I was.

"Don't worry," he said. "Our plan is pretty much foolproof." His confidence was just what I needed. "In a few hours, you will be on the other side of the border, I promise you."

In Aaghgol, we stopped at the home of Hossein and Vazeir's parents. The wooden gate was frozen solid, imbedded in ice, but we squeezed through into the courtyard. On either side of the yard was a low structure made of stone and mud, one of them a barn for the cattle. In the middle of the courtyard sat a heap of dung, mostly covered with snow. I followed Hossein through one of the doors on the north side of the yard, into a room that had neither heater nor stove. We sat on a woollen carpet where Hossein supplied me with a pair of thick woollen socks, then a white sheet with a hole on top, like a poncho. I slipped it over everything that I had on, and secured the socks over my old ones by tying the string that was laced around the top of each sock. Another brother appeared with what I imagined might be my last meal. He was a dead ringer for Hossein. He set down flatbread, feta cheese, and a big mug of hot tea. There was more for the journey, more bread, boiled eggs, and walnuts.

"You'll need them," Hossein said.

Shortly, the brother returned again, this time with two men similarly sheathed in white, as I was. One was still a youth, the other not much taller, looked fifty but was probably closer to forty. He was a wild, brooding character with a weathered face and a moustache that narrowed to points near his ears. I didn't know whether to laugh or cry, because I had the disturbing feeling that I was expected to put my life in his hands. What choice did I have? I had run out of patience waiting for the other guide to return. I shook his hand, uttered some pleasantries, but he didn't say a word.

So, this was the legendary smuggler. His name was Rajab.

26

NO MAN'S LAND

The boy was Rajab's nephew, about sixteen, with the Lame Reza. He reminded me instantly of my own son, Shahrokh. This was going to be his first mission into Turkey, learning the smuggling business. As pleasant and polite as he was, I didn't like the idea of training someone on my time. With my money. And my life at stake

After brief introductions, the two left. I would meet up with them in the next village, Vazeir explained. At the sound of an approaching vehicle, Vazeir and Hossein rushed outside, leaving me alone to listen to some kind of ruckus, an argument that I couldn't understand. Hossein hurried back in and led me through a small door in the wall behind me. Suddenly, I was in a barn, in near-total darkness. I could hear livestock scurrying away at the sound of us intruders.

"Stay here until I come back for you," Hossein said. If he hadn't remained calm, I don't know what I would have thought. "We'll take you to the next village where Rajab will be waiting. Reza will follow up after that. Separate is best while it's light out. Too many people attract attention."

He instructed me in what to do in case things went wrong. If he didn't return in ten minutes, or if I heard gunshots, or a serious commotion outside, I was to exit through another door, which he pointed out in the gloom.

"You'll see a trail. Run to the next village." He explained all this very coolly, as if it were nothing more or less than part of the tried-and-tested plan. Before I could quiz him about it, or ask him to bid his brothers goodbye, he was gone. I was reassured for the moment, but deeper down I wondered if things were falling apart. The voices I could hear were too fierce for a family argument. Then I heard two gunshots. I had to decide quickly if this was what Hossein had meant. I had a strong urge to get out of the barn so I wouldn't be found hiding in there. I slipped through the door and bolted through the snow towards the trail. The frigid air sucked deep into my lungs.

Outside, I felt much safer. If I was forced to hide, it would have been easier. It was ravine country, steep slopes littered with snow-covered boulders that forced the trail to twist and turn. I stopped to listen for anybody following me, but all was quiet and crisp in that clear cold evening. It must have been forty below zero, and I was sweating.

The village came into view, small and desolate, only a few lights twinkling, but at least a sign of life. Since I was fresh out of instructions, I waited behind a low stone wall, watching for some sign. Ten, fifteen minutes went by, and then I saw what looked like Reza approaching from the village, but I couldn't be sure. Before he saw me, he stopped to take a piss. I called to him, and nearly frightened him to death.

"What happened to Hossein?" I asked.

"He can't come. But he wished you good luck."

"What now?" I asked.

"I'll tell my uncle you're here," he said, and vanished into the village. A few minutes later he returned with Uncle Rajab. Finally, we were together.

Rajab led the way, a continuation of the same trail out the back side of the village. How far it was, I had no idea, and Rajab didn't exactly give us a flight briefing. In fact, he didn't speak at all, not a word. He saved his energy for his relentlessly swift and steady pace, following the contours through the hills. I tried to keep up with him. I wanted to

ask him about Hossein. Not a chance. When Reza and I found ourselves lagging well behind, I asked him if he knew what had happened
in the village.

"Why did I have to leave through the barn?" I said. "Is that normal?"

He shrugged. "The Revolutionary Guard raids sometimes," he said.
"They search the houses."

"For human cargo?" I asked.

He nodded. "They know what's going on."

"They know Hossein and Vazeir?" I said, dumbfounded.

Reza nodded again.

"So that big commotion—"

"They shot to scare away the kids who were snooping around."

We caught up with Rajab, who was waiting for us with a stern hand
signal to stop talking, so I assumed we were close to the border. Not
one word from him since we'd left. I began to wonder if he could even
talk. He proceeded more cautiously, planting his feet in the footprints
made by the last person to pass that way. We heard voices behind us
and stopped to listen—husky grunts of approaching horses. Since
Rajab made no attempt to hide, I held my ground and watched as two
horses appeared, steam exploding from their nostrils. There was a single rider on the lead horse, and one man on foot. They ignored Reza
and I, but stopped next to Rajab and appeared to offer him a ride, but
he waved them through. Such a casual encounter, it surprised me.

"That got my heart racing," I confessed to Rajab.

He smiled and turned again and hustled up the trail. I let Reza
catch up to me, and asked him if he knew the men. He didn't, but he
was sure Uncle Rajab did. These smugglers probably plied this route
every night.

"What are they packing?" I asked.

"Whisky," he said. "And vodka and beer."

"And selling it on the black market," I said. "They must be making
a fortune." Reza nodded. "What about the gendarmes at the border
guard?" I asked.

"They bribe them," Reza said.

"The guards aren't going to turn down a regular supply of whisky, are they?" I said.

Reza seemed to like the attention I was giving him, as if he wasn't used to it. "Smuggling is a very good job," he said. "It's dangerous, but if you're careful, nothing will happen to you. Many people in my village have become rich doing this. Some have moved to the city and become successful businessmen."

"Don't people get killed doing this?" I asked. "Or arrested?"

"A few," he said. "They vanish. Nobody knows what happens to them. Some got shot in gunfights with the border guards, and I know of two who were tried and sent to jail, but compared to the many who have become rich, they hardly count. If I can do it long enough to buy a car, I might quit after that."

"Better be careful," I said. "People buy one car, then they want two, maybe three. That's the way it goes." I worried that he might not be strong enough to turn his back on greed, which could be fatal.

We caught up to Rajab, who wanted us to hold our position behind a large rock while he advanced alone. We were approaching a road used by the border patrol, Reza explained.

"The border?" I asked.

Reza nodded.

Standing still, I felt much colder. In fact, I'd never been so cold. It made my eyes water, Reza's too, and I could see how the droplets froze on his eyelashes before they could fall to his cheeks. His nostrils, too, were white with frost. A scarf over my mouth had become tough as cardboard. To keep the blood circulating we jumped up and down.

Rajab returned and signalled us forward. We followed him down a slope into what must have been marshland during the summer. It was flatter down there, and brighter and more exposed. Reza and I followed him step by step, like two lion cubs sticking close to their mother. We were heading for the protective shadows at the base of a steep slope, but I couldn't see anything that resembled border towers.

When Rajab flattened himself into the deep snow, we did the same, not daring to make a sound. I realized for the first time that my life was entirely in the hands of this mysterious character. I watched him, Colt revolver in one hand, binoculars in the other. After scanning the valley with the field glasses, he advanced along the base of the hill that blocked our view of the road in that direction, but also offered us equal invisibility from any vehicle that might be patrolling from that direction. Finally, I could make out the road bed cutting across the marsh, raised slightly above the snowscape. We would have to get across it without being seen, but how—running or crawling? I would soon find out.

At Rajab's command, we dropped into the snow amongst a bramble of leafless shrubs. Then we were up again, running towards the road, but before we reached it Rajab dived behind a low rock. There was no way that rock could hide three people, but there we were. I heard a vehicle, then saw headlights. It was making frequent stops to shine its spotlight through an atmosphere getting murky with ice crystals. We had no choice but to wait for it to pass, our white camouflage the only thing that could save us now.

As the vehicle came closer, I could see that it was a military jeep. I put my head in the snow and heard it pass. When it was nearly out of sight, Rajab made a dash towards the road, pulling up just below the shoulder and lying low in more brush. The width of the road and a hundred metres of open terrain on the other side seemed like an impossibly vast expanse. Rajab must have felt it wasn't yet safe to make a run for it, and he was right, because the headlights swung around and came back towards us. So, there we were, barely protected by skimpy little clusters of twigs. I held my breath, listening to the steady approach of the rumbling engine and the crunching of the tires over crisp snow. I don't know about Reza and Rajab, but I tried to become invisible by force of will, flattening myself as deeply as I could into the snow. My mind's eye flooded with images of my family, very possibly the last glimpse of them I'd ever have.

The jeep passed and slowly faded away.

I raised my head to see Rajab poised like a cat, his eyes focused on the other side of the road. He sprinted, low like a panther with dead aim on its prey. Suddenly, he was safely on the other side. There was no time to reconsider—no consideration of stiff muscles and frozen clothes and biting breath that stung the throat and burned the eyes— I just ran. And I didn't stop when we got to the other side, just kept on running, slogging through heavy snow until we arrived at a concrete cairn that read "Iran." I collapsed on the other side and saw "Turkey." *I was free!*

I would have shouted for joy, except that Rajab was making big "shut the hell up" hand signals and pointing to a revolving spotlight in the distance. How far away it was, I couldn't determine. The dim undulations of the landscape and the beacon's reflection off the snow made it impossible to say—200 yards or 2 kilometres?

"Turkish guards," Reza said. "Guards and commandos. Operations base."

Our sprint across the road seemed like nothing, suddenly. Turkish commandos weren't your regular border guards. They were seriously armed soldiers battling Kurdish rebels in the region. Furthermore, there was no trail through this no man's land, none that I could see. I knew now why Rajab wasn't celebrating. He just pushed on, but more cautiously than ever, dropping to his knees every few steps to listen— for what? I couldn't hear a thing. I held my breath for fear it was making too much noise, that's how tense I was. That and the pounding of my heart.

The land in front of us fell away towards a small river, frozen except for a narrow section of open water in the middle. Descending to the river's edge, we lost sight of the beacon. Rajab wasted no time hoisting me over his shoulder and carrying me across. I remembered what Hossein had said about burrowing his way into Turkey, if he had to. Reza had to cross by himself, and managed, with some whining. His teeth chattered so hard I could hear them fifteen metres away. Rajab congratulated him with a pat on the shoulder, then without wasting a minute he forged ahead up the slope. Reza didn't even have time to complain about his wet feet turning to ice.

When the guard post came into view again, it seemed to be no more than one or two hundred metres away. Rajab began darting left, then right, as if he was uncertain on which side to slip past the tower. Why were we approaching the post in the first place? Why weren't we avoiding it entirely?

Frozen and dumbfounded as I was, I kept close behind Rajab, exactly in his footsteps, springing when he did and stepping and dropping to the snow as he did. I had no mind of my own, and in an odd way it was liberating. He was my god—he could save us or destroy us. His lunging and loping became even more erratic, zigzagging and collapsing, then crawling and crouching and more zigzagging. We must have travelled five metres for every one that took us any closer to the post. Hearing howling, we lay still. What were they—wolves? Jackals? I recognized the bark of domesticated dogs, which meant there was a village nearby, probably adjacent to the command post. I hoped the dogs were reacting to the predators, not sniffing us out. Suddenly, a single shot rang out from the tower.

We scrambled towards the protection of rocks, ducking more shots until we fell face down in the snow. A burst of machine-gun fire strafed the air above our heads—we didn't dare to lift our heads. How many minutes did we lie there? I was certain this was the end of the line; I just wasn't sure how it would come or what it would feel like.

With fingers numb and stiff, I burrowed deeper into the snow, hoping to give myself a slightly better margin of protection. As the gunfire intensified, Rajab, who was much more in the open than I, nestled himself closer to a rock. He couldn't risk any sort of movement, even though he was camouflaged in white. Surrendering seemed like an option, better than dying a certain death by gunfire or of exposure to the cold. When the firing stopped for a minute, I heard Rajab's teeth crunching. I lifted my head. He signalled me with an open palm up and down: "Be patient." What a guy. He hadn't lost his perspective. To him, this near-death experience was just another stepping stone on the way. Another river to cross. What a small mind I had, I thought. What little faith. I was wasting my time dreaming of the home life I'd once had, family and food and friendships. It all seemed so far away, perhaps even a dream I'd once had.

For half an hour, the gunshots would be sporadic, then they'd explode in a flurry, then a single shot, then a volley. It was impossible to tell if the assault was easing or worsening. During a lull, Rajab threw a chunk of snow towards Reza. The kid moved, raised his head and saw Rajab wave to him, but Reza didn't wave back. Rajab was up again, running low in his catlike style in the direction of the tower, then dropped out of sight. I was right behind him, into another frozen creek bed where he was lying still.

We heard more firing, as if Reza's movements had alerted them. As soon as Reza appeared, Rajab was on his feet again, doubled over, crossing the creek with me on his heels. We used our momentum to scramble up the bank, where we only had a hundred more metres to reach the guardhouse. Why were we headed for the guardhouse? It seemed insane, but we were still running, all the way, somehow not being shot, until we pressed ourselves flat against the wall of the fort, safe for the moment because gunmen in the tower had no angle on us; they couldn't have seen us.

From our position, we could see Reza struggling to cross the ice. He was stumbling and falling and crawling and holding out his hand for help as if the ordeal had sapped him. I sensed Rajab bolstering himself for a return dash to save Reza, and when I got set to run, that tough Turk held up his mitted palm in my face. "Stay here." He leapt into the darkness.

Not even a professional dancer could have moved with such speed and grace. He was at Reza's side in seconds, lifting him to his feet and draping the boy's left arm over his shoulder and supporting him around the waist with a tight grip on his bulky clothes, dragging him. I watched in horror, shaking with cold, certain that they were going to be shot. But somehow they made it.

The boy was breathing hard and groaning from the cold or from despair, or perhaps a bullet wound. We held him upright, let him rest for a couple of minutes, then dragged him behind the guard post towards the village, a matter of only a few metres.

This comprised crumbling mud buildings, typical of mountain villages, with their piles of dung and goat horn root used for fuel. Two mustachioed inhabitants saw us lay Reza down behind one of the houses. The sound of gunfire had attracted them, no doubt, but when they recognized Rajab, they ran to shake his hand, as if they were old friends. They wasted no time lifting Reza by the arms and legs and hauling him towards a house deeper into the village. As Rajab and I followed them, he offered me his hand in a gesture of congratulations.

"You are free now," Rajab said. "But no celebrating yet, please."

They carried Reza inside a low stone house. Rajab and I removed our frozen gear and draped it over the porch railing. I was left in an unheated room, literally vibrating from the cold, while Rajab followed after the others. I looked at my watch: 11:20 p.m. I noticed bedding piled against one wall. A single window was covered with a sheet of floral plastic that once might have served as a tablecloth. A teenage boy joined me—barefoot, if you can imagine—and wearing a worn-out track suit. He fed dung into the stove standing in the middle of the room and tried to light it. On the third or fourth match, it caught, and almost immediately I could feel warmth start to build up in the room. That godforsaken place quickly felt like a five-star hotel.

Two young men entered with food. Thank God! Flatbread cooked in milk and crowned with an egg baked on top, looking like polished gold. And feta cheese mixed with dried vegetables, and tea. I'd never needed nourishment so badly. They introduced themselves in Turkish, although they were Kurds. They were brothers, Ahmed and his younger brother, Abdollah.

"How is Reza?" I asked.

"All right," Ahmed said. "Some blisters. And something wrong with his right leg. He can't feel it. But it's no big deal. We have a doctor. He will heal him, don't worry."

I'd never tasted such nutty bread and such aromatic cheese. I ate like a hungry cat. The younger brother poured me steaming tea from a stained old pot into a heavy blue-glazed mug.

"You are lucky to be alive," Abdollah said. "Turkish forces have been randomly attacking Kurdish rebels along the border, all the way from Syria. This is the fourth straight night of shooting."

"They thought we were Kurds," I said.

"They're trying to send a message—go somewhere else, some another country."

After preparing my bed, they left me to sleep. This hovel was pretty much at the bottom end of the hospitality scale, but what luxury! A palace couldn't have served me any better. Nor could anyone have been more generous. These people were committed to freedom, and not only to their own, but also to the freedom of those who were passing through. I felt honoured to be amongst them. What a feeling to be exhausted but warmed through and well fed. And most important, to be beyond the reach of Iranian Intelligence for the first time in years. Sleep came quick and deep.

I woke up at 6 a.m. to a room that was freezing again. With my head buried in the blankets, I could only think of my childhood winter mornings, curled up like a baby in the womb, listening to the wind worrying the windowpane. I could hear the same sound, the sound of the room in which I was born.

At first light, Ahmed and Abdollah invited me next door for breakfast. With Rajab were the brothers' parents. On the far side of the room I could see Reza still asleep, his ears red as beets and his face dark with cold burns. I wondered how he was feeling after his first successful training run. We sat with our feet under the *korsee*, a low table covered with blankets and warmed with burned-down charcoals that served as a communal foot warmer. Grateful doesn't begin to describe how I felt to be amongst this motley collection of beautiful people.

At the first sign of breakfast ending, I sipped the last of my tea and thanked everyone for their hospitality. It was obvious that Reza wouldn't be travelling on with us, so I approached him and placed a hand on his forehead as a thank-you and goodbye. He opened his eyes, smiled, and apologized for the trouble he'd caused. He showed me his legs and feet wrapped in rags. Frostbite, I imagined. Or had he been shot in the leg? I did nothing to disturb the conspiracy of silence around it.

"I'll never forget our adventure," he said. "I'll never forget you."

I leaned down and kissed him on both cheeks, feeling a lot like a father bidding his son farewell, he was that much like my own son. "Go back to school, Reza," I whispered. "There must be an easier way to make your fortune."

Dogubayazit was the largest Turkish city in the region adjacent to the Iranian border. That's where we headed, by car. Rajab and I and the two brothers, Ahmed and Abdollah.

27

SO CLOSE BUT YET SO FAR

———

I was free. Out of the cage. And feeling more fantastic than I had a right to feel. Without travel documents, without an identity, my family was still a world away. It was December 23, 1993, a sunny and cold Thursday morning as we set out for the city of Dogubayazit, a forty-five-minute drive down a snowy mountain road—Rajab, Ahmed, Abdollah and I.

What a place Dogubayazit was—a maze of alleys feeding off a few main commercial arteries. We stopped in the market area, where Ahmed led me into a small smoke shop that had a public telephone. I called Akram.

"I'm in Dogubayazit," I said.

She fell silent, which meant she was crying, which got me crying, too. Ahmed and the shopkeeper looked at me.

"I'm okay," I told Akram. "I'll talk to you later."

"Be careful," she said. That was it, she hung up.

"Hello?"

That was odd, I thought. Not one happy word from her. But I had other things to worry about, like crossing Turkey and getting passage out of the country without legal documents. The brothers wanted to put me on a bus that was headed for Ankara, the capital, in two hours, but Rajab objected.

"Not safe," Rajab said. "Fighting everywhere. The army is looking for Kurdish rebels. Travelling without proper papers would be crazy. You need a better plan. We can't talk here."

The brothers led us away from the busy market to the southern part of town, down narrow alleys to the house of their brother, Jamal. It was a typical concrete-walled compound with two wooden doors leading to a courtyard. Jamal wasn't home, but his wife greeted us with a shy smile. It was a delight to see such a fine woman, her Turkish-Kurdish dress worn over loose pants that reached her toes, and her five-year-old son clinging to it, shyly.

I followed Ahmed through the sitting room into a backroom where we consumed a meal of bread, butter, cheese, and scrambled eggs. In fact, we ate like wild animals. After Rajab had sipped the last of his tea, he handed the little boy a twenty-lira note, a custom in that country to reward the family through the child.

"My job is finished," Rajab told me. "You have to manage the rest of the way yourself. Just one word of warning—don't be in a hurry."

I thanked him, and gave him the only valuable object I had with me: my pilot's knife. I paid him the balance of his fee, and a bit extra to show my appreciation, but when I searched my pockets, I was short a few hundred dollars. It could only have been stolen back in the village, while I slept. The thief had to have been one of the brothers—Ahmed, Abdollah, or the youngest one, but I said nothing, since I still needed their help.

Rajab stashed the money in his pocket without counting it, then took a good look at the knife. "Thank you," he said. No show of emotion, but he shook my hand firmly and said, "Goodbye." As the door closed behind him, I realized that I still knew nothing about him, and wondered if he even cared what people thought of him, and if my good wishes mattered to him at all. He wasn't the least sentimental; he was an expert smuggler who needed no advice from anyone. But he was a good man, and I wished he could have taken me all the way to Ankara or Istanbul.

Jamal didn't show up until after Abdollah returned home. He was surprised to see a stranger in his house, yet he greeted me with a warm smile. I got right down to business, asking about the best way to reach Ankara without travel documents. He knew a bus driver who, if paid well enough, would hide me in the sleeping compartment normally occupied by the second driver. I thanked him, but I needed other options.

I called my friend Maksüt Demir, in Istanbul. I'd phoned him before leaving Tehran, the only person to whom I'd confided my plan. He'd already saved Shahram from deportation; perhaps he could do something for me, too.

"I have been expecting your call, Sharifi," he said.

He gave me the number of the Canadian embassy, and a lawyer who worked at the United Nations in Ankara. "I hope they can help you," Maksüt said.

Meanwhile, I called another old friend, whom I'd known for as long as I'd known Maksüt. Ahmet Ergönen was still in the air force, a colonel (later he made brigadier general), and still second in command of an air base about 500 kilometres from Dogubayazit.

"If you can get to Diyarbakir, Sharifi, I can help you, yes," he said. "I can send you to Ankara by plane."

"But how do I get there?" I asked. "How do I get out of here?"

"Listen, Sharifi," he said. I could tell he wasn't optimistic. "That area is dangerous, even for us. Tensions between Turkish forces and Kurdish rebels are heating up. Almost anyone is a target, and anyone without identification is a suspect. I'm sorry, but I can't help you with that."

He got the numbers of the place I was in and hung up. A few minutes later, Colonel Ahmet's wife, Filiz, phoned back to add her apologies for being unable to assist me. She confirmed her husband's concern for me in trying to move through this region of Turkey without identity papers, but it was good to hear the voices of caring friends.

I spent that first night in Dogubayazit chatting with Jamal and watching television. You could tell this was a country with a secular government. Iran and Turkey are both Islamic countries, but Turkey's television programs reflected the considerable freedoms enjoyed by the Turkish people—women with or without the veil mix with well-dressed men singing and dancing together, showing that they have equal rights in their country.

The next morning, I used Maksüt's references to seek help from the Canadian embassy and the UN. I got nothing but the same sympathetic but unhelpful responses. "First, get to Ankara, then we can consider your case."

Ahmed and I spent the day walking around the city, freshly dusted with a light snowfall. I was restless, thinking often of my wife and how I'd led her to believe that I was almost on a plane heading to Canada. Wet and shivering, I followed Ahmed into a tea house in the market opposite the city hall. We were greeted by a blast of warmth from a wood-burning stove in the middle of the room. The place was packed with people chatting, drinking tea, and playing backgammon. Sipping tea at a window table, we finally hit on a solution to my dilemma. Jamal would travel to Istanbul to arrange a fake passport. It was expensive, US$2000, but I handed over the money without a second thought.

"If you need more," I said, "you can contact my friend Maksüt in Istanbul."

The obvious disadvantage of this plan was having to remain in Dogubayazit until Jamal returned.

On Christmas morning, Jamal introduced me to a public bath located behind the city hall. We stripped down, wrapped towels around our waists, and entered a large steam room with showers on each side, and a massage platform in the centre. Two men were getting the treatment, the masseurs pounding them like slabs of meat.

After a shower, I asked Ahmed if I could get a massage. "Sure, why not?" he shrugged. A few minutes later, I was one of those slabs of meat on the block. Lying on my back, I could see a small circle of sky through a domed window high in the ceiling. The masseur flipped me over onto my stomach, then pulled my left arm far to the right, then my right arm to the left. I signalled him to stop when he stressed my vertebrae, then it was a head-to-toe massage like I'd never experienced before. Later, Jamal took me to a photo shop in the market for the mug shots he would take with him to Istanbul. He left by bus that afternoon, promising to return in three or four days.

I became aware what a political tinderbox the city was, ready to blow up. Kurdish liberation forces were everywhere, but so were Turkish soldiers and their tanks. The army was waiting for any excuse to suppress any acts of Kurdish self-determination. One shot from a sniper, I thought, and this town could become a battlefield. And the next day it happened just as I feared it would. Someone must have tossed a match onto the kindling, because all hell broke loose, gun battles that raged until four in the morning. We heard it all from where we were huddled in a backroom of Jamal's house. In the morning, Ahmed slipped out to buy bread, returning twenty minutes later empty-handed.

"Nothing open," he said. "All boarded up, windows smashed, a few people trying to clean up. The city is in a virtual state of martial law." He didn't see any casualties, but plenty of buildings riddled with bullets, even the city hall.

Jamal called from Istanbul, needing another six hundred dollars, which I told him I would arrange with Maksüt. Jamal warned me that his return might be delayed, since traffic to the eastern part of the country wasn't getting past Arzanjan until the situation cooled off. Making things worse was the lack of news; television reports didn't even mention the battle. I didn't learn anything about it until Jamal unexpectedly showed up a few days later. He handed over my passport.

Sure, it was an official-looking document, and it had someone's name on it, but the photo was only crudely pasted into position. I had serious doubts about its ability to see me through, but I kept them to myself, for the moment. Jamal's kids were all over him as he recounted details of his trip to the big city, and passed out gifts including warm jackets that he had bought for everyone. Jamal's youngest showed off his gear with such joy as I've never seen on anyone's face. He wanted his mother to take him outside to use the pull-toilet across the snowy courtyard, never mind that he could have more comfortably used the heated one in the backroom. He simply wanted to wear his jacket outside.

Eventually, Jamal drew me aside to talk strategy. "You'll leave tomorrow," he said. "Turkish Intelligence are checking everyone's documents, searching suitcases, everything. And not just once, but many times along the way."

I could have waited, but for how long? I was tired of waiting. I called Maksüt to give him the update and my estimated time of arrival in Ankara, all going smoothly. He was excited, and looking forward to seeing me. He was going to fly from Istanbul to Ankara to meet me, and he gave me his phone number in Ankara, and told me to call him when I arrived. He would meet me at the bus terminal.

That night, I couldn't sleep for imagining what could go wrong, and how I'd react if it did go wrong. If I was caught and deported to Iran, my family might never hear from me again. I wasted the entire night in this state of insane anxiety, and by dawn, the room was freezing. I looked outside—everything in a deep freeze. The small apple tree in the yard was so heavily frosted that it looked as if it was in bloom. I took an aspirin from a small bottle I kept in my jacket pocket.

After breakfast, I asked Ahmed to take me to a clothing shop in the market where I could undergo a kind of makeover. A teenage salesman helped me into the black trousers and grey jacket of a businessman. Add a blue shirt with a matching tie and a pair of black shoes, and suddenly I was respectable. At the point of paying, I noticed more money missing, about three hundred dollars. Saying nothing about it, I just paid up and left the shop. Then, I put it to Ahmed—money had been stolen from me. He was quick to blame his oldest nephew. I didn't buy his story, but what could I do about it?

Once back at Jamal's, I began my rounds of thank-you-and-good-bye, starting with Jamal, expressing my gratitude to him and his wife. Then, Ahmed, facing him, fixing him with a direct stare to see how he'd react. He seemed uncomfortable, all right, but I thanked him for his companionship, even gave him some money to buy a gift for his fiancée.

"I could give you more," I said, "if I hadn't lost all that money."

I offered a small sum to Jamal's wife, but tradition wouldn't allow her to accept it until given the go-ahead by her husband. Another amount I gave to Jamal, in the event my phone bills exceeded what I'd given him to cover them. He insisted on accompanying me to the bus station.

"*Allahaismarladik,*" I said, climbing into the bus. "Goodbye Jamal."

"*Güle, güle,*" he said. "Goodbye, and have a nice trip."

I found a window seat four rows behind the driver, my home for the next 1166 kilometres, all the way from the eastern part of Turkey to Ankara, which lay in the geographical centre of the country. When the driver put the bus in gear, I waved to Jamal, my heart pounding. So many things could go wrong. Jamal followed the bus for a few steps, then disappeared from view.

An odd thing happens to me when someone I love or admire vanishes from my sight. Their whole life seems to crystallize in my mind into one organic design that makes total sense. Perhaps because my own life was such a mess.

We were soon beyond the city limits and rolling down the main road. Many vehicles, large and small, had pulled over to install chains on their tires. Our driver pulled over too, but only to flag down an approaching bus to chat with the driver. Moving once more, the co-driver came around with a bottle of cologne, a little splash into our waiting palms. Taking my cues from my seatmate, who rubbed his perfumed hands together, then washed his face from his forehead down to his chin, I did likewise.

The bus didn't smell pleasant for long, however, as every second passenger lit a cigarette. I was offered one, but declined. My neighbour would inhale, then start talking on the exhale, about how poorly maintained the road was because the government didn't care about this part of the country. The reason they didn't clear the snow, he joked, was because nobody could see the road to begin with. I smiled but said nothing, wanting to remain as anonymous as possible. I didn't mind him talking, but I made it clear that I wasn't interested in answering his questions. My accent would have given me away immediately. So, I closed my eyes, pretending sleep, only occasionally grunting a yes or no. Finally, he fell asleep, and I took a shift watching the passing landscape. There wasn't much to see with a blizzard raging and the glass frosting up on the inside.

I started to pray. After all, something had been working in my favour to see me this far, so why not give thanks? I asked to be forgiven for failing to more regularly acknowledge my many blessings. I had not thanked God nearly enough for protecting me from wolves, gunfire, the cold, and potential thieves at every turn. The miles humming by beneath the wheels of the bus, separating me from everything I knew, made me feel nostalgic for my country, or for what used to be my country.

"Checkpoint coming up!" the driver yelled.

The bus stopped in front of a small military installation surrounded by barbed wire and manned by a pair of soldiers on each side, their rifles trained on the bus. The driver jumped down with his documents in hand and followed a soldier into a small office. Peculiar, I thought, that the soldier has no visible rank on his shoulder or sleeves. An official-looking civilian climbed aboard and stood there examining the human cargo. A pistol hung from a holster on his belt. Armed soldiers stood guard at the doors, front and back, eyeing us as if we were subhuman. Most passengers already had their identification at the ready. I wasn't so enthusiastic about the process, since my passport was such a pathetically bad fake . . . and after all the thousands I'd spent on it. Then I realized that I couldn't remember my new name, so I checked, but my hand was visibly shaking. No way was I going to make eye contact; the official would see right through me. When it was my turn, I held my passport out, open at the photo page, thinking, okay, this is it, he must be able to hear my heart pounding, and any second he'd see me sweating. I couldn't help recalling a better time, when we travelled across borders with our heads held high, our passports a welcome and respected document. Now, we were all treated like criminals. He lifted his eyebrow and looked at me, then at the picture on the passport. Another look, back and forth, and a second later he flipped to another page, and another.

"Date of entry?" he asked.

"Page seventeen," I said. "Two weeks ago."

He turned to page seventeen. "Your entry point is Istanbul. What are you doing here?"

"Business," I said. "Importing goods to Iran by road. I was in Dogubayazit to check on the stuff and load the truck. Now I'm going to Ankara, and then Istanbul to check out other stuff."

He handed me my passport. "Have a nice trip."

I heaved such a sigh of relief, almost sobbed, I was so giddy. In the aftermath, my neighbour looked at me. He wanted to know more about me, but fortunately the guards started shouting, "Luggage check!"

Some satchels they just glanced through, others they dumped upside down, throwing things into the aisle and leaving them there as they swaggered past us and off the bus. While this was going on, two more guards checked the baggage compartment beneath us. I watched them stick their noses into the co-driver's sleeping compartment, and recalled how Jamal had wanted me to hide there, and how Rajab had said that that was a crazy idea. We were detained there for two and a half hours, tired and hungry, until finally they gave us the green light to continue on our way. The smokers lit up, and I leaned back, lulled by the gentle swaying of the bus until I fell into a deep sleep. My neighbour woke me. It was morning.

"Another checkpoint coming up."

Two armed men entered the bus and again asked for our documents. I didn't have time to become anxious. He examined the first page and handed it back. That was it? Whew! No baggage check either, inside or out. Back on the road again. Saved again. The checkpoints continued to come with annoying frequency, some even lengthier than others, but none as thorough as that first experience, until we approached the city of Arzeroom.

A pair of soldiers studied each of us closely, one by one, carefully, perhaps because it was getting dark again. I wouldn't have withstood such scrutiny at that first check. No passports were demanded, only our baggage checked, and this time it was every bag off the bus and thoroughly inspected. We wasted about an hour there.

Half an hour later, we stopped at a restaurant where some ate and some prayed. Leaving the restaurant, I noticed it was snowing. The inclement weather made the road more slippery, which meant that the driver had to work especially hard to avoid winding up in a ditch. Soon, we and almost every other vehicle on the road were pulling over to install snow chains. We stopped in the city of Arzanjan for tea and a short rest, after which we completed the trip to Ankara without further interruptions. At least, not until we were entering the city. A single, tired-looking soldier climbed into the bus and selected a few passengers to question. He passed me by without even looking at my fake passport.

I had made it to Ankara, the capital of Turkey, a city with which I was familiar from having been posted there in 1976, seventeen years earlier. We arrived at the bus terminal at 7 a.m. My first task was to phone Maksüt and let him know I'd arrived.

We met outside the main gate of the terminal, Maksüt and someone I didn't know. My friend had lost a lot of hair, and what remained, little strands, was white with only a few hairs speckled in. His eyes, though, were as kind as ever, and his face creased into the warmest smile in the world. We hugged and kissed each other on the cheeks, then studied each other closely, both of us struggling to find the words, like two long-lost brothers.

"Hos geldiniz, Sharifi," he said. "Welcome."

He introduced Cebe, his brother-in-law, who led us back to his car and drove us to Maksüt's hotel. He'd flown in from Istanbul the night before. We enjoyed a civilized breakfast before heading to the United Nations, where I would apply for political asylum.

28

THE NEVER-ENDING STORY

On Thursday, January 5, 1994, at 9:30 a.m., accompanied by Maksüt, I joined a crowd waiting in the street in front of the United Nations offices in Ankara. There were Afghanis and Iranians. Iraqis, Pakistanis, and Russians. From the looks of it, I might have a three months' wait just to get an interview.

Maksüt had a lawyer friend, Nadim Yuca, working there, so he made an initial foray into the building to speak to him, and returned half an hour later with a grin on his face. My name would get preferential treatment. I wouldn't have to wait six months like some of those poor bastards standing in the cold. Maksüt briefed me on the kinds of questions I'd be asked. Once I'd finished, he wanted me to join him back at the hotel. Sure enough, it wasn't long before I heard my name called over the loudspeaker.

I was directed into an office below street level, a windowless suite where a woman photographed me and asked me to fill in application forms, after which she led me to another room for my first interview. An hour later, I was on file with UN number 5–3272. They gave me a letter allocating me another number, the ID by which the Turkish police would know me. In two weeks I was to return for my main interview.

The next day, Maksüt took me to get registered at the foreigners' section of the police department. Again, a very crowded place. Maksüt tried to exert his influence, as he had at the UN, but this time his name didn't make anyone stand to attention, so we had to hang around for a couple of hours. While I held down my place in the lineup, Maksüt wandered about, lost in his own thoughts, reading hallway notices, examining maps, pretty much exhausting his patience, at which point he suggested we get the heck out of there. I could return tomorrow and get registered. He had too many things to do, since he had to fly back to Istanbul the next day.

The Canadian embassy was next on our list. Akram had long ago sent me their application forms, so they should have been on file, all filled out, and sure enough, it didn't take long to see someone and get installed in their process. The trouble was that before we left there, I was told that I might have to wait six to eight months for an answer. The last thing Maksüt could do for me was to recommend a reasonably priced hotel where I could lodge indefinitely. Not only did we not find such a place, but I couldn't even find a room for the night; no one would take me without proper ID. My fake passport? No, too risky after being reported to UN and Turkish police. It could create more problems, I thought. One hotel manager threatened to call the police if I didn't leave his lobby immediately. He called me "an illegal immigrant," and I suppose he was right.

I had two options for staying in Ankara. The first was to rent a room from a Turkish family, and the other was to try for the refugee camp run by the UN, but that required more official letters, which were impossible to obtain that night. Seeing that I was stressing out, Maksüt called up Cebe, his brother-in-law, and told him that we were on our way over. We arrived just in time for dinner, but I was so exhausted that they made up my bed immediately. I didn't sleep long before waking up in a highly anxious state, and pretty much stayed that way all night.

In the morning, Maksüt suggested I join him in Istanbul. I was speechless. He had discussed the idea with his wife, by phone. I could report to the police in Istanbul, just as well as in Ankara. I didn't have words to thank him enough. While Maksüt was catching his flight back to Istanbul, Cebe drove me to the station in time to catch the one o'clock bus. For 458 kilometres, I would put up with the second-hand smoke from twenty-eight chain-smokers, and without complaint, I can tell you. Yes, there were checkpoints, but I had no major problems, and we pulled into Istanbul by mid-evening.

I took a taxi to Maksüt's apartment. His wife, Emel, ran to me with open arms, as if I was her long-lost brother. *"Hos geldiniz,"* she said, "Welcome." Maksüt wasn't home from work yet, and neither was their son, Gökhan, nor their daughter, Gökcen. One was at work, and the other at university.

Emel wanted to know everything. I stuck to the good news, the countless ways that I'd been given a lease on life, including this latest salvation. To her, it was "what friends were for, no?" She described Shahram's visit with them, and how he'd told them about my prison experience, including the torture I'd been subjected to. My ordeal had upset her terribly. Why do all bad things happen to good people? she wanted to know.

When Maksüt came home, he was tired, but smiling, and he, too, welcomed me into their house and to their table, which was all laid out. After his second glass of *raki*, Turkish vodka, my host fell asleep at the table, even before his daughter arrived home from school. I couldn't believe how Gökcen had grown into such a beautiful and mature woman. We had so much to talk about after seventeen years, but most of it would have to wait till the next day. Gökhan was kindly overnighting with a friend, so they put me on a sofa bed in his room.

In the morning, Maksüt accompanied me to police headquarters to help me register as a foreigner in Turkey. He once knew an officer there, but finding him in that maze of offices wasn't easy. The official read my letter from the UN, and then listened as Maksüt explained my case, all to no avail. He couldn't help. I had applied in Ankara, and so that's where I would have to wait until the authorities decided where I should reside. Maksüt virtually pleaded with him for some option other than this bureaucratic runaround.

"I can pretend I know nothing about his staying with you," he said. "Just make sure the police don't find out."

I was worried sick again. Maksüt told me not to worry. I would stay with them until I got an answer from the Canadian embassy. In the meantime, Maksüt would contact his friend at the UN to help resolve this problem. God bless Maksüt. He told me to consider my stay in Istanbul a holiday, and to enjoy it. But how could I do that, when I knew I was creating problems for my friend?

"Don't think another thing about it," he said.

I phoned Akram in Vancouver with ideas about putting a Canadian immigration lawyer on my case, but she was a step ahead of me: a lawyer had already faxed the embassy in Ankara. She sounded sad, as if she had something on her mind, but was frightened to say it. I didn't want to pressure her to say anything that she wasn't willing to share.

A few days later, I bused it back to Ankara for my second UN interview. I had only recently noticed that my initial letter prohibited travel outside Ankara, so I had yet another reason to fret the whole way. Maksüt's tailor, Hayri Misiroğlu, had arranged for me to connect with his son in Ankara, a young man named Murat. We arranged a rendezvous under the protective camouflage of hustle and bustle in the busy town centre, and found refuge from the cold in a bakery café.

Murat was tall, strong, and polite, and even spoke a bit of English. The plan was for me to bunk at his place, where he lived with two other students. They were both good-natured fellows, so I was relieved to have found a pleasant place to park my tired body.

The next morning, I waited for two hours at the UN for my name to be called out. I was directed to a small room where a young woman named Zeynep put aside her piles of paperwork, and asked me to sit down. She began with simple questions, name, job, any specializations. She wanted to know why I'd defected, of course, and how difficult my life was before my escape. I answered her questions, making it clear that, although I loved my country and had fought for it, I had no life there. Worse, I had a short life expectancy if I stayed there. But most important, my family had already fled to Canada. I was suspicious of her sad expression, because bureaucrats were famous for faking sympathy that came with bad news. I was surprised when she truly seemed to lament the human tragedies so common in this part of the world. She felt sure that my file would be well received, and she encouraged me to feel optimistic.

"Good luck, Mr. Sharifirad," she said.

That was it. I thanked her very much, and left.

I stayed one more night with Murat and his friends. It was refreshing to be with energetic young people who liked to tell jokes and stories of outrageous encounters with girlfriends. But the next day, it was another stinking bus trip back to Istanbul. My seatmate chain-smoked the entire way, and he never lit up without first offering me one. Twenty times I had to graciously decline. Who could hate a fellow who showed such generosity?

I spent twenty-five days with Maksüt, waiting for news from the Canadian embassy. Each morning, Emel went off to her teaching job and returned in the afternoon. Gōkhan hung out mostly with friends, coming home occasionally to play chess on his computer. He was completely involved in chess, working out new moves against online opponents. I soon learned that he was one of the best players in the country, having competed internationally.

Gōkcen attended university, arriving home every night with heaps of books, and never failing to make me a fruit salad before settling down to do her homework. Maksüt had an irregular travel schedule; he was often away from home for days at a time. To him, relaxation consisted of collapsing on the couch with one or two glasses of *raki* as he watched soccer on television, often falling asleep before the game was over.

I couldn't maintain my optimism unless I got out of the house every day, so I left in the morning, walking to the covered market in the town centre, then back again, an eight-hour expedition. Only on Maksüt's days off did I go farther afield, to clubs, pubs, churches and mosques, museums and historical sites, to shopping centres and expensive restaurants. Maksüt knew how to live, and he knew how to play the perfect host, never letting me spend a penny of my own money. "No, no, Sharifi, you are my guest," he would say. "Enjoy your holiday."

In mid-February, the Canadian embassy called to advise me of an interview in Istanbul in two days. The consulate was lodged in an old church, dimly lit and almost bare of furniture. Of course, the interviewer, Elizabet Huff, senior policy adviser, citizenship and immigration, had to start from scratch, so I cast my mind back to the beginning of the war with Iraq.

"I don't want to hear about the war," she said. "Just tell me about the conditions of your life in Iran, and why it's untenable, and why Canada is your only option."

I was thrown off my plan, not being able to recount the dramatic backstory that led to my personal disaster. So, I jumped right to my imprisonment, the torture, and the ongoing persecution. Then I described my family's misadventures trying to reach Vancouver, and then the nightmare I'd just been through with Rajab, adding little details that enhanced the jeopardy. You'd think that, telling the story so often, I wouldn't get so emotional, but I was exhausted by the end of my narration.

"You don't look like you've been through hell," she said.

What did she mean by that? She excused herself to confer with her boss, while I worried. She returned ten minutes later, carrying documents, and with the okay to send me to the American Hospital for a checkup. "If everything goes smoothly," she said, "you'll be in Canada before me."

I couldn't believe it. Couldn't believe it! No more paperwork, no warnings or caveats. I wanted to give her a hug, but it probably wasn't appropriate. I asked for her Canadian phone number, and just like that, she gave it to me! So much openness, absolutely no paranoia— I was overwhelmed. She wished me luck, and that was it. I left the old church building and headed to the hospital to get that medical appointment, and then to return to Maksüt's place to call Akram.

I arrived for my appointment at the American Hospital a few days later. The place was crammed with people waiting to hear their names called out. My examination lasted two hours. The results would be sent to the Canadian embassy without me having a chance to see them. With no further interviews called for, and Akram's lawyer apparently pursuing my progress, step by step, I only had to await word from the embassy.

As the waiting dragged on, I worried that I might have failed the medical, and I grew pessimistic and moody. One day, Maksüt asked me abruptly when I was leaving. What could I say? Maksüt's rudeness upset Emel, and she apologized, and also for his habit of monopolizing the television with his soccer obsession, which prevented me from watching my favourite programs.

"You know him," she said, "and how kind he is—no need to let one fit of bad temper ruin everything. The fact is, you're not bothering us at all. If sometimes we ask why the Canadians are delaying, it is only because we're thinking of Akram and your kids in Vancouver, and how hard it must be for them waiting for you. You are welcome to stay here for as long as it takes, because you are like a brother to us."

The next day we all got out of the city, to the ski resorts of Bursa. The following weekend, Maksüt was going to take me to visit his father and brother in a small town called Uzunkopru, 235 kilometres west of Istanbul. Emel felt sure that the embassy would have called with good news by the time I got back.

Off we went: Maksüt, Emel, Gökcen, and I, and for two days we hung out at the ski resort, by day soaking up the wild, gorgeous landscape, by night being catered to by Sami Gündüz, the husband of Maksüt's aunt. The fun included a wedding on our first night there. I knew no one, but that didn't prevent me from having a good time.

The next day, we caught up with Ayse, a woman who had been like a mother to Akram and I when we were stationed in Merzifon in 1976. Ayse was also the mother of Remzi Armen, a pilot in the Turkish Air Force. Sami and his family continued to pour on the hospitality as only

Turks can. This was just the diversion I needed to take my mind off waiting.

Two days later, after returning to Istanbul, Maksüt and I departed again to see his father Suleyman, a fine old man who spoke little, but whose heart was solid gold. He lived alone, remaining loyal to his wife who'd died many years earlier. On the way back to Istanbul, Maksüt listened non-stop to a radio broadcast of soccer matches.

"When I finally make it to Canada," I told him, "I'm not going to watch or listen to a soccer game again. I've had enough of that to last me a lifetime."

He laughed, but he didn't change the station.

Arriving in Istanbul, I watched Emel's expression for a sign of news, but there was none. I phoned Ahmet Ergönen in Ankara, to see if he knew where I might spend ten days while I cleared up my registration process and immigration status with the Immigration Police Station. He called me back later that same evening with a plan for staying briefly with his daughter, Gökce, a university student, and then at the guest house of an oil company executive, but only for ten days. The next morning, I returned to Ankara.

My three days with Gökce were enjoyable, since she reminded me of my own daughter. Then it was the guest house at the executive's place. But after ten days I hadn't heard anything from the embassy, or the UN. Fortunately I was allowed to remain in my room for four more days. During my daily police check-ins, the officer in charge came to know and like me for my punctuality. He advised me that in twenty-five days I would have to relocate from Ankara to another city. I was getting desperate.

I called my wife, pressuring her to push the immigration lawyer harder.

"What's he doing for his money?" I asked her.

Again, I sensed that something else was bothering her, and this time I insisted she tell me. So, I guess I asked for it. Besides the news that Shahrokh had broken his arm in a wresting match at school, that Shahram needed knee surgery, and that Mahrokh had been hurt while play fighting with Shahrokh, she told me that for the past three months, she'd been to the hospital repeatedly. Akram started crying, almost blaming me for all the troubles she'd been through. Then it came gushing out: how sick and tired she was of providing for three kids, unable to answer their questions—"How is Daddy?" and "When is Daddy arriving?" She was blubbering, claiming she wanted to die, which got me crying, too.

"The minute you arrive, Yadi, I'm taking a break," she said. "I'm done taking care of the kids."

What I wouldn't have given to trade places with her.

"Please," I begged her, "you just have to tough out these last few weeks. Soon all our miseries will be behind us." I said goodbye to her with tears still running down my face.

After returning from my daily police visit, I phoned the Canadian embassy. What harm could it do? The Canadians wouldn't shout me out of the building, like they had Akram in the Tehran passport office. I identified myself, explained my case and how I'd been waiting for three months, all interviews and medical check completed, but so far not a word from anyone. It only took a moment for the official on the other end of the line to pull up my file.

"Sharifirad," she said. "Yes. Your application has been approved, and your immigration documents are sitting here ready for you to pick up anytime."

"Excuse me?" I said. "I can come now? Today?"

"Anytime," she said. "Is there anything else?"

It occurred to me on the way to the embassy in the taxi that she might have mistaken my file for Shahram's. Why else would they not have called? Prepared for that possibility, I presented myself at embassy reception. A short while later, a woman carrying a file invited me into a small office.

"You have your exit permission from the Turkish police?"

"No," I replied.

"Well, you'll have to get it," she said. They couldn't give me the documents until I had police clearance to leave Turkey. I also had to arrange my air passage to Canada, which I could purchase myself, or wait a week while they made the arrangements.

"A week? No way," I said. "I'll purchase the ticket today."

"Fine," she said, and she handed me a letter addressed to the police, requiring my exit permit. "Good luck," she said.

I went directly to a travel agency and bought a ticket for Istanbul–Amsterdam–Vancouver. Amazingly, a return ticket on KLM was cheaper than a one-way. I didn't ask any questions. I left the office, striding down the street like a new man. Everything appeared more wonderful, from the weather, to the people, to the automotive bedlam at rush hour. No more worry about moving from Ankara, no more living in fear of the police. Every few minutes, I tapped my pocket to be sure my ticket to freedom was still there.

I thought of phoning Akram, but resisted the temptation until I had secured that police permission, and until my immigration documents were in my hands. She couldn't handle any more false hope.

I celebrated with a dinner in the Sheraton Hotel. Later, I phoned Maksüt, but he hadn't arrived home from work, so I shared my good news with Emel, who congratulated me and looked forward to seeing me back in Istanbul in a day or two.

29

"O CANADA!"

I abandoned my daily ritual of hiking to the police station to kill time, and took a cab. The refugee department was crowded as usual. I showed my embassy letter to the policeman, who had become something of a friend by this time. He advised me that I was at the wrong police station. The Foreign Ministry needed to process that letter. There was a police station there, and it was they who would write a letter, which I would then have to bring back here. "Can't it be phoned or faxed?" I asked. I was in a rush.

"No! Do it the way I told you," he said. The way he said it, I didn't dare ask him anything else, like, where the Foreign Ministry police station was located, and how I could get there.

At a nearby tea house, I phoned Maksüt. I wanted some advice before I got involved in more red tape, not to mention more endless lineups. He might even have connections at the Foreign Ministry. Maksüt knew a way that this cursed police letter could be obtained with minimum hassle. I was to talk to Rafik Kosmaz, a friend of his in the insurance business, who was also a former army colonel with influential friends within the government, including a close relative in the National Assembly. If it turned out that Rafik couldn't help me, I was to call back immediately. Good old Maksüt. He would call Rafik to let him know I was coming. I waited half an hour for Maksüt to do that, then phoned ahead. Rafik gave me directions and told me to come over right away. It wasn't far.

A woman answered the security buzzer and let me in. A smartly dressed gentleman stepped out from behind his desk, extended his hand in welcome, and introduced himself as Rafik. Maksüt had already explained everything, he told me, so I didn't have to go into detail. Nor did I have to struggle with my bad Turkish accent, because he spoke English. Rafik placed a call to somebody and explained my situation. I watched him write notes as he listened to instructions, adding his little "yes, yes, yes sirs," and ending with "thank you very much."

"You've got an appointment with the head of police at the Foreign Ministry at nine tomorrow morning," he said.

Done. Tremendous. I couldn't believe it! Rafik had no doubt that my problems were solved, and he wasted no time changing the subject to Maksüt, asking how we knew each other. I told him about our friendship going back almost twenty years, and described all that he'd done for me during the last three months. As for Rafik, he had met Maksüt when they were both students at the English Language School in the Armed Forces Educational Centre, but he had never met Maksüt's family. He questioned me on my choice of Canada, and I explained that my family was there, and he wished me good luck, and invited me to call again if I ran into any more problems.

The next day I was up early, adrenaline pumping through my veins. When I arrived at the police station, I was directed to the chief's office where I had to use my broken Turkish to explain the problem with my "permission." I told him that if I didn't get it within forty-eight hours, I would lose the cost of my ticket—$1200—and my money had run out. He listened to what I had to say, then called a lieutenant colonel into the office. The chief ordered him to "write a letter to the Security Police, and ask them to clear this gentleman's name so that he can leave the country—and do it immediately!" The lieutenant colonel asked me to follow him. I stood up and thanked the chief and bid him adieu, but he barely looked up. Up to the fourth floor we went, where the officer's secretary went to work on the letter. Forty-five minutes later, I had the blessed document in my hands.

I took a cab to the office of the General Security Police Station, Foreigners' Branch, the same station where I had been signing in for so many weeks. To deliver my letter to the proper authority, I was required to wait in the long line of refugees in the hallway. What if I didn't get my clearance before closing time? It was becoming a kind of Catch-22. They'd warned me that I'd outstayed my welcome in Ankara, and now that my necessary exit documents were in my hands, I was stuck in this constipated system. There were too many of us! After a couple of hours' anxious waiting, I was admitted to see the appropriate officer.

"How did you get this?" he asked, looking at my letter.

"From the chief of police, himself, sir," I said. "He arranged it."

"Sorry, but I can't prepare your document today," he said. "I have too many things to do before I can get to it."

Mentally, I was trembling. There was a limit to the amount of bureaucracy a person could take without going crazy.

"Come back tomorrow," he said.

I was on the verge of going berserk, and ruining everything. Today! I wanted the letter today!

"When you come," he said, "come here directly. The letter will be ready to pick up."

What could I say? Had I said anything, who knows what further setbacks I would have faced?

On the way home, I walked for a while with another young Iranian, who invited me back to the place he was staying with other Iranian refugees. It turned out to be one of Ankara's most desperately poor districts, really quite squalid. I counted my blessings for having friends like Maksüt and Ahmet. Upon leaving, I gave the young man every dollar I had to spare. At first he refused to accept the money, but I insisted.

Once downtown, I phoned Maksüt to tell him about my situation: if I obtained my clearance letter in the morning, I'd take the bus to

Istanbul and spend my last night in Turkey with him and his family. He would finally be released from all of Sharifi's problems forever! He laughed and said he was anxious to see me in Istanbul. I phoned as many people as I could to thank them for all they'd done. Many weren't home, so I left messages, and asked that they be passed on. For the rest of the day, I wandered around the market, returning to my hotel only as it was getting dark.

The next day, I woke early to pack, then stopped at a bakery for a box of their best pastries before taking a cab to the police station. I bypassed the usual lineup, entered the office to pick up my letter, greeted the officer who was chatting with his colleagues, and placed the pastry box on his desk.

"What is this?" he said.

"Some pastries," I said, "for your kindness and troubles."

"Well, thank you. But I haven't done your letter yet." He looked in the box. "I'll do it right away," he said.

Never underestimate the power of a gift.

It didn't take him long. Within a few minutes I had the letter in my hand. It was hard to believe that all my worrying was over and that I could finally fly to Canada and join my family in freedom. I thanked the roomful of officers and left, heading for my final stop, the Canadian embassy.

Coaxing the cab driver to take every shortcut he knew, it still took half an hour to get there. Once through the security check, I stepped up to the receptionist and asked for my immigration documents. She asked me for my police clearance and onward air ticket, and I presented both. She sounded excited for me, and invited me to take a seat while she collected my file. Why should I have been so nervous? But I was, shaking, because bureaucracy was so unpredictable.

"Ya-dol-lah." I heard my name called out as the receptionist approached with documents in her hands, giving them to me as she reminded me how important and valuable those papers were, as if I didn't realize it, my God! Along with my UN letter and the police clearance, I'd need to present them all at the airport. I thanked her and the guard standing there and left.

On the street, I was aware of so many more people I needed to thank, many of whom I could never thank enough, people who didn't know me, but who bent over backwards to keep my spirits up during the whole ordeal. I returned to my hotel to pack the last of my things, then took a taxi to the bus terminal in time for the 1 p.m. departure.

What a relief, as we pulled up to checkpoints on the way to Istanbul, not to have to worry about the police. I was now a man with an identity. And a country. I was going to be a Canadian. Not even the chain-smokers on the bus bothered me. In fact, when a cigarette was offered to me, I accepted and lit it up and contaminated the bus right along with all the other addicts. By nine o'clock, I was with Maksüt and Emel and their daughter, Gökcen, who had been waiting for me since six. Their celebratory dinner had gotten cold, but their welcome was warmer than ever.

Dinner became strangely quiet, though, and someone was always jumping in to break the awkward silence. As for me, I felt a strange mix of sadness and excitement. These people deserved so much from me, for all their patience, and for putting up with my troubles—even their son, Gökhan, who I hardly saw because he'd often stayed with friends so that I could sleep in his bedroom. I had become a member of their family, and there was no doubt that they would be in my heart forever, a part of my family as well.

After dinner, I phoned Akram and told her that I would be arriving the next day at around six in the evening. She didn't sound surprised or excited.

"How's the weather there?" I asked. "Is it cold?"

"No," she said. And that was it.

What else was there to say? But her lack of enthusiasm worried me. Had her feelings for me changed? It had been close to three years, after all, or was there more bad news? She had already kept much from me, perhaps to save me from worrying. I could understand that. I remembered when she had unloaded the news about the children and all their problems, and how she wasn't happy that she'd had to bear it all by herself. I wondered what was going on, my head swimming with questions that couldn't be answered until I saw her in Vancouver.

In the morning, I couldn't eat, but Emel forced me to take some nourishment. Maksüt drove me to the airport and accompanied me to the check-in counter, where I received my boarding pass. From there, it was immediately through the security checkpoint, with Maksüt following me, thanks to his flashing his pilot's ID. At passport control, I explained that I didn't have a passport, but instead had my official exit permit. The man didn't look very convinced. We were directed to his supervisor. Maksüt summarized my situation as the official read the letter, and without further questions he signed it and let me go, even wishing me a pleasant journey. We were then free to join other passengers waiting to board the plane.

Nothing was left for us but the goodbyes, and tears were lying in wait ready to make a mess of it, so we avoided them and just sat on a bench against the wall. Maksüt asked me if I needed anything from the duty-free shop, but I needed nothing. He stood up.

"I'll leave you now, my friend," he said. "And let you get ready for your flight."

I stood up and hugged him. Like brothers we were.

"Give Akram my regards," he said, his voice trembling. "And the kids."

"From the bottom of my heart, Maksüt, thank you," I said.

He hugged me more tightly.

"As long as my heart is beating," I said, "I will remember your generosity." And it was true. In the future, if anyone asked me who I had most to thank for my escape to freedom, I would say "Maksüt."

"Don't mention it," he said. "We've been friends for so many years. My heart spoke and all I did was listen. What else could I have done?"

He shook my hand again. "You'd have done the same for me," he said. "Take care of yourself, Sharifi."

He backed away, tears in his eyes, and turned around and walked through the security gate. I watched him exit into the larger terminal, watching him until I couldn't see him anymore.

God bless you, Maksüt.

At 9 a.m. the plane took off for Amsterdam. Flying again! It felt like flying again! I looked down upon many of the places I'd been, streets I'd driven along and neighbourhoods I'd explored. Once we were above the clouds and had levelled off, we were served breakfast, and then I began to jot down a few notes about my farewell with Maksüt.

I tried to sleep, but couldn't, not even with the help of a sleeping pill. I watched the screen displaying the progress of the flight from Istanbul to Amsterdam, but so many things were going on in my mind. Eventually, I must have fallen asleep, because next I knew a flight attendant was shaking me gently, informing me that we were approaching Amsterdam.

Amsterdam airport was another world. Shops and restaurants beckoned me, but the tight connection to my Vancouver flight left me no time to be a tourist. At the KLM desk, I presented my immigration document. "Nothing with a photo?" the official asked. I would have to return to Turkey, he said. I was horrified. They ushered me into a security office, where other officers attempted to contact the Canadian embassy for information on me. I would have to wait until they heard back. "Wait where?" I asked. I was free to wander around the airport until they had news. One thing was certain: I wouldn't be getting on the airplane, because it had already left.

I called Akram to explain this latest glitch. "Tomorrow," I said, "with any luck." She blamed me for everything, as usual, and I began to understand why she appeared so underwhelmed at my endless promises of showing up.

I couldn't do much walking around in the terminal, at least not if I expected them to find me if and when news came through. Sure enough, after three hours the security agent tracked me down, wondering where I'd been. Two Canadian diplomats had arrived to talk to me, he told me, but I couldn't be found. He informed me that a fax from the Canadian embassy in Turkey had explained everything. I would have to take a morning flight, but since I couldn't be released from the in-transit zone, I'd have to sleep in the passengers' lounge. KLM would provide me with food vouchers. The man was sorry that I'd missed my plane, but, he explained, he was only doing his job. Although he was off duty the next day, he promised to show up to help me on my way.

Relieved, I enjoyed a meal, then prowled around the airport until I couldn't stand it anymore, and joined other stranded passengers in the lounge, settling in for an uncomfortable night. I stretched out on the floor but couldn't sleep, so I read the paper, and then documented the day's events in my notebook. In the morning, the KLM agent showed up as promised to see me safely aboard the flight, and apologized once again before bidding me goodbye.

As the plane climbed into the sky, the positive G's—gravity and heaviness—on my body felt divine. I closed my eyes, thinking I might sleep all the way, but too many things were on my mind, painful feelings that I couldn't track to their roots. The more I tried to analyze what was bothering me, the less I understood it. Perhaps I was just so tired. Perhaps a beer would help. I ordered one, two, three, and by the fourth I was nodding off. Only the decreased pressure as the pilot dropped out of his cruising altitude woke me up. We were landing in Toronto.

We had an hour's wait to connect to the Vancouver flight. An official intercepted me at the customs gate. She ushered me into an immigration office to fill out some forms and answer a few questions. I was down to my last ounce of patience, and my last seventeen dollars of cash, so I couldn't have withstood another bureaucratic problem. Before we reboarded, I asked the woman to phone my wife with my arrival time in Vancouver.

It was dark and rainy when the flight took off from Toronto, heading west. I wasn't tired anymore, but I was dizzy with what seemed like lack of oxygen. Maybe my body was quitting after all it had been through. I fell into a kind of semi-dream state where I saw my kids, how they must have been getting ready to drive to the airport to greet me, and my wife, who had suffered so much because of me, and with so much unexplained and simply unexplainable. And raising three children on her own. With every hour that brought me closer to my family, my heart began to pound until I could actually hear it. I was worried that my nervous system had worn out; I was running on empty. I couldn't take any more, I couldn't wait anymore.

As the plane turned into its final approach to Vancouver International Airport, I realized I needed to prepare myself to see them. I wanted badly to appear normal and not break down in a dramatic public display of tears. I tried to remember my family as best I could, to become familiar with them again, so that I wouldn't be an emotional wreck. If only I could see them before they saw me; that way, I could take them in slowly, dilute what was sure to be too much joy for me all at once.

In the terminal, I recognized the rhythm of free people walking, the untroubled expressions on the faces of free people hurrying towards their wives and children, waiting for them in the arrivals lobby. My story suddenly began to overwhelm me, all the events leading up to this new-found freedom. All the crimes against us and the sacrifices we'd made. The guilt over the fall of my family's fortunes. The closer I got, the more my past seemed to shadow me, even following me through Customs and Immigration. But at the sight of my wife and children and their half-smiling faces, my past fled from me like a traitor into hiding. I ran towards them, pushing people aside, I must confess. Which of them should I embrace first? Bless those kids, they made way for their mother; her green eyes flooded with tears. The children stood staring at us, looking dumbstruck.

I felt Shahrokh's hand on my arm, greedy for attention. Reluctantly, Akram eased away to allow my attention to fall upon our little daughter hanging on to her mother's skirt. I picked her up and landed a thousand kisses on her face. I held her body against my heart to feel life. She was shy, and I understood perfectly. Who was this person? Was I her father? She probably wanted me to show some evidence, to present my documents. Prove it! I set her down and found myself between my two sons. They were boys when I had seen them last, and here they were now, handsome young men. I buried myself in their embrace, the three of us becoming a huddle of sobs, tasting tears on each other's cheeks.

Words were out of the question. I remember thinking with some amazement how, when you are sad, you cry, and when you are very happy, you cry, too. How foolish I was to think that I was through with crying! People were staring at us. Some touched, no doubt, at this outpouring of emotion, others simply curious, wondering why a cameraman from one of the local media outlets was filming us. It was Akram's idea, and I was heartened that she felt as strongly as I did that our story, which was climaxing there at the airport, was a history worth recording, especially since she didn't know the half of it. Just as I had no idea how much she had suffered in her own way.

Shahram drove us home, Shahrokh sitting next to him, while Akram, Mahrokh, and I snuggled in the back seat. We zigzagged through the beautiful city of Vancouver, over Lions Gate Bridge and onto Marine Drive into North Vancouver where my new home was located. It was a small one-bedroom apartment with a newspaper lying by the welcome mat, and inside, the smell of simmering *ghour-me-sabzi*, a stew of vegetables and meat served with rice. Behind the coat rack, a sports poster of someone named Wayne Gretzky, and in the living room, a television and leopard-skin sofa, and behind it on the wall, a photo of me.

Colonel Sharifirad kneeling on the tarmac in front of his F-5.

That was long ago.

EPILOGUE

The meaning of freedom is not known until it has been lost, and it is only then that we realize how precious it is. In this book, I tried my best to tell my story, but words cannot describe how tragic it is to leave a whole life behind unwillingly.

Many years have passed since my departure from Iran, but not much has changed there since then. Arrest, torture, and assassination of dissidents still persist. For instance, the killing of Zahra Kazemi in 2003, an Iranian-Canadian photo journalist, and the shooting of a young girl by the name of Neda Aghasoltan in 2009, during the presidential elections, are all well-known by the world.

People have realized their freedom has been stolen and fear is no longer keeping them from demonstrating in any activity that involves demanding democracy. These days more people are participating in street demonstrations and the younger generations are using the Internet as a way to break the silence about what's really going on in Iran between the people and their government.

Although this is a high hope to have, I wish to see the fall of this regime, and to see my people join together to achieve the freedom that was stolen from them almost thirty years ago.

Yadi Sharifirad
December 2009

Acknowledgements

I want to thank my wife, who is my hero in life for her support and patience throughout the ordeals of our life, as detailed in this book. I would also like to thank my two sons, Shahram and Shahrokh, for their help by reading and editing the early versions of my manuscript.

I give special thanks to my wonderful daughter, Mahi, for her typing skills since she put in many hours to transform my hand-written manuscript into its digital format. I should also mention that it definitely was not an easy life for my family, having to go through the ordeals that they went through along with me, and I am, and always will be, proud of them and their fighting spirit.

My special thanks to PJ Reece for his contribution and help for bringing this story to life. He was the first and the main source of my inspiration to translate my manuscript from Farsi into English.

I owe thanks to my friends Michael Angelo, Stephen Rybak, Timothy Kevin O'keeffe, and Jen Barsky for their occasional help throughout the process of writing this book.

I salute Michael Lee for connecting me to Barry Kennedy, to whom I owe immense gratitude for having introduced me to his agent, Peter Taylor.

Many thanks and appreciations go out to Peter Taylor, now my agent, for his efforts and recognition of the value of my book and for paving the way to bring it into print.

My gratitude and thanks to my editor, Janice Zawerbny, for her vision, experience, instructions, and encouragement. She asked all the right questions during the editing process, in order to make the book a better read.

Thanks to Wendy Thomas, managing editor, for her direction, and the whole staff at Thomas Allen Publishing who worked on my book.

My special thanks to a wonderful person, my publisher, Patrick Crean, whom I met only a few months ago yet I feel like I have known him all my life! I call him the guardian angel of my book and a brother of mine from a past life.

Thanks to my all-time friends, Professor Dr. Reza A., Mehrat H., and Morteza F., for their encouragement, unconditional support, and most importantly for always being my true friends.

Thanks,
Yadi